Peaches 'n Cream

Peaches 'n Cream

Compiled and Edited By
Brenda McKnight

Eakin Press   Austin, Texas

FIRST EDITION

Copyright © 1988
By Brenda McKnight

Published in the United States of America
By Eakin Press, P.O. Box 23069, Austin, Texas 78735

ISBN 0-89015-650-6

RECIPE CREDITS:
The book, *Southern Living Recipes*, 1984, may be purchased at bookstores or from Southern Living Books, P.O. Box 2463, Birmingham, Alabama 35280
Redbook Magazine, copyright 1983 by the Hearst Corporation. All rights reserved.

This book is dedicated to all peach lovers. Here is a book that is devoted to our favorite fruit, PEACHES.

One day my husband and I went to pick some peaches, and bought the orchard. So many of our customers have asked for peach recipes; therefore, I decided to compile this book.

It has been fun and I hope that you'll enjoy the recipes as much as I have enjoyed doing the research.

At the end of each recipe, I have tried to credit everyone that contributed to this book by listing their name and city in which they live, or the name of the corporation which so graciously gave me permission to reprint the recipe.

As you try each recipe, make your own notes about it. We all like to add our own touches. Thus as the years go by, you will have written your own recipe book and it will become yours and not mine.

Many, many thanks to everyone. Without you, this book would not exist.

Father of our Lord Jesus Christ

We invoke your blessing upon
this book of recipes which has
been done for the glory of God.

We know that the peach is your
handiwork and was given for our
pleasure and enjoyment.

May those who gave their
recipes for the use of this
fruit and those who receive
them be blessed of God.

We realize this is one of
your natural foods and is
nutritious for our bodies when
used properly.

God bless all who partake.
I ask in Jesus' Name.

Amen.

Evelyn Roberts

Contents

Acknowledgments

I would like to give special thanks to:

Mr.& Mrs. David Sisk and family—
   Cooking and tasting the adapted recipes to be sure that they were truly adaptable.

Mrs. David Sisk (Barbara)—
   Clerical support.

Janice Compton—
   Peaches Are Good For You.

Michael Ray Freeman—
   Poems.

Carol & Patsey McKnight—
   Help with research and clerical support.

Joy Moffitt Angel—
   for doing *The Taste of Texas Cookbook* which brought her publisher, Eakin Publications, Inc., to my attention and allowed the completion of this project.

Canning, Freezing, Jams & Preserves

PEACHES ARE GOOD FOR YOU

At first glance, the peach may appear to be a rather benign fruit, a juicy prelude to summer. But the peach packs more nutrition than its fuzzy exterior might indicate.

A carbohydrate-rich food, low in fat, sodium and calories (35 calories per 2-inch diameter peach; 4 per lb.), the peach is a good source of vitamin A, beneficial to the eyes and skin, and a fair source of vitamin C, useful in the healing of body tissues and claimed by some as a retardant to the common cold. In addition, the peach contains smaller amounts of the B vitamins, and iron. Peaches also contain a goodly amount of calcium not common in most fruit.

So eat up! Our best wishes for your good health as you enjoy our favorite fruit—the unequaled peach.

Janice Compton, Houston, Texas

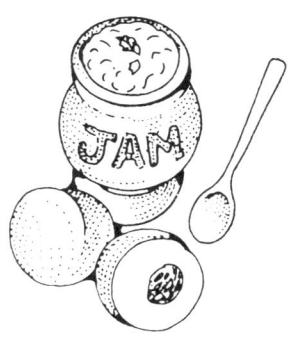

ANTIOXIDANT TREATMENT

Some fruits turn brown from being exposed to the air. To prevent browning, work quickly with only as much fruit as can be processed in one canner load. Treat the fruit with an antioxidant as soon as it is peeled or cut. Use one of the solutions listed below:

Salt-vinegar Solution: Add 2 tablespoons salt and 2 tablespoons vinegar to a gallon of water. Immerse cut fruit in the solution. Work quickly so it doesn't have to remain in solution more than 20 minutes. When all fruit is sliced, lift out of solution; rinse in clear water.

Ascorbic-Acid Solution: Ascorbic-acid or vitamin C crystals may be purchased in any drugstore, supermarket or health-food store. Dissolve crystals in 1 gallon of water. Immerse fruit in solution as it is peeled and cut.

Commercial Antioxidants are available in grocery stores. Follow directions on label.

FREEZING TEXAS PEACHES

FREEZING — To freeze peaches, choose firm, well-ripened fruit that is free of blemishes. Wash, peel and pit the fruit and slice into uniform sections. Before freezing, decide if you prefer a syrup or sugar pack. To sugar pack, sprinkle sugar over the peaches and let them stand a few minutes to draw the juice.

Peaches also freeze well in a medium syrup pack. Allow five cups of sugar to one quart of water. Dissolve the sugar in boiling water and chill the mixture before pouring it over the fruit. To prevent discoloration, add commercial ascorbic acid and citrus acid mixture or crystalline ascorbic acid according to manufacturer's directions as the fruit is being processed.

Choose containers that are moisture- and vapor-proof, odorless, tasteless and flexible. Put peaches into containers. Allow an inch of head space for the fruit packed in syrup, half an inch for fruit packed in dry sugar. Seal containers and label them with the date and name of the product. Freeze immediately at 0 degrees F or lower.

Reprinted by permission of Texas Department of Agriculture

FRESH FROZEN PEACHES

3 pounds ripe, unblemished
    peaches (about 12 medium
    size)
4½ teaspoons Sweet 'N Low

¾ teaspoon granulated ascorbic
    acid
3 cups cold water

Peel peaches by dipping first in boiling water, then in cold water. Slip off skins. Slice and pit peaches. (Yield will be approximately 6 cups.) Pack into 4 pint-size containers. Dissolve Sweet 'N Low and ascorbic acid in cold water. Pour ¾ cup sweetened liquid over each container of fruit, so fruit is covered, but leaving ½-inch head space. Seal tightly and freeze. Makes 4 pints.

Calories per cup: 75.

Reprinted by permission of Cumberland Packing Corporation

CANNING TERMS

Head space is the space that must be left between the food and the lid, to allow for expansion.

Release trapped air in canning jars. Insert a thin flat plastic or wooden utensil at the side of the jar; air bubbles will rise to the top.

Wipe jar rims before putting on lids. Food, droplets of syrup or liquid left on the jar will prevent airtight seal. Use clean damp cloth to wipe away sticky syrup.

Fill and close one jar at a time. This decreases the possibility of introducing microorganisms into filled jars waiting to be closed.

Canning Aids Required for Canning Peaches

• Knives should be made of good quality steel so they do not discolor the fruit. Keep knives sharp.
• Measuring cups and spoons are a must.
• Large kitchen pots and pans: large enough to hold the food to be cooked and plenty of boiling space.
• Long handled spoons — let you stir boiling liquids without getting burned.
• Colanders and sieves are helpful when washing and draining fruits. Use them to strain juices for syrups and jellies. Force cooked fruits through sieve to make sauces and butters.
• Clean towels are used to wipe rims of jars before you put on lids. Also, use towels under and around hot jars while filling them and after processing.
• Jar tongs or lifters fit snugly around neck of jar.
• Hot pads must be kept dry and handy.

CANNED PEACHES

**4 pounds firm, ripe peaches
(about 16 medium size)**

**2 cups water
1 tablespoon Sweet 'N Low**

Peel peaches by dipping first in boiling water, then in cold water. Slip off skins. Halve and pit peaches and combine with water in large saucepan; bring to a boil. Remove from heat and stir in Sweet 'N Low. Using a slotted spoon, pack peaches, cavity-side down and layers overlapping, into 4 hot, sterilized pint jars, leaving ½-inch head space. Seal, following manufacturer's directions. Process 25 minutes in boiling water bath. Cool before storing. Makes 4 pints. Calories per cup: 80.

Reprinted by permission of Cumberland Packing Corporation

PEACH HALVES

12 to 12½ pounds firm, ripe peaches

Soaking solution:

**8 cups water
1 tablespoon salt**

1 tablespoon vinegar

Light syrup: 2 cups sugar to 4 cups water

Prepare home canning jars and lids according to manufacturer's instructions.

Wash and drain peaches. Put fruit in wire basket or cheesecloth and lower into boiling water for ½ to 1 minute to loosen skin. Dip into cold water and drain. Peel, halve and pit peaches. Place halves in soaking solution. Combine sugar and water in a saucepan. Cook until sugar dissolves. Bring to a boil, but do not let syrup boil down. Rinse and pack, cut side down, into hot jars, one jar at a time, leaving ½-inch head space. Carefully cover fruit with boiling syrup, leaving ½-inch head space. Remove air bubbles with non-metallic spatula. Adjust caps.

Process 30 minutes in a boiling water bath canner.

Yield: about five 1½-pint jars. Variation: Peach nectar, pineapple juice or apple juice may be substituted for light syrup.

Reprinted by permission of Ball Corporation

PEACHES AND MELON BALLS

5 pounds peaches

Soaking solution:

8 cups water	4 cups water
2 tablespoons vinegar	2 cups sugar
2 tablespoons salt	¼ cup lemon juice
2 medium cantaloupes	

Prepare home canning jars and lids according to manufacturer's instructions.

Peel, pit and slice peaches; then place in soaking solution to prevent browning. Cut cantaloupes in half, remove seeds and cut melon into balls. Combine water, sugar and lemon juice in a large (6 to 8 quart) saucepot. Bring to a boil and add drained and rinsed peach slices and melon balls. Remove saucepot from heat and let mixture cool to room temperature. Remove fruit from syrup; set aside. Heat syrup to boiling. Pack fruit into hot jars, one jar at a time, leaving ½-inch head space. Remove syrup from heat and carefully pour over fruit, leaving ½-inch head space. Remove air bubbles with non-metallic spatula. Wipe jar rim clean, place lid on and screw band down evenly and firmly. Place closed jar in canner. Repeat for each jar.

Process 20 minutes in boiling water bath canner.

Yield: about 5 pint jars.

Reprinted by permission of Ball Corporation

PEACHES IN AMARETTO

10 pounds peaches

8 cups water	**Soaking solution:**
1 tablespoon salt	
1 tablespoon	3 cups water
vinegar or commercial ascorbic	2 cups sugar
acid mixture	½ cup Amaretto

Prepare home canning jars and lids according to manufacturer's instructions.

Peel peaches; cut into halves and remove pits. Place halves in soaking solution to prevent darkening. Rinse and drain. Cook a few peaches at a time in water until heated through. Drain and pack into hot jars, leaving ½-inch head space. Cook water and sugar until sugar dissolves. Carefully ladle over peaches, leaving ¾-inch head space. Add 2 tablespoons Amaretto to each quart jar, leaving

½-inch head space. Remove air bubbles with a non-metallic spatula. Adjust caps.

Process 25 minutes in boiling water bath canner.

Yield: about 4 quart jars.

Reprinted by permission of Ball Corporation

BRANDIED PEACHES

3 lbs. peaches	6 whole cloves
3 cups sugar	Brandy
3 cups water	

Select ripe, firm, unblemished peaches. Wipe away fuzz with a coarse towel. Combine sugar and water in saucepan and stir over low heat until it makes a thick syrup. Add cloves. Simmer peaches in syrup 5 minutes. Drain and place peaches in hot sterile jars. Pour 2 tablespoons brandy into each jar. Remove cloves and pour over fruit, filling within ½-inch of top. Seal and process in boiling water bath 15 minutes. Store in a cool dark place three months before using.

Yield: Six 6-oz. jars.

Reprinted by permission of Texas Department of Agriculture

BRANDIED PEACHES

8 pounds fresh peaches	1 lemon
1½ cups brown sugar	8 whole cloves
¼ cup water	1 tablespoon crystallized ginger
¼ cup vinegar	slivers
½ cup brandy	4 sticks cinnamon
1 orange	

Soaking solution:

8 cups water	1 tablespoon vinegar
1 tablespoon salt	

Prepare home canning jars and lids according to manufacturer's instructions.

Wash and drain peaches. Put fruit in wire basket or cheesecloth and lower into boiling water for ½ to 1 minute to loosen skin. Dip into cold water and drain. Peel, pit, and slice peaches. Place slices in soaking solution.

Combine sugar, water, and vinegar in saucepot. Bring to a boil. Add peaches and cook until they are hot through. Make a 2-inch layer of peaches in bottom of hot jar. Make a second layer of orange and lemon slice halves. Add 1 clove, 1 or 2 slivers of ginger, and half of a cinnamon stick. Make another layer of peaches, followed

6

again by fruit and spices. Fill remainder of jar to ½-inch of top with peaches. Repeat process for all jars.

Measure 1 cup of remaining syrup. Bring to a boil in small saucepan. Remove from heat. Add brandy. Carefully pour over fruit, leaving ½-inch head space. Remove air bubbles with non-metallic spatula. Wipe jar rim clean. Adjust caps.

Process 10 minutes in a boiling water bath canner.

Yield: Four 24-ounce jars.

Reprinted by permission of Ball Corporation

HONEY BRANDIED PEACHES

12 ripe large peaches
2 cups water
1 cup honey
3 tablespoons lemon juice

2 sticks (3 inches each) cinnamon, broken into pieces
¼ cup brandy

Prepare pint jars. Dip peaches into boiling water 30 seconds, then into cold water. Peel peaches; cut in half and remove pits (see note). Heat 2 cups water, the honey, lemon juice and cinnamon to boiling in 4-quart Dutch oven or kettle; add peaches. Heat to boiling; reduce heat. Cover and simmer 3 minutes. Remove from heat; stir in brandy.

Pack peaches in hot jars. Pour syrup to within ½-inch of tops of jars. Place at least 1 cinnamon piece in each jar; seal. Process in boiling water bath 20 minutes.

Yield: 3 pints.

Note: To prevent peaches from darkening during preparation, place halves in mixture of 2 tablespoons salt, 2 tablespoons lemon juice or vinegar and 1 gallon cold water. Rinse before packing.

Reprinted from Betty Crocker's Recipe Card Library, by permission of General Mills

FRUIT PUREE
(peach, apricot and pear)

Preparation: Wash. Remove peel and seed from very soft fruit. Chop fine or mash. Add about ½ cup sugar for each quart of raw fruit. Heat to boiling.

Hot pack: Pour into hot, clean glass jar to ½-inch of top.

Close and process containers in boiling water bath.

Pints and quarts: 20 minutes.

Remove containers from water bath and cool.

Reprinted by permission of Texas Agricultural Extension Service

SPICY PEACH BUTTER

8 cups sliced peaches, crushed
    or blended
4 cups sugar
¼ teaspoon salt

1 teaspoon cinnamon
½ teaspoon ginger
½ teaspoon allspice
¼ teaspoon ground cloves

Mix peaches, sugar and salt in a large kettle. Boil rapidly, stirring constantly to prevent scorching. As the butter becomes thick, lower heat to reduce spattering. Add spices. Continue cooking until butter is thick enough to almost flake off the spoon. Pour into hot sterilized jars to within ½-inch of top and seal.

Yield: 4 pints.

Reprinted by permission of Texas Department of Agriculture

PEACH BUTTER

18 large/medium peaches
1 cup brown sugar
1 cup honey

¼ teaspoon each salt, cloves,
    ginger, allspice, and nutmeg

Prepare home canning jars and lids according to manufacturer's instructions.

Pit, peel, and chop peaches. Cook in small amount of water until soft. Press through sieve or food mill, or puree in blender. Measure 2 quarts (8 cups) of pulp. In saucepot combine pulp, brown sugar, honey, and spices. Cook slowly over low heat. Stir frequently. Cook until butter is very thick. About 30 minutes. Carefully pour into hot jars, leaving ¼-inch head space. Adjust caps.

Process 10 minutes in boiling water bath canner.

Yield: about six 8-ounce jars.

Reprinted by permission of Ball Corporation

MAKING JAMS AND SPREADS

Delicious, low-calorie fruit jams can be prepared by substituting Sweet 'N Low instead of sugar. Because Sweet 'N Low provides only the sweetening and not the preserving qualities of sugar, jams and spreads made with Sweet 'N Low must be refrigerated and used within 2 weeks. However, they can be frozen until ready to use.

SWEET 'N LOW CONVERSION CHART

Remember: By using Sweet 'N Low you can reduce the sugar content of any of your favorite recipes with this simple conversion chart:

For Granulated Sugar	Use Sweet 'N Low
2 tablespoons	½ teaspoon
¼ cup	1 teaspoon
⅓ cup	1⅓ teaspoons
½ cup	2 teaspoons
1 cup	4 teaspoons

Reprinted by permission of Cumberland Packing

ACAPULCO PEACH AND PEPPER JAM

1½ cups cider vinegar
¼ cup fresh jalapeno chili peppers, quartered
3 pounds fresh peaches, finely chopped (6 cups)
6 cups sugar
1 teaspoon celery seed
1 teaspoon whole allspice
4 drops green food coloring
2 pouches (3 ounces) liquid pectin

Combine vinegar and jalapeno peppers in an electric blender. Process in stop and go fashion to desired fineness. Combine with peaches, sugar, celery seed and allspice in large kettle and bring to a boil. Reduce heat and simmer for 45 to 50 minutes, stirring frequently. Let cool 2 minutes then mix in food coloring and pectin. Ladle into hot, sterilized jars. Seal at once. Process in boiling water bath for 15 minutes, if desired. Cool. Makes 9½ cups.

Reprinted by permission of *The Houston Post*

PEACHY ORANGE JAM

3 large juice oranges
6 cups Domino granulated sugar
1 lemon
3 lbs. (about 12) medium firm ripe peaches

Grate the rinds of the oranges and lemon. Squeeze the juices and remove any seeds. Do not strain. Combine rinds and juices in a large heavy kettle or Dutch oven. Peel and chop peaches into citrus juices. Stir in sugar and bring to a boil over medium heat, stirring often. Reduce heat and let simmer slowly until thickened, about 35 – 45 minutes. Stir frequently. (Do not cover.) Pour into hot sterilized jars and seal at once.

Yield: about 5½ pints.

VARIATIONS: (1) Unpeeled nectarine may be substituted for peaches.

(2) Tropical Peachy Jam: When jam is almost thick, stir in 1 cup grated canned or packed coconut. Cook 10 minutes, stirring constantly.

Reprinted by permission of Amstar Corp., American Sugar Division

PEACH/PLUM JAM

4 cups peaches (about 3 lbs.)   **8 cups sugar**
5 cups red plums   **1 lemon, thinly sliced**

Peel and pit peaches. Pit plums. Cut fruits in small pieces or chop. Measure into large kettle. Add sugar and lemon (very thinly sliced) and stir to mix well. Boil rapidly, stirring constantly, until jellying point is reached or until thick. Remove from heat; skim and stir alternately for 5 minutes. Ladle into hot sterilized jars; seal. Makes 12 half-pints.

Reprinted by permission of Beverly Levandowski, Hempstead, Texas

PEACH AND RASPBERRY JAM

7 large peaches — peeled, pitted   **5 cups sugar**
and chopped (6 cups)   **1 pint raspberries, rinsed and**
2 tablespoons fresh lemon juice   **drained**

Place peaches, lemon juice and sugar into a Dutch oven. Slowly bring to a boil over low heat, stirring occasionally, until the sugar dissolves, 10–15 minutes. Increase the heat to moderate and boil, stirring occasionally, for 20 minutes. Remove from the heat and add the raspberries. Return to the heat and boil, stirring for 5 minutes. Skim off any foam.

Remove from the heat and test for thickness by dabbing about ½ teaspoon of the jam onto a chilled saucer and placing it in the freezer for 3 minutes. Push the jam gently with your finger. If the surface wrinkles, the jam is ready for processing. If it does not, the jam is too thin. Return to the heat and boil for another 5 minutes, then retest.

When the jam is properly thickened, ladle into 6 clean, dry, hot half-pint jars to fill them within ¼-inch of the top. Wipe the rims with a clean, damp cloth. Place lids on the jars and tighten the screw bands. Process in a boiling water bath for 15 minutes.

PEACH-WALNUT JAM

4 cups chopped peaches
½ cup chopped walnuts
¼ cup lemon juice

7 cups sugar
½ bottle liquid fruit pectin

Combine peaches, walnuts, lemon juice and sugar in large heavy saucepan; bring to a rolling boil. Boil hard for 1 minute, stirring constantly. Remove from heat; stir in fruit pectin immediately. Skim off foam, using metal spoon. Stir for 5 minutes or until slightly cooled to prevent fruit from floating. Skim well. Ladle jam quickly into sterilized glasses; cover with ⅛-inch layer of hot paraffin.

Reprinted by permission of Favorite Recipes Press, Nashville, Tennessee

PEACHY PEAR JAM

3½ cups mashed peaches and
  pears
6½ cups sugar
Juice of two lemons

½ teaspoon ground cinnamon
½ teaspoon ground nutmeg
½ bottle liquid fruit pectin

Mix all ingredients, except pectin. Place over high flame and bring to full rolling boil. Boil hard for 1 minute, stirring constantly. Remove from heat; stir in pectin. Skim. Stir and skim for 5 minutes. Pour into hot sterilized jars; seal. Makes 4 pints.

Reprinted by permission of Beverly Levandowski, Hempstead, Texas

PEACHY BLUEBERRY JAM

4 cups blueberries
4 cups peaches, peeled and pitted
½ cup water

5½ cups sugar
½ teaspoon salt

Chop peaches well and combine with berries and water in saucepan. Bring to a boil, cover and cook over low heat for 10 minutes, stirring occasionally. Increase heat and boil rapidly for 10 to 15 minutes. Pour into hot sterile jars. Seal.

Reprinted by permission of The Texas Blueberry Growers Association
The Adventures of Buckaroo Berry Cookbook

PEACH JAM

2 16-ounce cans sliced peaches,
  packed in its own juice

2 teaspoons unflavored gelatin
1 teaspoon Sweet 'N Low

Drain peaches and reserve juice. Chop peaches and set aside. Pour juice into a medium-size saucepan and sprinkle gelatin on top; let stand 1 minute. Cook over low heat 1−2 minutes until gelatin is completely dissolved. Add peaches and stir until blended. Puree ⅔ of mixture in a blender. Return to a saucepan, add Sweet

11

'N Low and mix well. Pour into 4 hot, sterilized, 8-ounce jars. Seal tightly and allow to cool. Freeze. Thaw before serving. Keeps in refrigerator up to 2 weeks. Makes four 8-ounce jars.

Calories per tablespoon: 5.

Reprinted by permission of Cumberland Packing Corporation

FREEZER PEACH JAM

4 cups peeled, coarsely chopped peaches

1 1¾-ounce package powdered fruit pectin

1 tablespoon sugar

1 tablespoon lemon juice

½ teaspoon ascorbic acid

Crush peaches in a medium saucepan; stir in remaining ingredients. Bring to a boil; cook 1 minute, stirring constantly. Remove from heat and stir 3 minutes. Spoon jam into freezer containers, leaving ½-inch head space. Cover at once with lids. Let stand at room temperature 24 hours; freeze. To serve, thaw jam at room temperature.

Yield: 2½ half-pints.

Approximately 11 calories and 7 milligrams sodium per tablespoon.

Reprinted by permission of North Carolina Department of Agriculture

NO-COOK SPICED PEACH JAM

2 pounds (about) fully ripe peaches

2 tablespoons lemon juice

1 teaspoon ascorbic acid crystals

½ teaspoon ground ginger

½ teaspoon ground nutmeg

4 cups sugar

1 cup Karo light corn syrup

¾ cup water

1 1¾-oz. package powdered fruit pectin

Peel and quarter peaches. Finely chop in food grinder, blender or processor. Measure 2 ¼ cups. Turn peaches into 4-quart bowl. Stir in lemon juice and ascorbic acid crystals. Add ginger and nutmeg; stir well. Add sugar and corn syrup, stirring thoroughly to dissolve sugar. Let stand 10 minutes. In small saucepan mix water and fruit pectin. Stirring constantly, bring to boil over medium heat and boil 1 minute. Pour into fruit mixture. Stir vigorously 3 minutes. (A few sugar crystals will remain.) Ladle into ½- or 1-pint freezer containers leaving ½-inch head space (no paraffin needed). Cover with tight lids. Let stand at room temperature until set. (It may take up to 24 hours.) Jam to be eaten within a week or two may be stored in refrigerator. Freeze remaining containers and transfer to refrigerator as needed. Makes about 7 (½-pint) containers.

Reprinted by permission of Best Foods, a unit of CPC North America

PEACH JAM

Peel and cut well-ripened peaches into small pieces. Place in a large kettle WITHOUT water. Heat slowly. When the peaches have begun to soften, crush them slightly; cook slowly about 20 minutes. Measure the peach pulp and for each cup of pulp, add 1 cup of sugar. Return to heat and cook until thick, about 20 more minutes. Pour into jars, seal and process in boiling water bath for 10 minutes.

Dorothy Williams, New Waverly, Texas

SPICY FRUIT 'N HONEY JAM

5 cups chopped, peeled fresh
   peaches or apples
⅓ cup honey
1 tablespoon lemon juice
¼ teaspoon ground cinnamon
Dash ground cloves
1 envelope Knox Unflavored
   Gelatin
¼ cup water

In medium saucepan, combine peaches, honey, lemon juice, cinnamon and cloves; cook 5 minutes, crushing peaches slightly. Bring to a boil, then boil rapidly, stirring constantly, 1 minute.

In small bowl, sprinkle unflavored gelatin over water; let stand 1 minute. Add to peach mixture; stir over low heat until gelatin is completely dissolved, about 5 minutes. Let stand 5 minutes. Ladle into jars; cover and cool slightly before refrigerating. Makes about 3 cups jam.

Tested recipe from The Lipton Kitchens
Reprinted by permission of Thomas J. Lipton, Inc.

HALF-CROCKED PEACH JAM

1½ lbs. fresh peaches
2 tablespoons lemon juice
1 1¾ oz. package powder fruit
   pectin
5½ cups sugar
Port, bourbon, brandy, or rum
   (optional)

Halve peaches and discard pits. Finely chop peaches to measure 3 cups; add lemon juice. In a 6–8 quart saucepan thoroughly mix peaches with powdered fruit pectin. Over high heat, cook and continually stir until mixture comes to a full boil. Add sugar and bring to a full rolling boil and boil hard 1 minute, stirring constantly. Remove from heat; skim off foam with a metal spoon. Stir and skim again in 5 minutes. Into hot ½-pint jars, pour 1 tablespoon of suggested liquor; add hot jam leaving ¼-inch head space. Stir, place lids and process 15 minutes in boiling water bath. Cool. Makes 3 ½ pints.

SPICED PEACH JAM

4 cups crushed peaches (about 7 or 8 med. size)
5 cups sugar (2 ¼ lbs.)
½ teaspoon ground cloves
½ teaspoon ground cinnamon
½ teaspoon ground allspice
1 box powdered pectin

Put peeled, pitted peaches into bowl. Crush fine with mesh-type potato masher or small can with both ends cut out. Put into 6-quart kettle. Measure sugar and set aside. Add spices and pectin to fruit. Mix well. Place over high heat. Stir until mixture comes to full rolling boil (when stirring, don't stop the boiling). Boil for 1 minute. Stir constantly. Take from heat. Alternately stir and skim (to remove foam) for 5 minutes. While stirring add a few drops of red food coloring to brighten color of jam. Pour into clean, hot, dry jars. Seal at once with self-sealing lids or cover at once with a ¼-inch layer of melted paraffin. Store in a cool, dry place.

Yield: 6½-pint jars.

Reprinted by permission of Texas Department of Agriculture

GINGERY PEACH JAM

3¼ pounds fully ripe peaches
¼ cup finely slivered Durkee Crystallized Ginger
6 cups sugar
1 1¾-oz. box powdered fruit pectin

Peel and pit peaches; grind or blend in blender container. Measure 4½ cups into a very large saucepan. Add ginger. Measure sugar and set aside. Add commercial pectin to fruit and mix well. Over high heat, stir until mixture comes to a boil. Immediately stir in sugar. Bring to a full rolling boil and boil hard for one minute, stirring constantly. Remove from heat and skim off foam with metal spoon. Ladle into sterilized jars, leaving ⅛-inch head space; adjust lids. Process in water bath 15 minutes (start counting processing time as soon as water comes to a rolling boil). Remove jars and cool. Makes 8 cups.

Reprinted by permission of Durkee Famous Foods Kitchens

PEACH CHAMPAGNE JELLY

1 pound fresh California peaches, pitted and sliced (2½ cups)
4 cups sugar
2 cups champagne or dry white wine
2 pouches (3 ounces each) liquid pectin

Combine peaches and sugar in a large saucepan. Heat slowly to boiling, stirring constantly, until sugar dissolves. Boil briskly 4 to 5 minutes or until peaches are tender. Let cool 10 minutes. Stir in champagne and liquid pectin. Skim off foam if necessary. Pour quickly into hot sterilized jars. Seal at once. Process in boiling water bath for 15 minutes, if desired. Cool. It may be necessary to gently invert jars to redistribute fruit as it begins to set (after about 3 hours). Makes 3 pints.

Reprinted by permission of California Tree Fruit Agreement

PEACH JELLY

3½ lbs. peaches, unpeeled and pitted
1 1¾-oz. package dry fruit pectin
½ cup lemon juice
6 cups sugar

Chop or grind peaches. Simmer for 10 minutes. Drip through jelly bag or cheesecloth lined sieve. Combine 3 cups juice, dry pectin, sugar, and lemon juice in pot. Cook over medium-low heat. Bring to rolling boil; boil 1 minute. Pour into clean, hot jar, leaving ½-inch head space. Seal. Makes 3 pints.

HONEYED PEACH PRESERVES

3 pounds peaches, peeled and quartered
4 cups sugar
1 cup honey
½ medium-size orange, quartered
½ teaspoon salt
¼ teaspoon almond extract

Combine first three ingredients in Dutch oven. Cover and let stand for 45 minutes. Position knife blade in food processor bowl. Add orange and top with cover. Process until finely chopped. Measure chopped orange and add an equal amount of water. Cook covered, about 10 minutes or until orange peel is soft. Set aside.

Bring peaches slowly to a boil, stirring frequently, until sugar dissolves. Bring to a rapid boil and cook 15 minutes, stirring constantly. Add orange mixture, return to a boil and cook about 25 minutes or until mixture registers 221 degrees on a candy thermometer; stir mixture frequently. Remove from heat, stir in salt and almond extract. Skim off foam with a metal spoon.

Quickly pour preserves into hot jars, leaving ¼-inch headroom; cover at once with metal lids and screw on bands. Process in boiling water bath for 15 minutes.

Yield: 5 half-pints.

Bob Muse, Houston, Texas

PEACH PRESERVES

4 pounds peaches
2 tablespoons lemon juice

1 1¾-ounce package powdered
   pectin
7 cups sugar

Prepare home canning jars and lids according to manufacturer's instructions. Peel and pit peaches; then thinly slice (about 4 cups, sliced). Combine peaches and lemon juice in a large (6 to 8 quarts) saucepot. Stir in pectin and bring to a full boil, stirring occasionally. Add the sugar and return to a full, rolling boil. Boil hard for 1 minute, stirring constantly. Remove from heat. Skim foam and carefully ladle into hot jar, leaving ¼-inch head space. Wipe jar rim clean, place lid on and screw band down evenly and firmly. Place closed jar in canner. Repeat for each jar.

Process 10 minutes in a boiling water bath canner.

Yield: about six 12-ounce jars.

Reprinted by permission of Ball Corporation

PEACH-ORANGE MARMALADE

2 quarts peeled, chopped
   peaches
¾ cup thinly sliced orange rind

1½ cups chopped orange sections
2 tablespoons lemon juice
5 cups sugar

Combine all ingredients in a large Dutch oven; slowly bring to a boil, stirring occasionally until sugar dissolves. Boil until mixture registers 230 degrees on a candy thermometer, stirring frequently to prevent sticking. Remove from heat and skim with a metal spoon. Quickly pour marmalade into hot sterilized jars, leaving ¼-inch headroom; cover at once with metal lids and screw bands tight. Process marmalade in boiling water bath 15 minutes.

Yield: 5 half-pints.

Bob Muse, Houston, Texas

SURPRISE PEACH MARMALADE

4 cups very ripe cantaloupe,
   crushed
4 cups very ripe peaches,
   crushed
6 cups sugar
¼ cup lemon juice

½ teaspoon ground nutmeg
¼ teaspoon cinnamon
¼ teaspoon salt
1 teaspoon grated lemon peel
1 tablespoon grated orange peel
½ cup pecans, finely chopped

Combine crushed cantaloupe and peaches in large jelly kettle. Simmer 20 minutes, stirring very often to prevent sticking. Add sugar and lemon juice. Boil until thick (45 minutes to 1 hour). Add remaining ingredients. Boil for 3 minutes. Ladle into hot jars and seal by either self-sealing lids or paraffin. If preferred, use self-sealing lids and process in water bath 5 – 8 minutes.

Yield: 6 pints.

Reprinted by permission of Texas Department of Agriculture

PEACH CONSERVE WITH RUM

1 orange
½ cup rum
2 quarts peeled and chopped
   peaches (about 12)
6½ cups sugar
¾ cup crushed pineapple

¼ cup chopped maraschino
   cherries
¼ cup lemon juice
½ teaspoon ground ginger
¼ teaspoon nutmeg

Prepare home canning jars and lids according to manufacturer's instructions. Remove peel from orange; cut into thin strips. Finely chop orange pulp, discarding seeds. Cook orange pulp and peel, in water to cover, until peel is tender. Place open container of rum in hot water. Combine chopped peaches, orange mixture, sugar, pineapple, cherries, lemon juice and spices in large (6- to 8-quart) saucepot. Cook and stir until thickened, almost to jellying point. Remove from heat. Stir in warm rum. Carefully ladle into hot jars, one at a time, leaving ¼-inch head space. Adjust caps. Process 10 minutes in boiling water bath canner.

Yield: about six 8-ounce jars.

Reprinted by permission of Ball Corporation

HEAVENLY CONSERVE DELIGHT

6 cups sliced fresh peaches
3 cups halved white seedless
   grapes
2 cups diced pineapple
2 cups diced peeled red plums

2 lemons, peeled, seeded and
   diced
1 cup orange juice
9 cups sugar

Combine all ingredients; let stand for several hours or overnight. Cook one-third of the mixture at a time until thick, stirring frequently. Pour into sterilized jars; seal. Process in hot water bath for 10 minutes to complete seal.

Yield: 7 pints.

Reprinted by permission of Favorite Recipes Press, Nashville, Tennessee

PEACH-CANTALOUPE CONSERVE

4 cups peaches (diced)
4 cups cantaloupe (diced)
4 lemons, juice and grated rind

6 cups sugar
1 cup English walnuts (blanched and chopped)

PEEL and dice peaches and cantaloupe. Combine all ingredients, except nut meats. Cook mixture until thick and clear: add nut meats and pour into sterilized Kerr jars to within ½ inch of top. Put on cap, screw band firmly tight. Process in boiling water bath 10 minutes.

Yield: Six 8-ounce jars.

Reprinted by permission of Kerr Glass Manufacturing Corporation
Kerr Home Canning and Freezing Book, 1983 Edition

PEACH CONSERVE

6 lbs. peaches, peeled and mashed
5 lbs. granulated sugar

1 cup chopped pecans (add last)
1 cup raisins
Rind and juices of 3 oranges

Cook slowly to avoid scorching. Cook until thick, add chopped pecans. Remove from fire. Pour into jelly glasses or jars. Place seals and rings onto jars. Process in boiling water bath for 10 minutes. Variation: Delete raisins and oranges. Add 25 maraschino cherries, cut in quarters, and juice of two lemons.

Dorothy Williams, New Waverly, Texas

CAMPBELL'S PEACH CONSERVE

1 16-ounce can sliced peaches
Mix:

1 pouch Campbell's Onion Soup

½ cup raisins
½ cup chopped walnuts
Slivered peel from ½ an orange
¼ cup orange juice

¼ cup packed brown sugar
1 tablespoon vinegar
2 teaspoons curry powder
½ teaspoon ground ginger

Drain peaches, reserving liquid; chop peaches. In 2-quart saucepan, combine peaches, peach liquid and remaining ingredients. Over medium heat, heat to boiling, stirring constantly. Reduce heat to low; simmer, uncovered, 10 minutes, stirring frequently. Serve warm or cover and chill until serving time, at least 4 hours.

Serve with ham, turkey or chicken.

Makes 2½ cups.

Reprinted by permission of Campbell Soup Company

TOMATO PEACH CHUTNEY

2 cups sugar
1½ cups distilled white vinegar
1 cup Karo light corn syrup
1 tablespoon minced ginger root
2 teaspoons uniodized salt
1½ teaspoons curry powder
1 teaspoon dry mustard
¼ teaspoon crushed, dried red
  pepper

1 clove garlic, minced or pressed
3 pounds firm, fully ripe
  tomatoes
3 pounds firm, fully ripe peaches
2 medium-large onions
1 large sweet green pepper
1 large sweet red pepper
1 cup golden raisins

In 5-quart stainless steel or enamel saucepot stir together sugar, vinegar, corn syrup, ginger, salt, curry powder, mustard, red pepper and garlic. Stirring occasionally, bring to boil over medium heat. Remove from heat. Dip tomatoes in boiling water about 1 minute. Remove and place in colander under cold running water. With a paring knife remove skins and cut away any white hard core. Cut into thin wedges. Measure 5 cups. Rinse, peel and pit peaches. Cut into thin wedges. Measure 5 cups. Peel onions; cut into thin wedges. Measure 2 cups. Rinse, split and remove white membrane and seeds from peppers. Cut in ½-inch pieces. Measure 2 cups. Bring syrup mixture to full boil over medium heat. Add vegetables, peaches and raisins. Return to full boil. Reduce heat. Stirring occasionally, boil actively, but gently, about 1 hour, stirring more frequently as mixture thickens, until syrup is thick and fruit and vegetables are translucent. Ladle into clean hot ½-pint jars, leaving ½-inch head space. Using non-metallic utensil, remove air bubbles. Wipe top edge with damp towel. Seal according to jar manufacturer's directions. Process in boiling water bath 10 minutes. Cool jars on wire rack or folded towel.

Makes 8 (½-pint) jars.

Reprinted by permission of Best Foods, a unit of CPC North America

PEACH CHUTNEY

3 pounds peaches, slightly
    underripe
Vinegar-water (1 quart water
    plus 1 tablespoon vinegar)
1 cup firmly packed light brown
    sugar
¾ cup seedless raisins

¾ cup honey
¾ cup Heinz Distilled White
    Vinegar
¼ teaspoon mace
6 whole cloves
1 3-inch cinnamon stick, broken
    up

Pour boiling water over peaches; let stand until skins can be easily removed. Dip in cold water; peel. Remove pits and red fibers; cut into chunks. Place immediately in vinegar-water to prevent browning. In saucepan combine brown sugar and next 4 ingredients. Add cloves and cinnamon tied in cheesecloth bag. Drain peaches; add to syrup. Simmer 2 hours, stirring occasionally. Remove spice bag. Continue simmering while quickly packing one clean hot jar at a time. Fill to within ½ inch of top, making sure syrup covers fruit. Seal each jar at once. Process 5 minutes in boiling-water bath.

Makes 4 – 5 half-pints.

Reprinted by permission of H. J. Heinz

PEACH HONEY

1 large orange
12 large peaches, peeled

sugar

Put orange, including peel and peaches through food chopper. Measure the mixture and add equal amount of sugar. Cook until desired consistency, approximately 20 minutes. Pour into hot sterilized jars; seal.

Makes 5 pints.

Reprinted by permission of Beverly Levandowski, Hempstead, Texas

PEACH SYRUP

4 lbs. peaches

7 cups sugar

Wash, peel and pit peaches. Puree in blender. In 10-quart pot combine peaches and sugar; heat at medium heat to full boil. Reduce heat; boil gently 10 – 12 minutes. Strain through jelly bag or cheesecloth lined sieve for several hours. Reheat juice and pour into hot jars leaving ½-inch head space. Adjust lids and process in boiling water bath. (Pints — 10 minutes, Quarts — 15 minutes.)

Makes 3 – 4 pints.

Reprinted by permission of Barbara Sisk, Hempstead, Texas

PEACH SAUCE

6 pounds firm, ripe peaches
Juice of one orange
½ cup honey

1 small piece crystallized ginger
or ¼ teaspoon ground ginger

Prepare home canning jars and lids according to manufacturer's instructions. Peel peaches; remove pits. Place in a soaking solution to prevent darkening. Puree half of the peaches in a blender or food processor. Slice or chop remaining peaches. Combine peach puree and slices, orange juice, honey, and ginger in a large saucepot. Bring to a boil; reduce heat and simmer about 30 minutes, stirring occasionally. Carefully pack into hot jars, leaving ½-inch head space. Adjust caps. Process 20 minutes in boiling water bath canner. Yield: about six 8-ounce jars.

Reprinted by permission of Ball Corporation

PEACH SPREAD

1 cup powdered fruit pectin
3½ cups sugar
4 cups pureed peaches

4 teaspoons ascorbic acid
½ cup light corn syrup
2 tablespoons lemon juice

Mix the pectin and ½ cup sugar. Add the pureed peaches and mix for 7 minutes. Add remaining ingredients and mix 3 minutes longer. Pour into containers, fasten lids. Let stand at room temperature 24 hours. Store in refrigerator or freezer.

Makes 6 half-pints.

Reprinted by permission of Beverly Levandowski, Hempstead, Texas

MIXED FRUIT PICKLE

15 ripe tomatoes, peeled and
    chopped
3 medium onions, chopped fine
3 peaches, chopped
3 pears, chopped fine
3 apples, chopped fine

2 cups finely chopped celery
2 cups cider vinegar
1¼ teaspoons pickling salt
3 tablespoons Durkee Pickling
    Spice (tied in bag)
3 cups sugar

Combine all ingredients in a large kettle and bring to a boil over medium-high heat. Reduce heat and simmer, uncovered, 3 hours, or until thick. Pack into hot sterilized pint jars, leaving ½-inch head space. Adjust caps and process 5 minutes in boiling water bath. (Start counting processing time when water returns to a boil.) Remove jars and set upright, several inches apart, to cool.

Makes 7 pints.

Reprinted by permission of Durkee Famous Foods Kitchens

PICKLED PEACHES

4 lbs. peaches (small)
2 cups vinegar
4 cups sugar

5 two-inch pieces of stick
  cinnamon
1 tablespoon whole cloves

Dip peaches quickly into boiling water, then cold water, and slip off the skins. Make a syrup of the vinegar, sugar and spices (tied loosely in a bag). Boil 5 minutes. Place the peaches into the syrup, a few at a time, and boil them until they are tender and somewhat clear. Let stand overnight in syrup. In the morning, remove the spice bag. Remove peaches and boil syrup until thickened. Pack peaches in clean, hot, sterilized jars. Cover with hot syrup. Seal. Process in boiling water bath for 15 minutes.

Kaye Applewhite, Magnolia, Texas

PEACH NECTAR

2 lbs. peaches
5 cups water

1 cup sugar
2 tablespoons lemon juice

Peel, pit and slice peaches to yield approximately 6 cups. In large pot combine peaches and water. Cook until soft, 8-10 minutes. Press peaches through sieve. Measure about 7 cups of puree. Add sugar. Heat and stir for 5 minutes. Pour into hot jars leaving ½-inch head space. Adjust lids and process in boiling water bath. (Pints — 10 minutes, Quarts — 15 minutes.)

Makes 4 pints.

Reprinted by permission of Barbara Sisk, Hempstead, Texas

PEACH PIE FILLING

10 lbs. peaches
Antioxidant solution
3 cups sugar
2 tablespoons ground cinnamon

½ teaspoon ground mace
2 tablespoons grated lemon peel
¼ cup lemon juice
1¼ cups tapioca

For this recipe you will need 10 pint or 5 quart jars. Clean and keep hot. Prepare lids according to manufacturer's directions. Wash peaches. Immerse 4 – 5 peaches at a time into gently boiling water for 30 seconds. Plunge into cold water; slip off skins. Slice peaches; discard pits. Immerse peach slices into antioxidant solution; set aside. In small bowl, combine 2 cups sugar, cinnamon, mace, lemon peel; set aside. Remove peach slices from solution; rinse with water. Place rinsed peach slices into 10-quart pot. Add sugar mixture and lemon juice. Let stand for 15 minutes until juices begin to flow. Stirring frequently, bring to boil over medium-low heat. Continue boiling until mixture reaches 212 degrees F. (100 degrees C.) on candy thermometer. In small mixing bowl combine 1 cup sugar with 1 cup tapioca. If peaches are really juicy add remaining tapioca. Stir into peaches. Stirring constantly, heat until temperature is again 212 degrees. Ladle hot filling into one hot jar at a time, leaving ½-inch head space. Release trapped air. Wipe rim of jar with clean, damp rag. Attach lid. Place in boiling water bath. (Pints — 20 minutes, Quarts — 25 minutes.)

PEACH RELISH

8 cups sliced, peeled Texas
    peaches (16 medium
    peaches)
1 cup raisins
1½ cups packed light brown
    sugar

¾ cup cider vinegar
1 teaspoon cinnamon
½ teaspoon ground cloves
2 teaspoons mustard seed
½ cup coarsely chopped pecans

Combine ingredients in a kettle or Dutch oven. Bring to a boil and cook, uncovered, stirring frequently for 45 minutes or until thick. Add pecans and cook 2 minutes. Fill 6 hot sterilized ½-pint jars to within ½ inch of top and seal. Store, covered in refrigerator, and use within 2-3 weeks. Good with light meats and poultry.

Makes 6 ½-pint jars.

Reprinted by permission of Texas Department of Agriculture

MEXICAN PICKLED PEACH RELISH

3 pounds ripe tomatoes (about
    7 medium)
2 cups sliced celery
2 cups chopped onion
2 green peppers, seeded and
    chopped (1½ cups)

3 fresh peaches, sliced
1 cup white vinegar
1½ teaspoons salt
1½ teaspoons mixed pickling
    spice, tied in a cloth bag
1 cup sugar

Peel tomatoes. Chop and measure to get 1½ quarts tomato pulp. Put in large heavy pan (at least 8-quart size) with celery, onion, peppers, peaches, vinegar, salt, pickling spice and sugar. Bring to a boil; boil slowly, stirring often, until thickened, about 2 hours. Remove bag of spices and discard. Pour relish into hot sterilized pint jars, leaving ¼-inch head space. Adjust caps. Process 10 minutes in boiling water bath. Seal tightly. Cool and store.

Makes about 5 pints.

Note: Recipe may be doubled, but boiling time will need to be increased to thicken relish.

Main Dishes

PEACHY COOKING

Cooking with peaches is easy as pie,
There's more than that,
Just give it a try!

Try a peach kuchen, frost or conserve,
A melba, a torte, or tasty preserve.
And if a main dish is more to your wish,
Try peaches with lamb or chicken or fish.
The vegetable section is ready to please,
Sample golden carrots or tarragon peas.
There's blintzes, kabobs, flambes and bars,
With jams and jellies to fill mason jars.
Dumplings or quiches, twists, scones or puffs,
When cooking with peaches,
Pies just aren't enough!

Patsey McKnight, Houston, Texas

BEEF BRISKET AND SPICED PEACHES

1 fresh beef brisket, 3 to 5 pounds
Water
1 tablespoon salt
6 whole allspice
1 bay leaf
1 29-ounce can spiced peaches
1 tablespoon cornstarch
8 to 12 whole cloves

Cover beef brisket with water in a large frying pan or Dutch oven. Add salt, allspice and bay leaf; cover tightly and simmer 40 to 50 minutes per pound until meat is tender. Drain peaches; reserve liquid and stir into cornstarch to blend. Cook, stirring constantly, until thickened. Add spiced peaches to sauce and cook slowly 2 minutes. Place brisket on rack in open roasting pan and decorate with whole cloves. Brush with sauce from spiced peaches and bake in a moderate oven (350 degrees F.) 30 minutes, brushing with sauce once or twice during baking. Serve peaches in sauce with brisket.

Reprinted by permission of
Consumer Services Department, National Live Stock and Meat Board

BEEF TOP ROUND ROAST

4- to 6-pound beef top round
   roast
Bay Laurel Peaches (see next
   recipe)

Place roast, fat side up, on rack in open roasting pan. Insert meat thermometer so bulb is centered in the thickest part. Do not add water. Do not cover. Roast in a slow oven (325 degrees F.) to rare or medium. Brush with syrup from Bay Laurel Peaches during last 20 minutes of roasting. Remove from oven at 135 degrees F. for rare; 155 degrees F. for medium. Allow approximately 25 to 30 minutes per pound, depending on desired doneness. Allow roast to "set" in a warm place 15 to 20 minutes after removing from oven. Since roasts continue to cook during this time, they usually rise approximately 5 degrees F. in internal temperature, reaching 140 degrees F. for rare; 160 degrees F. for medium. Serve Bay Laurel Peaches with the roast.

Rotisserie Directions

Insert rotisserie rod lengthwise through center of roast. Balance roast and tighten spit forks to fasten meat securely so that it turns only with the rod. Insert roast meat thermometer at a slight angle, so the tip is in the center of the roast but not resting in fat or on rotisserie rod. Place on rotisserie and roast at moderate temperature to rare or medium.

Microwave Directions

Place 3½- to 4-pound roast, fat side down, on rack in microwave-safe dish. Do not add water. Cover with wax paper. Cook at 30 percent power (approximately 200 watts). Allow 18 to 22 minutes per pound. Cook roast for half the cooking time, rotating dish a half turn during this cooking period. Turn roast fat side up, rotate dish a half turn and continue cooking, covered with wax paper, for remainder of cooking time or until meat thermometer registers 5 to 10 degrees below doneness desired, rotating a half turn during this time. Cover roast with foil tent and allow to "set" at room temperature 15 to 20 minutes after removal from oven. Since roasts continue to cook during this time, they usually rise approximately 5 degrees F. in internal temperature, reaching 140 degrees F. for rare; 160 degrees F. for medium.

Bay Laurel Peaches

1 29-ounce can cling peach halves	2 tablespoons butter
1 bay leaf	1 teaspoon sugar
¼ cup tarragon vinegar	½ teaspoon paprika
	½ teaspoon onion salt

Place peaches (including syrup) and bay leaf in a saucepan; bring to a boil. Cool to lukewarm. Meanwhile, combine vinegar, butter, sugar, paprika and onion salt. Remove peaches from syrup and place cut side up in 8 × 8-inch baking dish. Add syrup to vinegar mixture, stirring to combine; spoon over peach halves. Bake in slow oven (325 degrees F.) 12 to 15 minutes or until heated through. Baste and serve warm.

Microwave Directions

Place peaches (including syrup) and bay leaf in 8 × 8-inch glass baking dish. Cook on HIGH for 3 minutes. Stir and cool to lukewarm. Combine remaining ingredients in glass measuring cup. Cook on HIGH 50 seconds; stir in peach syrup. Spoon over peach halves and cook at HIGH 90 seconds to heat through. Baste.

Reprinted by permission of
Test Kitchens and Editorial Service, National Live Stock and Meat Board

BEEF SHORT RIBS WITH SPICED PEACHES

3 pounds beef short ribs	⅛ teaspoon pepper
2 cups water	¼ cup sugar
2 tablespoons salt	1 stick cinnamon
2 tablespoons lemon juice	1 11-oz. package dried peaches

Brown short ribs in large skillet. Drain away fat. Place meat in slow cooker. Add remaining ingredients, cover and cook on low for 8 hours. Serve with peaches and accumulated juices. 6 servings.

BEEF STEW WITH PEACHES AND WHITE WINE

2½ lbs. lean beef, cut into 1-inch cubes
2 tablespoons vegetable oil
2 cloves garlic
2 carrots, cut into 1-inch cubes
2 onions, cut into wedges
1 teaspoon salt

¾ cup dry white wine
¾ cup apple cider
2 peaches — peeled, pitted and cut into 1-inch cubes
¼ cup all-purpose flour into ¼ cup water, mixed to a paste

In large skillet brown meat. Place meat, garlic, carrots, onions, salt and wine in slow cooker. Pour cider into skillet and stir to pick up browned bits. Add cider to slow cooker. Cover and cook on low temperature about 8 hours. Add peaches the last 3 hours of cooking. Pour accumulated juices into saucepan. Add flour paste; heat; stirring constantly, until mixture thickens. Return mixture to meat and vegetables and serve at once. 6 servings.

Beverly Levandowski, Hempstead, Texas

PEACH-GLAZED CORNED BEEF

3- to 3½-lb. corned beef brisket, well trimmed
1 tablespoon whole mixed pickling spice
1 medium onion, finely chopped (about ½ cup)

½ cup peach preserves
1 tablespoon lemon juice or vinegar
¼ teaspoon dry mustard or ground ginger
⅛ teaspoon salt

Place corned beef brisket in Dutch oven; cover with water. Add pickling spices. Heat to boiling; reduce heat. Cover and simmer until tender, 2¼ – 3½ hours. Cool beef in broth at room temperature 1 hour. Place beef in shallow roasting pan. Mix remaining ingredients and spread over beef. Roast uncovered in 325-degree oven until hot and glazed, about 30 minutes. Cut beef across grain into thin slices.

Adapted by Barbara Sisk from Apricot-Glazed Corned Beef. Reprinted from Betty Crocker's Recipe Card Library, by permission of General Mills

LIVER AND ONIONS WITH PEACHES

3 tablespoons margarine
2 bacon strips, chopped
1 medium onion, thinly sliced
¾ pound calves' liver (¼-inch slices, seasoned and floured)

1 large peach, peeled, pitted and thinly sliced
½ cup peach nectar, hot
2 teaspoons cornstarch blended with 1 tablespoon nectar

Melt margarine in 12-inch skillet. Fry bacon over medium to high heat for a few seconds, stirring. Add onions and fry 30 seconds more, stirring briskly. Add liver and fry 2 minutes, turning pieces to cook evenly. Add peach and fry 1 minute, tossing gently. Add nectar and fry 1 minute. Add cornstarch and peach nectar; stir in quickly but gently to blend and thicken. Serve hot.

Reprinted by permission of Beverly Levandowski, Hempstead, Texas

CHINESE STEAMED FISH

2 pounds firm white fish fillets
Pepper
2 teaspoons cornstarch
2 teaspoons soy sauce
2 teaspoons vegetable oil
2 teaspoons sherry

1 tablespoon finely chopped
  green onion
1 thin slice ginger root, finely
  minced (¼ teaspoon)
1 large clove garlic, minced
1 fresh California peach, pitted
  and sliced (1 cup)

Cut fish lengthwise into 2-inch wide strips. Sprinkle with pepper as desired. Mix fish with cornstarch, soy sauce, oil and sherry in a bowl. Arrange fish strips in spirals on a shallow dish and sprinkle with green onion, minced ginger, garlic and sliced peaches. For steaming, place low rack or trivet in bottom of 10- to 12-inch skillet. Pour hot water into bottom of pan, under rack, and bring to a boil. Place plate of fish on rack. Cover skillet. Steam for 10 to 15 minutes or until fish is cooked. Transfer fish spirals and peaches to serving dish using wide spatula and spoon sauce over as desired. 4 servings.

Reprinted by permission of *The Houston Post*

PEACH FISH

3 – 4 tablespoons margarine
½ teaspoon parsley
¼ teaspoon basil
¼ teaspoon anise seed, crushed

1½ cups sliced peaches
1 lb. thin fish fillets, seasoned
1 teaspoon lemon juice

Melt margarine in large skillet. Add spices and peaches and toss. Add fish and fry 1 minute, covered. Spoon peaches and pan juices over top. Turn fish and sprinkle with lemon juice. Fry 2 minutes more, spoon peaches and pan juices over fish. Serve hot.

Reprinted by permission of Beverly Levandowski, Hempstead, Texas

FRIED SHARK WITH PEACHES

1¼ pounds shark fillets (1-inch thick), cut in 4 serving-size pieces
Salt and pepper
Juice of 1 Sunkist lemon
⅓ cup fine dry bread crumbs (seasoned or plain)
2 tablespoons butter or margarine
2 tablespoons salad oil
1 teaspoon cornstarch
1 8¾-oz. can sliced peaches in heavy syrup, undrained
Grated peel of ½ Sunkist lemon
Whole salted cashew nuts
Lemon wedges
Parsley

Sprinkle fish with salt, pepper and juice of ½ lemon; let stand 5 to 10 minutes. Coat fish with bread crumbs. In large skillet, heat butter and oil. Sauté fish (5 to 6 minutes on each side) until lightly browned and fish flakes easily with fork. Remove fish to serving dish; keep warm. Combine cornstarch with remaining juice of ½ lemon; gradually blend into pan drippings. Stir in peach syrup. Add peaches and lemon peel. Bring to boil, stirring constantly until thickened; spoon over fish. Sprinkle with cashews. Garnish with lemon wedges and parsley. Makes 4 servings.

NOTE: If shark fillets are unavailable, substitute any one of the following 1-inch thick fish steaks: salmon, halibut or swordfish.

Reprinted by permission of Sunkist Growers, Inc.

SHRIMP MOROCCAN

1 29-oz. can cling peach halves
¼ cup butter
½ pound fresh mushrooms, sliced
1 dozen large shrimp, shelled
1 clove garlic, crushed
⅓ cup medium dry sherry
Hot cooked rice
Lemon slices for garnish
Parsley for garnish

Drain peaches, reserving ½ cup syrup. Sauté mushrooms in butter in a large skillet. Push mushrooms to one side or remove from pan; add shrimp and garlic. Cook until shrimp turn pink. Add peach halves, sherry and ½ cup peach syrup. Heat through. Serve immediately with rice. Garnish with lemon slices and parsley. Makes 4 servings.

NOTE: Prepare rice in advance, toss with a little chopped parsley if desired, and keep warm until ready to serve.

Reprinted by permission of *The Houston Post*

CORAL AND JADE STIR-FRY

½ pound medium-size shrimp, peeled and deveined
2 tablespoons cornstarch, divided
3 tablespoons Kikkoman naturally brewed soy sauce, divided
½ teaspoon sugar
1 clove garlic, minced
1 16-oz. can California cling peach slices in juice or extra light syrup
1 teaspoon distilled white vinegar
4 ounces fresh* snow peas
2 tablespoons vegetable oil, divided
1 onion, chunked
1 tablespoon slivered fresh ginger root

Rinse shrimp and pat dry with paper towels. Combine 1 tablespoon each cornstarch and soy sauce with sugar and garlic; stir in shrimp. Let stand 15 minutes. Meanwhile, drain peaches, reserving ¼ cup juice. Add enough water to reserved juice to measure 1 cup; stir in remaining cornstarch, soy sauce and vinegar and set aside. Cut peaches crosswise in half. Remove tips and strings from snow peas. Heat 1 tablespoon oil in wok or large skillet over high heat. Add shrimp and stir-fry 1 minute; remove. Heat remaining oil in same wok. Add onion, snow peas and ginger; stir-fry 4 minutes. Stir in shrimp and soy sauce mixture; cook and stir until sauce boils and thickens. Stir in peaches and heat through. Serve immediately. Makes 4 to 6 servings.

*Substitute 1 6-oz. package pea pods, thawed and drained. Stir-fry onion and ginger 3 minutes. Add pea pods to wok with soy sauce mixture.

Reprinted by permission of Kikkoman International, Inc.

PEACH JAMBALAYA

1 green pepper, diced
1 onion, sliced
2 tomatoes, chopped
2 cloves garlic, minced
1 teaspoon thyme
¼ pound ham, diced
¾ pound spicy or smoked sausage, sliced
2 tablespoons oil
1 tablespoon tomato paste
1 cup chicken broth
8 fresh California peaches, sliced
¼ pound shrimp, shelled, deveined
Salt and pepper to taste
3 cups cooked rice

Sauté green pepper, onion, tomatoes, garlic, thyme, ham and sausage in oil about 5 minutes. Add tomato paste and chicken broth; simmer 5 minutes. Add peaches and shrimp; cover and simmer 5 minutes until shrimp turns pink. Salt and pepper to taste. Serve over hot rice. 4 servings.

Reprinted by permission of *The Houston Post*

SHRIMP AND PEACH STIR-FRY

4 tablespoons peanut or
vegetable oil
1 pound large shrimp, shelled,
deveined
½ pound broccoli, stems
diagonally sliced, flowerettes
cut into bite-size pieces

1 8-oz. can water chestnuts,
drained, sliced
2 fresh peaches, sliced
3 green onions, diagonally sliced
Glossy Sauce (recipe follows)

Heat 2 tablespoons oil in wok or large skillet. Add shrimp and stir-fry until tender, about 4 to 5 minutes. Remove from wok; set aside. Add 2 tablespoons oil and stir-fry broccoli until tender-crisp, about 4 to 5 minutes. Add shrimp, water chestnuts, peaches and onions to wok and heat through. Stir in Glossy Sauce and cook just until thick and glossy. Makes 4 servings.

Glossy Sauce

Blend 1½ tablespoons cornstarch with ¾ cup chicken broth, ⅓ cup sherry, 2 teaspoons soy sauce, ½ teaspoon fresh ginger root, minced, and 1 teaspoon sugar.

LAMB PATTIES WITH LEMON BUTTER

2 lbs. ground lean lamb
2 teaspoons salt
½ teaspoon pepper
12 slices bacon

Lemon Butter (recipe follows)
Chopped parsley
6 canned peach halves
Honey

Combine lamb, salt and pepper. Shape into 12 patties, 1-inch thick. Wrap each with a slice of bacon. Arrange on broiler rack and broil 3–4 inches from broiler for 8 minutes on each side. Place lamb patties on a warm platter; spread with lemon butter. Sprinkle with chopped parsley. Drain peach halves; brush with honey and broil for 10 minutes. Garnish platter with broiled peaches. 6 servings.

Lemon Butter

Blend 6 tablespoons melted butter with 3 tablespoons lemon juice and a dash of garlic salt.

LAMB SHOULDER WITH PEACH STUFFING

1 (3 – 4 lb.) square cut shoulder
   of lamb
2 tablespoons chopped onion
½ cup chopped celery
2 tablespoons butter or
   margarine
1 teaspoon salt
¼ teaspoon ground ginger
2 tablespoons brown sugar
2 cups peaches; peeled, pitted
   and chopped
1 cup bread crumbs
¼ cup milk

Have bones removed from roast to form a pocket. Sauté onion and celery in butter. Add remaining ingredients; toss. Fill pocket in roast with stuffing, skewer edges together. Place fat side up, on rack in shallow pan. Roast uncovered at 325 degrees for 2½ hours. Serves 6 – 8.

Beverly Levandowski, Hempstead, Texas

CHINESE SPICY PORK WITH PEACHES

1 pound boneless pork loin,
   trimmed
3 tablespoons soy sauce
1½ teaspoons sugar
1 tablespoon cornstarch
1 tablespoon minced garlic
1 tablespoon minced fresh ginger
   root
1 tablespoon green onion,
   minced
¼ to ½ teaspoon crushed red
   pepper
¼ cup peanut oil
Sauce (recipe follows)
2 large fresh peaches, scrubbed
   and sliced (2 cups)

Slice pork against the grain into thin (⅛-inch) slices. Blend soy sauce, sugar and cornstarch until smooth. Toss well with pork to coat. Marinate at least 1 hour. Combine garlic, ginger, green onion and crushed red pepper. Heat oil in wok or large skillet until very hot. Add garlic mixture and stir-fry 5 seconds before adding pork slices. Continue stir-frying 2 to 3 minutes or until pork is just cooked, adding more oil if necessary. Add Sauce and peaches and bring mixture to a boil. Toss briefly and transfer to a heated serving dish. Garnish with extra chopped green onion. Makes 4 servings.

Sauce

Combine 2 teaspoons soy sauce, 2 teaspoons sugar, 2 tablespoons dry sherry, 1 tablespoon hoisin sauce and 1 teaspoon roasted sesame oil until smooth.

BAKED PORK AND PEACH BUNS

¼ pound smoked ham, diced
1 small fresh California peach,
   diced (about ¾ cup)
2 tablespoons minced green
   onion
2 tablespoons catsup
1 tablespoon brown sugar

1 tablespoon soy sauce
2 teaspoons cornstarch
¼ cup water
1 small clove garlic, minced
¼ teaspoon ground ginger
2 10-oz. packages refrigerator
   biscuits

Combine ham, peach, green onion, catsup, brown sugar, soy sauce, cornstarch, water, garlic and ginger in saucepan. Cook, stirring constantly, until mixture comes to a boil and is thickened. Roll refrigerator biscuits out on lightly floured surface into 4½-inch rounds. Place about 1 tablespoon filling in center of each round. Pull edges of dough up around filling, enclosing it inside. Pinch to seal. Place buns with smooth, round side up about 2 inches apart on baking sheet. Bake in 400-degree oven for 10 minutes or until golden brown. Makes 20 buns.

Recipe adapted from Baked Pork and Nectarine Buns.
Reprinted by permission of California Tree Fruit Agreement

MEATLOAF SURPRISE

1 lb. ground ham
½ lb. ground pork
¼ cup crushed saltine crackers
1 egg
½ cup milk
½ teaspoon salt

½ teaspoon thyme
¼ teaspoon pepper
1 cup finely chopped onion
1 16-oz can peach slices, reserve
   syrup
½ cup chopped fresh parsley

In large mixing bowl, blend all ingredients except onion, peaches and parsley. Moisten a piece of waxed paper, 18 inches long. Pat meat mixture to make a rectangle 9 by 12 inches. Spread onions evenly over top of meat. Coarsely chop the drained peaches. Sprinkle over onions. Sprinkle parsley over all. Roll as for a jelly roll starting with a 9-inch side, making a compact roll. Simply lift up the waxed paper to start meat rolling. Place meat roll in lightly greased 9 by 5 inch bread pan. Bake at 350 degrees F. for 50 minutes. Meanwhile boil juice down from canned peaches to measure ¼ cup. Brush meatloaf halfway through baking with this juice. Allow to stand 10 minutes before serving. Makes 4 – 6 servings.

BEST HAM LOAF

1½ pounds ground ham
½ pound ground fresh pork
2 eggs, slightly beaten
½ cup milk
1 cup soft bread crumbs

1 teaspoon dry mustard
2 tablespoons chopped onion
⅛ teaspoon pepper
1 1-lb. can peach halves or
   1 8½-oz. pineapple tidbits

Preheat oven to 350 degrees F. Combine all ingredients; mix well. Press lightly into greased loaf pan, 9 × 5 × 3 inches, and bake for 1 hour. Slice for serving. Makes one 2-pound loaf.

Upside-down loaf: Sprinkle ½ cup brown sugar in bottom of greased loaf pan. Drain one 8½-oz. can pineapple tidbits or a 1-pound can peach halves; arrange in bottom of loaf pan, then top with ham loaf mixture.

Reprinted by permission of Oscar Mayer

EASTER BAKED SMOKED HAM

5- to 7-pound smoked half ham   Syrup from Spicy Peaches (see
                                     next recipe)

Place ham, fat side up, on rack in an open roasting pan. Insert roast meat thermometer so the bulb is centered in the thickest part. Be careful that bulb does not rest in fat or on bone. Do not add water. Do not cover. Roast in a slow oven, 325 degrees F., until the meat thermometer registers 130 to 140 degrees F. for a "fully cooked half ham" (18 – 22 minutes per pound); 160 degrees F. for a "cook-before-eating" half ham (22 to 25 minutes per pound). Brush ham with syrup from Spicy Peaches for last 20 minutes of baking time.

Spicy Peaches

1 29-oz. can cling peach slices
1 cup apple jelly
1 tablespoon lemon juice

1 teaspoon grated lemon rind
½ teaspoon ground allspice
¼ teaspoon mint extract

Drain peaches, saving syrup. Combine syrup with apple jelly, lemon juice, lemon rind, allspice and mint extract. Bring to boil. Reduce heat and continue cooking for 20 minutes or until mixture is reduced to 1½ cups. Add peaches; simmer 10 minutes. Remove from heat and when cool refrigerate several hours or overnight. Serve peaches hot or cold. Yield: 3½ cups sauce.

**Recipe reprinted by permission of
Test Kitchens and Editorial Services, National Live Stock and Meat Board**

FRUIT-STUFFED HAM

6 to 8 lb. (half) fully cooked, bone-in ham
1 8¼-oz. can crushed pineapple, drained
½ cup chopped dried peaches
¼ cup raisins
¼ cup chopped toasted almonds
1 10- or 12-oz. jar peach preserves
1 tablespoon grated lemon rind
1 tablespoon lemon juice
2 teaspoons prepared mustard

Remove bone from ham by cutting around bone from the back and front; pull bone out from the back side of the ham. Combine pineapple, peaches, raisins and almonds. Stuff into opening in ham. Place ham on rack in shallow roasting pan. Insert meat thermometer, placing tip in thickest part of meat. Bake at 325 degrees F. for 1 to 1½ hours or until internal temperature reaches about 120 degrees F. Remove rind; score fat into diamond pattern. Stud with cloves. Combine preserves, rind, juice and mustard, mixing until well blended. Brush scored surface of ham with preserve mixture. Continue to bake, brushing every 10 to 15 minutes with preserve mixture, until internal temperature reaches 140 degrees F. Makes 8 to 10 servings.

Reprinted by permission of M&M/Mars. A division of Mars, Inc.

HARVEST HAM BALLS

1 egg, beaten
½ cup soft bread crumbs
½ cup milk
1 tablespoon brown sugar
⅛ teaspoon ground cloves
1 lb. ground cooked ham
8 canned peach halves, drained
Green celery tops or parsley

Combine egg, crumbs, milk, sugar, cloves and ham; shape into 8 balls. Place peach halves, hollow sides up, in greased shallow baking dish. Nest a ham ball in each peach half. Bake in moderate oven (350°) 25 minutes. Garnish with celery. Makes 8 servings.

Beverly Levandowski, Hempstead, Texas

GLAZED HAM WITH PEACHES

2 slices fully cooked, center, smoked ham, 1-inch thick (about 3½ pounds)
½ cup packed brown sugar
¾ teaspoon dry mustard
¼ teaspoon ground allspice
1 16-oz. can peach halves, drained (reserve syrup)
3 tablespoons orange-flavored liqueur
2 tablespoons packed brown sugar
2 tablespoons butter or margarine
Lemon leaves or parsley

Cut ham slices ¼-inch deep in diamond pattern. Place in ungreased jelly roll pan, 15½ × 10¼ × 1 inch. Mix ½ cup brown sugar, the mustard and allspice. Add enough syrup (about 1 tablespoon) to make paste; spread over ham. Bake uncovered for 30 minutes at 325 degrees.

About 10 minutes before serving, cut each peach half in two. Heat peaches in liqueur, 2 tablespoons brown sugar and the butter over medium heat, stirring constantly, until sugar is dissolved and peaches are coated. Arrange the peaches around the ham; garnish with lemon leaves. Serve peach sauce with ham. 8 – 10 servings.

Reprinted from Betty Crocker's Recipe Card Library, by permission of General Mills

HONEY-GLAZED HAM — SPICY STUFFED PEACHES

7- to 10-pound boneless "fully-cooked" smoked ham

Honey Glaze — Spicy Stuffed Peaches*
1 tablespoon chopped walnuts

Place ham on rack in an open roasting pan. Insert roast meat thermometer so the bulb is centered in the thickest part. Do not add water. Do not cover. Roast in a slow oven (325 degrees F.) until meat thermometer registers 130 to 140 degrees F. (Allow 15 to 18 minutes per pound.) Meanwhile prepare Honey Glaze and Spicy Stuffed Peaches. Approximately 30 minutes before ham is done, spread glaze over ham and sprinkle with walnuts. Place Spicy Stuffed Peaches around ham in roasting pan or in separate baking dish. Return ham and peaches to oven and continue baking.

*Honey Glaze — Spicy Stuffed Peaches

1 29-oz. can cling peach halves
1 8-oz. can crushed pineapple in unsweetened juice
1 tablespoon cornstarch
⅛ teaspoon cinnamon

⅛ teaspoon nutmeg
Dash ground cloves
2 tablespoons honey
3 tablespoons chopped walnuts
2 tablespoons raisins

For honey glaze, drain peaches and pineapple; reserve ½ cup of syrup and ½ cup juice. Combine cornstarch, cinnamon, nutmeg and cloves in small saucepan. Gradually add reserved peach syrup and pineapple juice to blend; stir in honey. Bring to boil over medium heat and cook, stirring constantly, until thickened and clear. For Spicy Stuffed Peaches, combine pineapple, walnuts and raisins: stir in ⅓ cup honey glaze. Place an equal amount of fruit mixture in each peach half. Bake as directed.

Reprinted by permission of
Consumer Services Department, National Live Stock and Meat Board

PEACH GLAZED JUBILEE HAM (JUBILEE HAM & CRISPY PEACHES)

Oscar Mayer Jubilee Ham
1 1-lb. can peach halves
2 tablespoons brown sugar

1 teaspoon lemon juice
¼ teaspoon ground cloves
Grapenuts

Bake ham according to label directions. Meanwhile, drain peaches, reserving ½ cup liquid. Combine liquid, brown sugar, lemon juice and cloves in saucepan. Heat just to boiling, reduce heat and cook slowly 5 minutes. Thirty minutes before end of baking time, score ham and spoon glaze over top. Continue baking until ham reaches serving temperature (130 degrees on meat thermometer). For peach garnish, roll peach halves in Grapenuts. Fill centers with a spoonful of Spicy Cherry Sauce.

Spicy Cherry Sauce:

1 1 lb.-5 oz. can cherry pie filling
⅛ teaspoon cinnamon

⅛ teaspoon ground cloves

Combine all ingredients in saucepan. Cook over medium heat, stirring occasionally, 5 minutes, or until heated through. Serve warm. Makes 2½ cups.

Reprinted by permission of Oscar Mayer

PEACHY HAM PIE

1 1-lb. can sliced peaches,
    drained
2 cups diced, cooked ham
1 cup stuffing mix
1 cup finely chopped celery

2 eggs, slightly beaten
¼ cup French's America's
    Favorite Yellow Mustard
1 1¼-oz. envelope French's
    Cheese Sauce Mix

Set aside 8 to 10 peach slices; chop remaining slices. In a large bowl combine chopped peaches with ham, stuffing mix, celery, eggs and mustard. Prepare cheese sauce mix according to package directions. Stir into ham mixture, pour into well-greased 8-inch pie pan. Bake at 350 degrees for 25 minutes. Arrange sliced peaches on top of pie; bake 5 minutes longer. 4 to 6 servings.

Reprinted by permission of FRENCH'S, The R.T. French Company

UNCLE BEN'S WILD NEW BRANDIED HAM AND PEACH STUFFING

1 6-oz. package Uncle Ben's long
    grain and wild rice
1½ cups chopped celery
½ cup chopped celery leaves
1½ cups diced cooked ham
1 cup quartered dried peaches

1 cup slivered almonds
¼ lb. (1 stick) butter or
    margarine
⅔ cup brandy
1 8-oz. package herb stuffing mix
1 cup hot water

Cook Uncle Ben's long grain and wild rice as directed on package. Meanwhile, sauté celery, celery leaves, ham, peaches and almonds in butter 2 minutes. Heat brandy; flame and pour over celery-ham mixture; stir gently until flame dies. Add herb stuffing mix and hot water; mix well. Add hot cooked rice; mix.

Reprinted by permission of Uncle Ben's Inc., Houston, Texas

UPSIDE DOWN LOAVES

1 pound Oscar Mayer Ham,
    ground (3 cups)
½ cup bread crumbs
2 eggs, slightly beaten

1 tablespoon onion
⅛ teaspoon allspice
1 1 lb.-13 oz. can peach halves
Brown sugar

Preheat oven to 350 degrees F. Combine ham, bread crumbs, eggs and onion. Grease a 6-cup muffin pan, or 6 custard cups. Place a peach half, cut side up, in each cup; sprinkle with brown sugar. Press ham mixture into cups. Bake 45 minutes.

Recipe courtesy of Oscar Mayer

PEACH GLAZED PORK RIBS

4 to 4½ lbs. pork ribs, cut into
    serving pieces
1 to 1½ cups picante sauce

1 ½ cups peach preserves
¼ cup soy sauce

Place ribs in shallow roasting pan with meaty side up. Bake uncovered in 350-degree oven 45 minutes. Heat picante sauce, preserves and soy sauce to boiling, stirring constantly. Brush pork with about ½ cup of the sauce; bake until tender, 45–60 minutes. Baste ribs several times while baking.

PEACH TERIYAKI PORK

Serve up an elegant entree!

Place a loin of boneless pork on a rack in a shallow pan. Rub with salt and pepper. Sprinkle on rosemary. Roast at 350 degrees for 2–2½ hours. Mix ½ cup each of ketchup and soy sauce, ¼ cup honey, 1 crushed garlic clove. Use as basting last 45 minutes. Transfer to a heated platter. Surround meat with peach slices and/or halves.

PORK WITH PEACHES

2½ lb. lean pork, cut into 1-inch cubes
2 tablespoons vegetable oil
1 tablespoon sugar
1½ teaspoons salt
2 teaspoons paprika

1½ cups apple cider
4 peaches peeled, pitted and cut in 1-inch cubes
¼ cup all-purpose flour in ¼ cup water, mixed to make paste

Brown pork in hot oil in large skillet. Drain away fat. Place meat in slow cooker with sugar, salt and paprika. Add cider to skillet and stir to pick up browned bits. Add to slow cooker. Cover and cook 8 hours. Add peaches the last 3 hours of cooking. Pour off juices and thicken in a saucepan with flour paste. Return to slow cooker. Serve immediately. 6 servings.

Beverly Levandowski, Hempstead, Texas

PORK WITH PEACHES

3 tablespoons margarine
½ teaspoon cinnamon
¼ teaspoon nutmeg
⅛ teaspoon ground cloves
1 lb. lean pork, ⅛" sliced and seasoned
1 peach, peeled, pitted and sliced

¼ cup dry white wine, hot
¼ cup peach nectar, hot
2 tablespoons honey
2 tablespoons sour cream
2 tablespoons cornstarch blended with 1 tablespoon nectar

Melt margarine in large skillet. Put in spices and pork; fry for 2½ minutes, stirring briskly. Add peaches, fry 1 minute, stirring gently. Add wine and nectar, fry 1 minute more; stirring gently. Add honey and sour cream; blend. Add cornstarch and nectar mixture. Stir gently; until thickened.

Beverly Levandowski, Hempstead, Texas

CORN-STUFFED PORK CHOPS WITH PICKLED PEACHES

4 center-cut loin or rib pork chops, each 1-inch thick
5 tablespoons butter
1 medium onion, chopped
¼ cup chopped celery
1 cup soft bread crumbs
¾ cup canned whole kernel corn, drained

½ teaspoon dried sage leaves
¼ teaspoon salt
¼ teaspoon freshly ground pepper
2 medium onions, thinly sliced
8 cloves
1 29-oz. jar whole yellow cling spiced peaches with liquid, cut in half, pitted

Trim fat from meat; cut a pocket in the middle of each chop, starting from the outer edge and going toward the bone. Sauté meat in 3 tablespoons of the butter in 6-quart pressure cooker until brown on both sides; remove meat. Add remaining butter; sauté chopped onion and celery. Stir in bread crumbs, corn, sage, salt and pepper. Spoon stuffing into pockets of meat, packing tightly. Secure openings with wooden picks.

Place rack in pressure cooker; arrange meat on rack; place onion slices over meat. Place a clove in each peach half; arrange peaches around meat. Pour ½ cup of the peach liquid over meat. Secure lid according to manufacturer's instructions. Place cooker on high heat; bring up pressure to 15 pounds. Reduce heat to maintain pressure; cook 15 minutes. Reduce pressure immediately. Arrange meat and peaches on platter; serve with pan juices.

PEACHY GLAZED PORK KABOBS

¼ cup French's America's Favorite Yellow Mustard
¼ cup orange marmalade
2 tablespoons soy sauce
¼ teaspoon French's Poultry Seasoning

1½ to 2 pounds pork shoulder chops
3 green peppers
1 l-lb. can peach halves, drained

Stir together mustard, marmalade, soy sauce, and poultry seasoning. Cut pork and peppers into l-inch squares. Cut each peach half in 2 pieces. Alternate pork, peppers, and peaches on 4 or 5 skewers, brush with mustard mixture. Grill over hot coals 20 to 30 minutes, or until pork is thoroughly cooked. Turn occasionally and brush with additional mustard mixture. 4 or 5 servings.

Reprinted by permission of FRENCH'S, The R.T. French Company

PEACHY PORK CHOPS

4 pork loin chops, ½-inch thick
1 teaspoon salt
4 canned peach halves, drained (reserve 2 tablespoons syrup)

1 tablespoon soy sauce
¼ cup whole berry cranberry sauce
1 tablespoon packed brown sugar

Heat oven to 375 degrees. Place pork loin chops in ungreased baking dish, ll¾x7½x1¾ inches; sprinkle both sides with salt. Mix reserved syrup and soy sauce; brush over pork chops. Cover and bake 40 minutes. Mix cranberry sauce and brown sugar. Remove pork chops from oven; turn. Top each pork chop with peach half and 1 tablespoon cranberry mixture. Bake uncovered, basting once, until chops are tender, 15 to 20 minutes. 4 servings.

Reprinted from Betty Crocker's Recipe Card Library, by permission of General Mills

PEACHY PORK CHOPS

6 lean pork chops (about 2 pounds)
½ teaspoon freshly ground pepper
1 1-lb. can juice-packed peach halves

3 packets Sweet 'N Low
2 teaspoons lemon juice
¼ teaspoon cinnamon
¼ teaspoon ginger
3 whole cloves
2 teaspoons all-purpose flour

Carefully trim away any visible fat from chops. Season chops with pepper and brown in large non-stick skillet. Drain off fat. Drain peaches, reserving ½ cup juice. Combine juice with Sweet 'N Low, lemon juice, and spices. Pour over pork; cover tightly. Simmer gently over very low heat, about 45 minutes, or until pork is well cooked, turning chops once. Remove chops to serving platter and keep warm. Add peaches to liquid in skillet. Cover and heat through, about 5 minutes. Place one peach half on each chop. Mix flour with remaining juice and stir into pan juices. Heat and stir until sauce thickens, about 5 minutes. Remove cloves. Pour sauce over chops.

Nutritional information per serving (1 pork chop) — Calories: 180. Protein: 18 gm. Carbohydrate: 7 gm. Fat: 9 gm. Sodium: 400 mg.

Reprinted by permission of Cumberland Packing Corporation

PEACHYQUE PORK CHOPS

10 to 12 unpeeled fresh Texas peaches
2 cups pureed pulp from 4 to 5 fresh, unpeeled Texas peaches (of the above)
4 tablespoons lemon juice
¼ cup soy sauce

⅓ cup honey
1 large clove garlic, minced
⅛ teaspoon ginger
⅛ teaspoon pepper
12 pork chops (about 1-inch thick)
1 tablespoon lemon rind, grated

Cut peaches in half and remove pits from peaches. Crush or puree in blender to make 2 cups pulp. Blend 1 cup of pulp with 1 tablespoon lemon juice. Cover and refrigerate for sauce. Mix second cup pulp with remaining lemon juice, soy sauce, honey, garlic, ginger and pepper. Pour over pork chops. Let stand several hours, turning several times. Drain, save marinade. Place pork chops on grill; cook for about 15 to 25 minutes, turning for a more even cooking. The last 10 minutes, baste often with marinade. At the same time when placing meat on the grill, cut rest of peaches in half, remove pits. Lay halves on double thickness of foil. Sprinkle with lemon rind. Brush with marinade. Place on grill about 20 to 25 minutes or until pork chops are done. Serve as garnish with chops. Add reserved 1 cup peach-lemon juice mixture to remaining marinade. Heat and serve with meat. Serves 12.

Reprinted by permission of Texas Department of Agriculture

PORK CHOPS IMPERIAL

3 to 4 pork chops (1 to 1½ pounds)
2 tablespoons vegetable oil
1 8-oz. can sliced peaches (drain; reserve syrup)
1 cup chicken broth
1 teaspoon salt
½ teaspoon curry powder
½ teaspoon seasoned pepper
⅛ teaspoon garlic powder
1 tablespoon cornstarch
1 tablespoon snipped parsley
1½ cups hot cooked rice

In a skillet brown pork chops in oil on both sides. Drain off all fat. Add peach syrup, broth, and seasonings to skillet. Stir to loosen brown particles. Cover and simmer 30 minutes or until chops are tender. Dissolve cornstarch in 1 tablespoon water; stir into pan juices. Add peaches; cook, stirring, until mixture thickens. Sprinkle with parsley. Serve over beds of fluffy rice. Makes 3 servings.

Reprinted by permission of Rice Council for Market Development Home Economics Department

PORK EXTRAORDINAIRE

6 pork top loin chops (boneless)*
¼ cup flour
1 teaspoon salt
¼ teaspoon ground black pepper
2 tablespoons butter or margarine
1 tablespoon vegetable oil
¼ cup firmly packed brown sugar
1 teaspoon ground cinnamon
1 16-oz. can sliced peaches, drained
⅓ cup slivered almonds, toasted
¼ cup brandy
⅓ cup half-and-half (cream and milk)
3 cups hot cooked rice

Dredge pork in flour seasoned with salt and pepper. Heat butter and oil in large skillet. Add chops; brown over high heat 3 to 4 minutes per side. Discard fat. Reduce heat. Sprinkle pork with sugar and cinnamon. Add 2 tablespoons water to skillet. Cover and cook over medium-low heat 25 minutes, or until pork is tender. Add peaches and almonds. Warm brandy. Ignite and pour over pork. Spoon flaming pan juices over chops until flame subsides. Add half-and-half; simmer a few minutes to thicken sauce. Serve over beds of fluffy rice. Makes 6 servings.

*Or use pork sirloin cutlets.

Reprinted by permission of Rice Council for Market Development Home Economics Department

SUPER STUFFED PORK CHOPS

6 pork rib chops, cut 1½ inches
thick
1 small onion, chopped
3 tablespoons butter or
margarine
1 3-oz. package cream cheese
1 2¼-oz. can sliced ripe olives,
chopped

2 teaspoons lemon juice
½ teaspoon salt
⅛ teaspoon pepper
2 cups toasted ¼-inch bread
cubes
Salt and pepper
Country Curried Peaches*

Make a pocket in each chop by cutting into the chop with a small, sharp knife on rib side parallel to the surface of the chop. Be careful not to cut through the opposite side. Lightly brown onion in butter or margarine. Remove from heat. Add cream cheese, olives, lemon juice, salt and pepper, stirring to combine. Stir in bread cubes. Fill pocket in each chop with approximately ¼ cup stuffing, distributing evenly. Place chops on rack in broiler pan (or on outdoor grill over ash-covered coals) so surface of meat is 5 to 7 inches from heat and broil 10 minutes; turn and broil 10 minutes. Season chops on both sides with salt and pepper. Brush top side with the syrup from curried peaches and continue broiling 10 to 15 minutes or until done, brushing with the syrup and turning occasionally. 6 servings.

*Country Curried Peaches

1 29-oz. can cling peach halves
2 teaspoons tarragon vinegar
1 teaspoon curry powder
¼ teaspoon cinnamon

¼ teaspoon poppy seed
¼ teaspoon salt
1 teaspoon grated lemon peel

Drain peaches; reserve syrup. In saucepan combine syrup, vinegar, curry powder, cinnamon, poppy seed, salt and grated lemon peel; heat to boiling, stirring to combine. Add peach halves, heat to simmering. Serve hot, or place peaches and syrup in covered container in refrigerator overnight. Serve cold or reheated.

Reprinted by permission of Consumer Services Department, National Live Stock and Meat Board

SAUSAGE AND BROILED PEACH GRILL

2 lbs. Eckrich Smoked Sausage
8 peach halves
Sugar

Cinnamon
Butter

Split 3-inch lengths of Eckrich Smoked Sausage and put on rack in broiler, about 3 inches from the heat, so that the broiling will be done slowly. Turn sausage so that it will brown evenly.

44

After turning, sprinkle peaches with sugar, cinnamon and dot with butter. Place around the sausage on the grill. Broil until sausage is done and the peaches are delicately browned. GOES WITH EVERY-THING!

Reprinted by permission of Peter Eckrich

SAUSAGE EXTRAORDINAIRE

1 pound fully cooked sausage,
  cut into ¼-inch thick slices
1 large onion, cut into wedges
1 green pepper, cut into l-inch
  squares
2 tablespoons oil
2 7¾-oz. jars Gerber Junior
  Peaches

2 tablespoons sweet pickle relish
¼ cup cold water
1 tablespoon cornstarch
2 teaspoons prepared mustard
½ teaspoon salt
Dash pepper

In large skillet, cook sausage, onion, and green pepper in hot oil until onion is tender (about 5 minutes). Drain off fat. Add peaches and relish. Bring to boiling; reduce heat and simmer, covered, 5 minutes. In small bowl combine cold water and cornstarch. Stir in mustard, salt, and pepper. Stir into sausage mixture and cook, stirring constantly, for 2 minutes more. Serve over rice or noodles. Yield: 4½ cups.

Reprinted by permission of Gerber Products Company

SAUSAGE PEACH BALLS

1 lb. Jimmy Dean Sausage
2 cups soft bread crumbs
8 canned peach halves
Peach syrup

2 tablespoons fresh minced onion
1 egg, beaten
24 whole cloves
Salt and pepper to taste

Combine sausage, onion, bread crumbs, salt, pepper and beaten egg. Form into 8 balls. Drain peach halves, reserving syrup, and arrange in a shallow greased baking dish. Stick 4 cloves around edge of each peach half. Place sausage in center. Bake in 350-degree F. oven for 45 minutes.

Reprinted by permission of Jimmy Dean Meat Company, Inc.

SAUSAGE SAN MIGUEL

6 ounces smoked country-style
  link sausage
1 small onion, sliced
1 8-oz. can sliced peaches,
  including syrup
⅓ large green pepper, cut in 1-
  inch squares
1 tablespoon sweet pickle relish

1 teaspoon prepared mustard
1 teaspoon cornstarch
⅛ teaspoon each, salt and
  seasoned pepper
2½ tablespoons chicken broth or
  water
1 cup hot cooked rice

Cover and cook sausage in ¼ cup water about 5 minutes; remove from water and cut in thin slices. Combine sausage and onion in a small skillet. Cook until onion is tender crisp. Add peaches, green pepper, and sweet pickle relish. Simmer about 5 minutes. Blend mustard, cornstarch, and seasonings with chicken broth. Pour into meat mixture. Cook, stirring, until clear and thickened, about 2 minutes. Serve over beds of fluffy rice. Makes 2 servings.

Reprinted by permission of Co-Op Power

TASTY SAUSAGE AND PEACHES

12 ounces "fully-cooked"
  smoked link sausage
1 16-oz. can sliced cling peaches
2 tablespoons brown sugar

2 tablespoons butter or
  margarine
1 teaspoon lemon juice
⅛ teaspoon cinnamon
Dash nutmeg

Cut sausage into 4 equal pieces; cut each piece in half lengthwise. Drain peach syrup into an 11¾x7½-inch microwave-safe baking dish; reserve peaches. Add brown sugar, butter, lemon juice, cinnamon and nutmeg. Microwave at HIGH 2 minutes, stirring after 1 minute. Place sausage around sides of dish and peaches in center. Cover with waxed paper and microwave at HIGH 5 minutes, inverting sausage and rotating dish ¼ turn after 2½ minutes. 4 servings.

Reprinted by permission of
Test Kitchens and Editorial Services, National Live Stock and Meat Board

FRUIT-FILLED OMELETS

Filling:
1 pint fresh strawberries, hulled
  and sliced

2 medium peaches, sliced
  (2 cups)
2 teaspoons sugar
¼ teaspoon ground cinnamon

In medium bowl combine strawberries, peaches, sugar and cinnamon; mix well. Let stand at room temperature 30 minutes.

Omelets:

8 eggs	4 tablespoons butter or
½ cup milk	margarine, divided
3 tablespoons sugar	1 cup vanilla yogurt

In small bowl beat eggs, milk and sugar with an egg beater or wire whisk until light and frothy. In small skillet melt 1 tablespoon butter; pour in ½ cup of the egg mixture. With spatula, carefully push cooked portions at edges toward center so uncooked portion flows underneath. Slide pan rapidly back and forth over heat to keep eggs from sticking. While top is still moist spread ½ cup fruit filling over half the omelet. With pancake turner fold omelet in half and turn out onto heated plate with quick flip of the wrist. Top with yogurt and a fresh strawberry, if desired. Repeat with remaining butter, egg and fruit mixture. Makes 4 servings.

Reprinted by permission of United Fresh Fruit and Vegetable Association

SOUR CREAM OMELET WITH MARINATED FRUIT SAUCE

Marinated Fruit Sauce:	½ teaspoon whole allspice
½ cup sugar	½ cup Kirsch liqueur
1 tablespoon cornstarch	2½ cups tart cherries, thawed,
1 cup cherry juice or water	drained
1 tablespoon lemon juice	2 cups mandarin oranges,
2 cinnamon sticks	drained
½ teaspoon whole cloves	2 cups sliced peaches, drained

In a saucepan combine sugar, cornstarch, cherry juice or water, lemon juice and cinnamon sticks. Tie cloves and allspice in cheese-cloth and add to mixture. Bring marinade mixture to a boil over moderate heat; lower heat and simmer covered for 5 minutes. Stir occasionally. Remove from heat and cool. Remove the spice bag and cinnamon sticks. Stir in Kirsch. Pour the marinade over drained fruit, cover and refrigerate several hours.

NOTE: Other fruits may be substituted for the mandarin oranges and peaches.

Omelet:

Prepare a 3-egg omelet. Before folding, fill with 2 tablespoons sour cream (cream cheese, whipped, may be substituted). Warm the needed amount of marinated fruit. Gently pour ⅓ cup of fruit mixture over sour cream filled omelet.

Reprinted by permission of National Red Cherry Institute

PEACHES AND CREAM OMELET

2 eggs
2 tablespoons water
¼ teaspoon salt
1 tablespoon butter

½ cup dairy sour cream
½ cup sliced cling peaches, well
    drained

Mix eggs, water and salt with a fork. Heat butter in omelet pan or skillet (approx. 8-in.) until just hot enough to sizzle a drop of water. Pour in egg mixture. Mixture should set at edges at once. With a pancake turner, carefully draw cooked portions at edges toward center, so that uncooked portions flow to the bottom. Tilt skillet as it is necessary to hasten flow of uncooked eggs. Slide pan rapidly back and forth over the heat to keep mixture in motion and sliding freely. While the top is still moist and creamy-looking, spread half of sour cream on omelet. Place approximately ⅓ cup peach slices on half of omelet. With a pancake turner, fold in half, turning out onto platter with a quick flip of the wrist. Spread remaining sour cream on top of omelet. Garnish with remaining peach slices. Makes 1 serving.

Reprinted by permission of American Egg Board

PEACHY STIR FRIED TURKEY

3 cups sliced celery
3 tablespoons butter or
    margarine
2 cups diced cooked turkey
1 10-oz. package frozen peas,
    partially thawed

¼ cup honey
1 to 2 tablespoons French's
    Worcestershire Sauce
1 1-lb. can sliced cling peaches,
    drained

Cook celery in butter in skillet for 5 to 10 minutes. Add turkey and peas; cook and stir 5 minutes longer. Add honey, Worcestershire sauce, and drained peaches; heat 5 minutes. Serve on rice. 4 to 6 servings.

Reprinted by permission of FRENCH'S, The R. T. French Company

MUFFRIENDS

6 ounces cooked chicken meat,
    cubed
1 8-ounce package cream cheese,
    softened
½ cup shredded almonds
1 tablespoon mayonnaise

1 tablespoon peach chutney,
    minced
½ teaspoon curry powder
Salt and pepper
6 Bays English Muffins

Combine chicken, cream cheese, almonds, mayonnaise, peach chutney and curry powder in a medium bowl. Divide mixture evenly among muffin halves. Spread to cover the entire cut surface. Broil until bubbling. Serves 6 – 12.

Reprinted by permission of BAYS ENGLISH MUFFINS. Vivian Burger, Mentor, OH

MEXICAN CHICKEN WITH CORIANDER AND PEACHES

2 whole chicken breasts, boned, skinned and split
2 thin slices fresh ginger root, crushed a bit
1 green onion, quartered
Water
1 cup cherry tomatoes, halved
½ cucumber (½ cup) pared, cored and sliced
2 large fresh peaches, pitted and cut into wedges (2 cups)
Leafy lettuce
1 small bunch cilantro (fresh coriander or Chinese parsley), stems removed, torn slightly, or ½ cup minced fresh parsley
Spicy Sauce (recipe follows)

Combine chicken, ginger and green onion in saucepan. Add enough water to cover chicken by 1 inch. Bring to a boil over high heat; reduce heat to simmer 10 to 12 minutes, uncovered, or until done. Drain chicken and plunge into ice water (this seals in juices and keeps chicken moist). Chill, submerged, 15 minutes. Drain or pat dry. Shred chicken to measure 2 cups. Arrange chicken, tomatoes, cucumber and peaches in an attractive manner in lettuce-lined serving bowl or platter. Sprinkle with cilantro. Serve Spicy Sauce on side. Makes 4 servings.

Spicy Sauce

Combine 1 cup tomato puree, 2 tablespoons cider vinegar, 4 tablespoons red salsa picante, ½ to 1 teaspoon minced garlic in jar. Shake to combine. Makes 1⅓ cups.

CHICKEN AND PEACHES PIQUANT

12 pieces of chicken (2½ to 3 lbs.)
¼ teaspoon ground black pepper
¾ cup catsup
1 16-oz. can sliced peaches (drain, reserve syrup)
¼ cup soy sauce
1 large onion, sliced
1 large green pepper, cut in squares
4 teaspoons cornstarch
3 cups hot cooked rice

Sprinkle chicken with pepper. Place skin side up in lightly buttered shallow 2½-quart casserole. Bake, uncovered, at 450 degrees, for 20 minutes. Mix catsup and peach syrup with enough water to make 2½ cups. Add soy sauce; pour over chicken, top with onion rings. Cover and bake 30 minutes longer. Add green pepper, peaches, and cornstarch dissolved in ¼ cup water. Replace cover and bake

10 more minutes. Serve over bed of fluffy rice. Pass additional soy sauce, if desired. Makes 6 servings.

Sarah Murphy, Blessing, Texas

BAKED CHICKEN AND PEACHES

3 whole chicken breasts
3 whole chicken legs
1 16-oz. can peach halves in light
  syrup

2 tablespoons orange juice
1 tablespoon soy sauce
Dash of ginger
Pepper to taste

Rinse chicken breasts and legs under cold water; pat dry. Cut each breast in half; cut legs at joints into drumsticks and thighs. Place chicken in single layer in shallow baking pan. Drain peaches; reserve syrup. Set peach halves aside. Stir orange juice, soy sauce and ginger into reserved syrup. Season chicken with pepper. Bake in preheated 400-degree oven for 1 hour or until chicken is tender, basting every 15 minutes with syrup and pan juices. Place peach halves in pan; brush with pan juices. Bake for 5 minutes longer or until hot. Arrange chicken and peaches on serving platter. Pour pan juices into saucepan; boil to reduce liquid by half. Spoon over chicken. Yield: 6 servings.

Reprinted by permission of Favorite Recipes Press, Nashville, Tennessee

BARBECUED PEACH CHICKEN

⅓ cup brewed soy sauce
¼ cup sauterne (white wine)
¼ cup brown sugar (packed)
2 tablespoons lemon juice
1 clove garlic, pressed
⅛ teaspoon powdered ginger

4 frying chicken halves (about 1
  pound each)
6 fresh California peaches
2 tablespoons catsup
2 tablespoons oil

Combine soy sauce, sauterne, sugar, lemon juice, garlic and ginger; mix well. Place chicken halves in a 9 × 13 × 2-inch baking pan. Pour marinade over and turn once to coat all sides. Refrigerate 2 hours or longer, turning occasionally. Shortly before cooking, coarsely dice 2 peaches into blender jar and blend smooth to measure 1 cup (or puree peaches using sieve). Drain marinade from chicken and add to it the blended peaches, catsup and oil. Place chicken on grill over glowing charcoal.* Grill slowly, turning often, 50 to 60 minutes, until chicken is done. During last 20 minutes of cooking, baste chicken frequently with the peach marinade. Place remaining peaches, cut in halves, on grill the last 10 minutes of cooking, basting with the marinade. Makes 4 servings.

*Or, on broiler rack in oven at least 8 inches from source of heat.

Recipe adapted from and reprinted by permission of
California Tree Fruit Agreement's, Barbecued Nectarine Chicken

CHICKEN WITH PEACHES

1 broiler-fryer, 2½ to 3½ lbs.,
   cut up and skinned
½ teaspoon Morton Lite salt
   mixture
½ cup flour

1 1 lb.-13 oz. can peach halves
   or slices
¼ cup unsalted polyunsaturated
   margarine
⅓ cup orange juice
½ cup walnuts

Wash chicken and pat dry. Sprinkle with salt and coat with flour, shaking off excess. Place in medium shallow baking dish. Drain peaches, saving ¾ cup of syrup. Melt margarine in small saucepan; stir in orange juice and peach syrup. Pour over chicken. Bake at 375 degrees, basting several times with juices in dish, for 1 hour. Add peaches and walnuts and continue baking, basting once, for 15 minutes, or until chicken is tender and glazed. Makes 4 servings.

Reprinted by permission of Morton Salt Division of Morton Thiokol, Inc.

CHICKEN WITH PEACHES AND CREAM SAUCE

3 whole chicken breasts, halved,
   boned and skinned
Salt and pepper
1 tablespoon butter or margarine
1 tablespoon oil
¼ cup dry white wine or chicken
   broth

1 tablespoon orange marmalade
¼ teaspoon crumbled dried
   tarragon
1 16-oz. can cling peach slices,
   drained
¼ cup heavy cream or half and
   half

Season chicken lightly with salt and pepper. Melt butter in a large frying pan; add oil and lightly brown chicken in hot fat. Combine wine, marmalade and tarragon; add to pan. Cover pan, reduce heat and simmer 10–12 minutes. Add peach slices and cook 5–8 minutes more, until chicken is cooked through. (Don't overcook.)

Using a slotted spoon, remove chicken and peaches to a serving dish; keep warm. Add cream to liquid in pan and bring to boil. Cook and stir until sauce is reduced and slightly thickened. Season to taste with salt and pepper. Pour sauce over chicken and peaches. Serves 4–6.

Reprinted by permission of Cling Peach Advisory Board

CHICKEN WITH SWEET-SOUR SAUCE

Sauce:

1 cup orange juice
1½ cups peaches, sliced (canned, fresh or frozen)
2 tablespoons brown sugar

2 tablespoons vinegar
1 teaspoon dry mustard
2 dashes Worcestershire sauce
1 clove garlic, minced

6 each fryer legs and thighs or 1 chicken or 2 breasts and 4 thighs, disjointed
½ cup flour
1 teaspoon salt
⅛ teaspoon pepper

Cooking oil to depth of ½ inch in large frypan
½ cup bamboo shoots, drained well
6 servings cooked rice

Heat oil in frying pan while dredging chicken in flour, salt, and pepper. Brown chicken. Combine sauce ingredients and simmer 10 minutes. Remove chicken when it is browned and pour off oil. Replace chicken and pour sauce over chicken. Cover and simmer about 30 – 35 minutes over low heat to prevent scorching. Test chicken for doneness. Add drained bamboo shoots and simmer for 15 minutes more. Serve over rice. Yield: 6 servings.

Reprinted by permission of Texas Department of Agriculture

CRUNCHY CHICKEN WITH PEACH SAUCE

⅓ cup dark corn syrup
¼ cup spicy brown mustard
2 whole chicken breasts, skinned, boned, cut in 1-inch cubes, ¼-inch thick
2 egg whites

4 tablespoons cornstarch
2 tablespoons water
3 cups finely chopped pecans
1 quart (about) corn oil
Peach Sauce (recipe follows)

In small bowl stir together corn syrup and mustard. Add chicken; toss to coat well. Cover; refrigerate several hours or overnight. In small bowl beat egg whites lightly but not until frothy. Gradually stir in cornstarch and water until smooth. Dip chicken pieces, a few at a time, into cornstarch mixture; then coat with pecans. Dry on waxed paper-lined trays while coating remainder. Pour corn oil into heavy 3-quart saucepan. Heat over medium heat. Add chicken pieces, a few at a time, fry about 1 minute or until golden brown. Drain on paper towels. Serve with Peach Sauce. Makes 8 servings as an hors d'oeuvre, or 4 as a main dish.

Peach Sauce

2 cups fresh or frozen peach
  slices, thawed
¾ cup dark corn syrup
¼ cup cider vinegar

¼ cup finely chopped onion
¼ teaspoon ground cinnamon
⅛ teaspoon ground nutmeg

In 2-quart saucepan stir together peaches, corn syrup, vinegar, onion, cinnamon and nutmeg. Stirring occasionally, bring to a boil over medium heat and boil gently 15 minutes. Place fruit mixture, about ½ at a time, in blender container; cover. Blend on medium speed 5 to 10 seconds or just until coarsely chopped. Store in tightly covered container in refrigerator. Serve with Pecan-Coated Chicken. Makes about 3 cups.

Reprinted by permission of The National Pecan Marketing Council, Inc.

LO-CAL PEACHY CHICKEN

6 chicken breasts
6 drumsticks
1 16-oz. can diet peach slices

1 teaspoon onion salt
1 tablespoon soy sauce
1 tablespoon lemon juice

Arrange chicken, skin side down, in 12 × 8 × 2-inch pan. Drain peaches; reserve juice. Combine onion salt, soy sauce and reserved peach syrup; add lemon juice. Brush half the mixture over chicken. Bake at 400 degrees for 1 hour, brushing chicken with juice mixture every 15 minutes. Add peach slices; bake for 5 minutes longer.

Reprinted by permission of Favorite Recipes Press, Nashville, Tennessee

PEACH BAKED CHICKEN BREASTS

6 boneless chicken breast halves
Salt and white pepper
6 thin slices baked ham
1 cup shredded Swiss cheese
1 tablespoon dried chives

1 21-oz. can Wilderness Peach
  Fruit Filling
1 tablespoon Dijon-style mustard
1/16 teaspoon garlic powder
melted butter or margarine
parsley sprigs (optional)

Pound chicken breast with flat side of mallet until even in thickness; sprinkle lightly with salt and pepper. Layer ham, cheese and chives on chicken; roll up, tucking in ends. Secure with string or wooden picks. Mix peach fruit filling, mustard and garlic powder; spoon into glass baking dish. Arrange chicken on top; brush with butter. Bake at 350 degrees until chicken is done, about 40 minutes. Garnish with parsley. 6 servings.

Reprinted by permission of Wilderness Foods, Inc.

PEACH-LEMON CHICKEN

1½ cups peaches (sliced)
1 clove garlic, pressed
1 tablespoon cornstarch
2 teaspoons Worchestershire
   sauce

2 teaspoons Dijon mustard
1 teaspoon rosemary, crumbled
3 whole chicken breasts, split
1 teaspoon salt
1 small lemon, thinly sliced

Drain juice from peaches, reserving juice. Combine reserved juice with garlic, cornstarch, Worchestershire sauce, mustard and rosemary and ¼ cup water. Arrange chicken in shallow dish, skin side up. Sprinkle with salt. Broil until browned. Stir sauce. Pour over chicken. Bake in 400-degree oven for 30 minutes. Arrange peaches and lemon slices around chicken, spoon sauce over all. Bake 5 minutes more.

Barbara Sisk, Hempstead Texas

PEACH-LUSCIOUS CHICKEN

1 broiler-fryer chicken, cut in
   parts
1 teaspoon garlic salt

1 teaspoon pepper
Peach Sauce (recipe follows)

In large, shallow, non-stick baking pan, place chicken, skin side up. Sprinkle garlic salt and pepper on chicken. Cook, uncovered, in 450-degree oven for 25 minutes. Drain any accumulated fat from baking pan and discard. Turn chicken and pour Peach Sauce over chicken. Lower oven temperature to 350 degrees and continue cooking for 15 minutes. Baste chicken with peach sauce and cook 15 minutes more or until peach sauce has thickened and formed glaze on chicken and fork can be inserted in chicken with ease. Makes 4 servings.

Peach Sauce:

In saucepan, place 1 12-oz. jar Peach Jelly and melt over low heat. Mix 1 cup boiling water with 2 teaspoons chicken bouillon granules and add melted jelly. Stir in ½ cup chopped onion, ⅓ cup red wine vinegar, 1 tablespoon soy sauce, 1 teaspoon ground ginger and 1 teaspoon Chinese Five Spices mixture. Simmer 10 minutes.

Adapted from and reprinted by permission of
Doris Gibson's Plum Luscious Chicken, Kentucky

STIR-FRY CHICKEN WITH PEACHES

1 2½- to 3-lb. chicken, cut in 8
    pieces
1 teaspoon salt
½ teaspoon poultry seasoning
3 tablespoons cornstarch
1 cup oil
1 tablespoon oil
1 clove garlic, peeled, crushed
8 oz. frozen unsweetened
    peaches, thawed

1 tablespoon sugar
2 tablespoons lemon juice
½ cup chicken broth
2 teaspoons cornstarch dissolved
    in 1 tablespoon water
1 10-oz. package frozen snow
    peas
3 cups hot cooked rice

Place chicken in shallow baking dish. Sprinkle with salt and poultry seasoning. Place dish on rack in wok over simmering water. Cover, steam chicken for 45 minutes. Remove from wok and blot chicken dry with paper towels. Rub cornstarch into each piece. Pour water from wok and wipe dry. Add 1 cup oil and heat almost to sizzling. Fry chicken pieces in oil, 2 or 3 at a time until lightly browned. Remove as browned and set aside. Pour oil from wok. Add 1 tablespoon of oil to wok. Add garlic and stir-fry until browned. Remove and discard garlic. Add thawed peaches and sugar. Stir until heated. Stir in lemon juice. Add broth, heat to boiling. Stir in dissolved cornstarch. Add snow peas, stirring them into the liquid. Cover, steam for 30 seconds. Return browned chicken to wok. Cover and steam for 30 seconds or until chicken is reheated. Serve over hot cooked rice. Makes 6 to 8 servings.

Reprinted by permission from
Wok Cookery by Ceil Dyer, © 1977 HP Books, Inc., Tucson, Arizona

TERIYAKI CHICKEN WITH PEACHES

¼ cup all-purpose flour
¼ teaspoon garlic powder
3 pounds frying chicken pieces

2 tablespoons vegetable oil
1 16-oz. can cling peach halves
½ cup Kikkoman Teriyaki Sauce

Mix together flour and garlic powder; coat chicken pieces thoroughly with mixture. Brown chicken on all sides in hot oil in Dutch oven or large skillet over medium heat. Drain off excess fat. Drain peaches; reserve ½ cup syrup. Combine syrup with teriyaki sauce and ¼ cup water; pour over chicken. Bring to boil; reduce heat and simmer, covered, 30 minutes. Turn chicken pieces over. Simmer, covered, 15 minutes longer, or until chicken is tender. Arrange peaches around chicken; heat through. Remove chicken and peaches to serving platter; keep warm. Skim off excess fat from pan juices and serve with chicken and peaches. Makes 4 to 6 servings.

Reprinted by permission of Kikkoman International, Inc.

WALNUT CHICKEN STIR FRY

6 large boned chicken breasts
2 16-oz. cans cling peach slices
    in juice or extra light syrup
2 large tomatoes
3 large stalks celery
2 cups fresh broccoli flowerettes
1 cup diagonally sliced green
    onions

¼ cup soy sauce
¼ cup medium-dry sherry
2 cloves garlic, minced
2 tablespoons cornstarch
⅓ cup light oil
1 tablespoon minced fresh
    ginger*
½ cup chopped toasted walnuts

Remove skin from chicken breasts. Cut into thin strips ½ inch wide by 1½ inches long. Drain peaches, reserving liquid for another use. Cut tomatoes into wedges and celery into ¼-inch diagonal slices. Set vegetables aside with broccoli and onions. Combine soy sauce, sherry, garlic and cornstarch. Heat oil in wok; stir in ginger and chicken, tossing until chicken has completely turned opaque. Stir in broccoli until it turns bright green. Add celery and onions and stir until coated with oil. Add peach slices and tomatoes. Pour soy mixture over all, stirring until thickened. Add walnuts, toss lightly and serve. Makes 6 servings.

*Or use 1½ teaspoons powdered ginger stirred into soy mixture.

Reprinted by permission of S.& W. Fine Foods, Inc. and Cling Peach Advisory Board

CHICKEN WITH PEACHES

¼ cup all-purpose flour
2 teaspoons curry powder
4 skinless, boneless chicken
    breast halves
2 tablespoons butter or
    margarine

1 16-oz. can sliced peaches in
    syrup
1 pouch Campbell's Onion
    Mushroom Soup Mix
¼ teaspoon ground ginger

In pie plate, stir together flour and curry powder; coat each chicken piece on all sides with flour mixture. In 10-inch skillet over medium-high heat cook chicken in butter until browned on all sides. Remove chicken to plate. Drain peaches, reserving syrup; add water to syrup to make 2 cups liquid. Stir liquid, soup mix and ginger into skillet. Heat to boiling, stirring constantly. Return chicken to skillet; reduce heat to low. Cover; simmer 15 minutes or until chicken is fork-tender. Stir in peaches; heat through. Makes 4 servings.

Reprinted by permission of Campbell Soup Company

PARTY CHICKEN TORTE

**12 slices white meat chicken roll
(about ½ lb.)
8 ounces soft cream cheese**

**2 tablespoons chopped walnuts
1 8-oz. can sliced peaches,
drained**

Combine cheese and walnuts. Spread cheese mixture on 9 slices chicken roll; stack slices in stacks of three. Top each stack with one of the remaining slices of chicken roll. Chill. Cut each stack in 8 wedges. Top each wedge with peach slice. Secure with toothpick. Makes 24.

PEACH STUFFED CHICKEN BREASTS

**3 chicken breasts
2 fresh peaches, peeled and diced
⅓ cup chopped onion**

**¼ cup cashews (optional)
¼ teaspoon ginger
2 tablespoons margarine**

Bone and skin chicken breasts and cut in half lengthwise. Pound to flatten. Combine peaches, onion, cashews and ginger. Place this filling on each piece of chicken, roll and secure with a toothpick. Melt margarine in baking pan and then place the stuffed chicken breasts in the pan. Bake at 350 degrees F. for 25 minutes; turn chicken and bake 20 minutes longer. May be served with fresh peach sauce if desired (see recipe below). Serves 6.

Fresh Peach Sauce

Combine 2 fresh peaches, peeled and sliced, with ¼ cup brown sugar, 2 teaspoons mustard, and 1 cup sour cream. Heat for 5 minutes.

Reprinted by permission of U.S. Department of Agriculture

Vegetables, Soups & Salads

E & B's

If you want the best peaches fit to please,
Just drive down Clarke Bottom Road to E & B's.
They usually open about mid-May,
So come on down without delay.
The peaches are plentiful and the owners are nice,
If you need any help, they are there, for advice.
One kind they have is Early Amber,
This peach is a big demander.
There are more kinds without a doubt,
Come and see what it's all about.
So tell your family and all of your friends,
To come and pick before peach season ends.

By Michael Freeman, Ennis Texas, July 1984

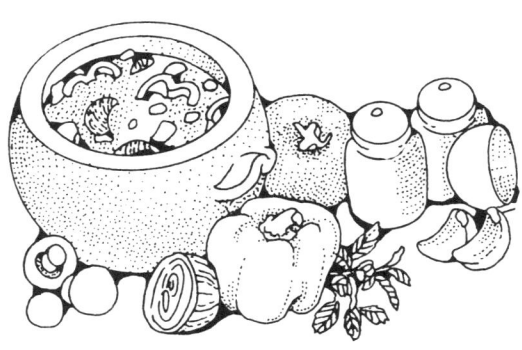

PEACHES AND PEAS TARRAGON

1 CAN (29 oz.) cling peach halves   1 tablespoon tarragon leaves
½ cube butter (1 stick)   1 10-oz. package frozen peas

Drain peaches, saving syrup. Melt butter in saucepan, add syrup and tarragon; heat for about 2 minutes. Place peach halves in baking pan. Drizzle one-half syrup mixture over peaches. Bake in 350-degree oven until heated through. Cook frozen peas according to package directions. Spoon cooked peas into prepared peach halves and serve.

Reprinted by permission of California Cling Peach Advisory Board

CABBAGE WITH PEACHES

1 head of cabbage   ½ teaspoon salt
1 peach — peeled, pitted and   3 tablespoons lemon juice
   sliced   2 tablespoons sugar (optional)
½ cup dairy sour cream
2 tablespoons butter or
   margarine

Cut cabbage into wedges. Cook in small amount of water until tender. Drain. Add peaches, sour cream, butter, salt and lemon juice. Heat until completely hot. 6 servings.

GOLDEN CARROTS

1 pint sliced carrots   ¼ cup peach marmalade
3 tablespoons butter or   1 tablespoon lemon juice
   margarine

Boil carrots for 10 minutes. Drain. Melt butter in saucepan; stir in peach marmalade and lemon juice. Add drained carrots. Cool and stir mixture for 8–10 minutes. Makes 4 servings.

GREEN BEANS WITH PEACHES

2 10-oz. packages frozen green   3 tablespoons butter
   beans   Salt and pepper to taste
1 pint CANNED peach slices

Cook beans according to package directions; drain. Add peaches and butter. Heat; season with salt and pepper.

Beverly Levandowski, Hempstead, Texas

PEACH-GLAZED BEETS

1 pint canned beets
4 tablespoons butter or
   margarine

¼ cup peach marmalade

Boil beets, uncovered, for at least 10 minutes; drain. Melt butter in saucepan; stir in peach marmalade. Add the beets. Cook and stir over low heat 6–8 minutes. Makes 4 servings.

Barbara Sisk, Hempstead, Texas

PEACHY BEETS

1 pint CANNED sliced peaches
½ cup water
⅓ cup cider vinegar
4 tablespoons brown sugar

1 tablespoon cornstarch
½ teaspoon salt
⅛ teaspoon ground ginger
2 1-lb. cans sliced beets, drained

Drain peaches, reserving juice. Mix juice from peaches with water and vinegar. Mix brown sugar, cornstarch, salt and ginger; add vinegar mixture. Cook until thickened, stirring constantly. Add beets, then heat to boiling. Just before serving add peaches to hot mixture. 8 servings.

Beverly Levandowski, Hempstead, Texas

PEACHY BUTTERNUT SQUASH BAKE

1 3–3½ lb. butternut squash
1 teaspoon salt
½ teaspoon black pepper
¼ cup water

3 tablespoons butter or
   margarine
½ pint peach preserves
¼–⅓ cup chopped pecans

Wash squash; remove seeds; cut in ½-inch slices. Overlap slices in 13 × 9 × 2-inch baking dish. Sprinkle salt and pepper onto squash. Add water; cover and bake at 400 degrees for 25–30 minutes (until squash is tender). In saucepan melt butter; add peach preserves. When squash is tender pour preserve mixture over squash; sprinkle with pecans. Bake 15 minutes more. 4–6 servings.

Barbara Sisk, Hempstead, Texas

FRESH PEACH-SQUASH CASSEROLE

2½ cups sliced, soft-skinned
   squash (yellow crookneck or
   zucchini)
1 cup sliced fresh peaches

2½ tablespoons butter
2 tablespoons brown sugar
Salt to taste

Place layer of squash then layer of fresh peaches in 2-quart casserole. Continue alternating layers of fruit and vegetable until all have been used. Sprinkle brown sugar and salt over the combination and dot with butter. Cover and bake in a 350-degrees F. oven from 45 minutes to an hour. Serves four.

Reprinted by permission of National Peach Council

SWEET POTATOES AND PEACHES

1 CAN (16 oz.) sliced cling
  peaches
1 tablespoon cornstarch
⅓ cup liquid brown sugar

1 cup (8 oz.) whole berry
  cranberry sauce
½ teaspoon cinnamon
2 tablespoons butter
2 17-oz. cans yams, drained

Drain peaches; reserve juice. Dissolve cornstarch in ¼ cup peach juice and set aside. In an 11-inch skillet, heat remaining juice, brown sugar, cranberry sauce, cinnamon and butter. When butter is melted, add cornstarch mixture. Stir over medium heat until thickened. Add yams and cover. Cook 10 minutes. Stir in peaches and cook 5 more minutes.

WILD RICE WITH PEACHES

1 cup wild rice
1 teaspoon salt
10 dried peaches

3 tablespoons melted butter
½ cup Jacquin's Peach Brandy

Wash the rice; put it into a pan, cover with cold water and boil for 15 minutes. Drain and rinse. Cover again with water, add salt, bring to a boil, cover pan and simmer until rice is tender. Meanwhile, pour boiling water over peaches to soften them; cut in small pieces. When rice is tender, drain and rinse again. Stir in peaches, melted butter and Jacquin's Peach Brandy; put in a casserole and bake in a 325-degree oven for 15 to 20 minutes.

Recipe adapted from and reprinted by permission of
Wild Rice with Apricots, Charles Jacquin et Cie., Inc.

PEACHY VEGETABLE SALAD

Yogurt-Dill Dressing:
1 8-ounce carton unflavored yogurt
2 tablespoons chopped red onion
½ teaspoon dill seed, crushed
¼ teaspoon salt
¼ teaspoon garlic powder

Vegetable-Peach Salad:
1 CAN (29 ounces) cling peach slices
1 bunch broccoli, cut into flowerettes
4 carrots, cut into 2-inch sticks
2 stalks celery, cut into 2-inch strips
¼ pound green beans, cut into 2-inch strips
4 mushrooms, thinly sliced

Dressing: Mix all ingredients in small bowl. Refrigerate at least 2 hours for flavors to blend.

Salad: Drain peaches; reserve. In large saucepan or vegetable steamer, place broccoli, carrots, celery and green beans. Place 1 inch of water in pan. Heat to boiling; reduce to simmer. Cook 5 minutes or until vegetables are crisp-tender. Drain. Rinse under cold water; pat dry. Arrange vegetables, drained peaches and mushrooms on serving platter. Drizzle dressing over vegetables. Makes 4 servings. Approximately 147 calories per serving.

Reprinted by permission of California Cling Peach Advisory Board

TURKEY FRUIT SALAD

2 cups cubed cooked turkey
1 8-ounce container lemon yogurt
1 teaspoon minced fresh mint
2 cups shredded lettuce
2 fresh pears, cut into ½-inch pieces
1 11-ounce can mandarin oranges, drained
2 fresh peaches, cut into ½-inch pieces
½ cup chopped walnuts or pecans

Blend yogurt and mint. Chill one hour. Combine remaining ingredients. Pour yogurt over salad. Toss well. Serve at once.

PEACHY TURKEY SALAD

1½ cups diced cooked Jennie-O turkey
½ cup sliced celery
¼ cup each sliced ripe and green stuffed olives
2 tablespoons chopped onion and pimentos
⅓ cup mayonnaise or salad dressing
¼ teaspoon prepared horseradish
1 1 lb.-13 oz. CAN (8 – 9 halves) peach halves, drained
⅓ cup thick French dressing

In medium bowl, combine all ingredients except peach halves, French dressing, and lettuce; chill about 2 hours. Marinate peach halves in French dressing; chill 1 hour. Fill peach halves with turkey mixture. Serve on lettuce. Drizzle with French dressing marinade, if desired. About 4 servings.

Reprinted by permission of Jennie-O Foods, Inc.

CALIFORNIA MARINATED SALAD

2 medium or large fresh California peaches
½ pound mushrooms, quartered
1 cup cherry tomatoes, halved
½ cup pitted ripe olives
⅓ cup green onion, cut into 1-inch lengths
1 6-ounce jar marinated
artichoke hearts
⅓ cup vegetable oil
¼ cup lemon juice
¼ teaspoon salt
¼ teaspoon pepper
1 teaspoon sugar
1 teaspoon tarragon, crumbled
½ teaspoon thyme, crumbled

Cut peaches into thick slices then cut each slice in half. Combine peaches with mushrooms, tomatoes, olives and onion in large salad bowl. Drain and save marinade from artichokes. Add artichokes to salad. Combine reserved marinade with oil, lemon juice, salt, pepper, sugar, tarragon and thyme in jar. Shake well and pour over salad. Cover and chill for at least 2 hours, tossing once or twice. Makes 6 (1-cup) servings.

Reprinted by permission of California Tree Fruit Agreement

LETTUCE FRUIT SILOS

1 head iceberg lettuce
2 envelopes plain gelatin
½ cup cold water
1 teaspoon prepared mustard
½ cup sugar
¼ teaspoon salt
2 cups boiling water
½ cup lemon juice
Few drops Tabasco sauce
1 16-oz. can cling peach slices
Radish slices

Core, rinse and drain lettuce well. Remove 6 to 8 outer leaves. Cut remaining lettuce lengthwise into halves; place cut sides down on chopping board. Shred across heart with sharp knife to make 1 cup. Place remainder and outer leaves in plastic bag or plastic crisper; chill. Soften gelatin in cold water; stir in mustard, sugar and salt. Add boiling water; stir until gelatin and sugar are completely dissolved. Stir in lemon juice and Tabasco. Set aside 1½ cups gelatin mixture. Chill remaining mixture until it mounds on spoon; fold in shredded lettuce. Turn into 6 or 8 individual molds; chill to a soft set. Meanwhile, drain peaches well. Chill reserved gelatin until mounds on spoon; fold in peaches. Turn into molds over lettuce layer. Chill until firm. Unmold on bed made of lettuce leaves. Garnish with radish slices. Makes 6 servings.

Calories per serving 111
Grams of protein per serving 4
Grams of carbohydrate per serving 24
Grams of fat per serving 0

Reprinted by permission of Pompeian, Inc.

PEA POD AND PEACH SALAD

¼ pound fresh Chinese pea pods, strings removed *or* 1 package (6-ounce) frozen pea pods
2 large fresh California peaches, sliced
2 stalks celery, cut into matchsticks
Chinese Dressing (recipe follows)
Sesame seeds (optional)

Bring large saucepan of water to boil. Add fresh pea pods and cook 30 seconds.* Rinse with cold water and drain well. Combine pea pods, peaches and celery in a bowl. Toss with Chinese Dressing and chill well before serving. Makes 4 to 6 servings.

Chinese Dressing: Combine ¼ cup white vinegar, 1 tablespoon soy sauce, 1 tablespoon sugar and ½ teaspoon ground ginger in electric blender. Whirl to blend. Continue blending, using slow speed, gradually adding ½ cup oil. Stir in 1 tablespoon toasted sesame seeds (optional).

*If using frozen pea pods, rinse with hot water to thaw. Drain well. Omit boiling step.

Reprinted by permission of California Tree Fruit Agreement

PEACHTREE SALAD

⅔ cup salad oil
⅓ cup Heinz Wine Vinegar
1 clove garlic, split
1 teaspoon sugar
½ teaspoon salt
⅛ teaspoon pepper

8 cups torn salad green, chilled
1 cup finely chopped parsley
1 cup sliced fresh or canned
   peaches
½ cup broken pecans

Combine first 6 ingredients in jar. Cover; shake vigorously. Chill to blend flavors. Remove garlic and shake again before tossing with salad greens, parsley, peaches and nuts. Makes 8 servings (about 8 cups).

Reprinted by permission of Heinz U.S.A.

ORIENTAL SALAD BOWL

½ pound green beans, halved
½ pound bean sprouts
2 fresh California peaches, sliced
½ cup cashews or peanuts or
   whole natural almonds

Lettuce
Hot and Sour Dressing and/or
   Ginger Dressing (recipe
   follows)

Bring 1 quart water to a boil in a saucepan. Add green beans and return to a boil. Cook 2 minutes or until tender-crisp. Put bean sprouts in colander. Pour green beans and cooking water over sprouts to soften. Drain well. Arrange green beans, bean sprouts, peaches and nuts on lettuce-lined platter. Serve with Hot and Sour Dressing or Ginger Dressing. Makes 2 to 4 servings.

Hot and Sour Dressing: Combine 3 tablespoons vinegar, 2 tablespoons peanut butter, 2 tablespoons soy sauce, 1 tablespoon sugar, 2 medium cloves garlic, 4 slices peeled fresh ginger root and ⅛ teaspoon cayenne pepper in electric blender container. Whirl to blend. Slowly add ½ cup oil while blending at low speed.

Ginger Dressing: Combine ¼ cup white vinegar, 1 tablespoon soy sauce, 1 tablespoon sugar, ¾ teaspoon ground ginger and ⅛ teaspoon pepper in electric blender. Whirl to blend. Continue blending, using slow speed, gradually adding ½ cup oil. Whirl in 2 or 3 sprigs parsley just until finely chopped.

Reprinted by permission of California Tree Fruit Agreement

PEACH TORTELLINI SALAD

1 12-ounce package fresh or frozen tortellini,* cooked, rinsed and drained

2 fresh California peaches, cut into chunks

⅓ cup chopped parsley (packed)
1 cup sliced celery
Basil Dressing (recipe follows)

Toss tortellini, peaches, parsley and celery with Basil Dressing in a large bowl. Chill. Makes 4 servings.

Basil Dressing: Combine 5 tablespoons white vinegar, 2 tablespoons sugar, 2 teaspoons basil, 1½ teaspoons thyme, 2 medium cloves garlic, ¾ teaspoon salt and ¼ teaspoon pepper in electric blender. Whirl to blend. Slowly add ½ cup vegetable oil while blending at low speed.

*If preferred, substitute 4 ounces shell macaroni, cooked and drained as directed on package, for the tortellini.

Reprinted by permission of California Tree Fruit Agreement

SIMPLY ELEGANT PEACH SALAD

2 16-oz. cans cling peach halves in juice or extra light syrup
2 tablespoons lemon juice
⅓ cup raspberry-flavored red wine vinegar*
1 tablespoon capers

2 tablespoons finely minced green onions
¼ teaspoon garlic salt
¼ teaspoon dry mint leaves
2 bunches watercress
Sour cream

Drain peaches, reserving 1 cup liquid. Combine reserved liquid with lemon juice, raspberry vinegar, capers, green onions, garlic salt and mint. Pour over peach halves, cover and chill 1 hour. Arrange watercress on large platter or 6 individual salad plates. Arrange peach halves on watercress, spooning marinade over each. Top each half with a dollop of sour cream to serve. Makes 6 servings.

*Or use ⅓ cup red wine vinegar with or without 2 tablespoons frozen raspberry juice.

Reprinted by permission of S & W Fine Foods, Inc. and Cling Peach Advisory Board

SUMMERTIME POTATO SALAD

2 pounds long white or round red
    potatoes
⅓ cup mayonnaise
⅓ cup dairy sour cream
2 tablespoons dried parsley
    flakes
2 tablespoons Kikkoman Soy
    Sauce

1 tablespoon prepared
    horseradish
½ teaspoon black pepper
4 hard-cooked eggs, peeled and
    cut into eighths
½ cup minced onions
Fresh California peach slices

Peel and cut potatoes in ¾-inch cubes. Cook in salted, boiling water about 6 minutes or until tender, being careful not to overcook. Drain thoroughly; transfer to large bowl and chill. Meanwhile, combine mayonnaise, sour cream, parsley, soy sauce, horseradish and pepper. Pour dressing over potatoes with eggs and onions; toss gently to mix well. Refrigerate about 3 hours for flavors to blend or until salad is chilled. To serve, turn salad out into serving bowl; arrange peach slices around edge of salad. Makes 6 to 8 servings.

Reprinted by permission of Kikkoman International, Inc.

SUPER SUMMER SALAD

2 cups thickly sliced peaches
2 tablespoons orange juice
6 cups torn fresh spinach
6 cups torn green leaf lettuce
1 cup shredded Swiss cheese

3 cups red or green seedless
    grapes
1 tablespoon poppy seeds
½ cup bottled sweet and spicy
    French or slaw dressing

Toss peaches and orange juice together in a large salad bowl; add spinach, lettuce, grapes, cheese and toss well. Stir together the dressing and poppy seeds; pour over the salad and toss well. Serve immediately. Makes about 10 servings.

Reprinted by permission of M&M/Mars, a division of Mars, Inc.

BOMBAY SALAD

1 cup dairy sour cream
⅓ cup Major Grey's chutney,
    finely chopped
1 teaspoon curry powder
1 tablespoon lime juice
⅓ cup toasted coconut, shredded
¼ cup toasted almonds, slivered

2 cups chicken or turkey, cooked
Leafy lettuce
3 medium fresh California
    peaches, sliced (2 cups)
4 fresh California plums, sliced
    (1¾ cups)
1 kiwi, pared, sliced

Combine sour cream, chutney, curry, lime juice, ¼ cup coconut and almonds until mixed. Mix ¾ cup of this dressing with chicken; chill. Line salad bowl or platter with lettuce and pile 1 quart torn lettuce in center. Pile chicken mixture into center of bowl. Arrange peaches, plums and kiwi in an attractive manner around chicken mixture. Sprinkle remaining toasted coconut over salad. Serve remaining dressing on the side. Makes 4 servings.

Reprinted by permission of California Tree Fruit Agreement

FRUIT CURRY

1 medium papaya (about 1 pound), pared, seeded, chopped
2 medium bananas, sliced
2 fresh peaches (about ½ pound), peeled, diced
1 8-oz. can pineapple chunks, drained
2 tablespoons lime juice

2 cups thinly sliced onions
2 tablespoons butter
½ cup milk
⅓ cup flaked coconut
¼ cup dark raisins
2 teaspoons curry powder
2 teaspoons minced, pared ginger root

Combine papaya, bananas, peaches, pineapple and lime juice in medium-size bowl. Sauté onions in butter in large saucepan until limp, about 5 minutes; stir in fruit and remaining ingredients. Heat to boiling. Reduce heat; simmer uncovered, stirring occasionally, until fruits are tender, 25 to 30 minutes. Cool. Serve warm or cold. Makes 8 servings.

ALOHA SALAD

1 17-oz. can S&W Bartlett Pear Halves, drained
1 8¼-oz. can S&W Seedless Grapes, drained
1 17-oz. can S&W Unpeeled Apricot Halves, drained

1 20½-oz. can S&W Sliced Pineapple, drained
1 17-oz. can S&W Freestone Peach Halves, drained
2 apples, sliced
2 bananas, sliced diagonally

Islander Dressing:

1 cup mayonnaise
1 tablespoon chopped candied ginger

1 cup lime, orange or raspberry sherbet
Lettuce (butterleaf or romaine)

Chill salad ingredients. Combine dressing ingredients; chill. Arrange fruits on lettuce-lined platter. Serve with dressing. Serves 6−8.

Reprinted by permission of S&W Fine Foods, Inc.

CHRISTMAS FRUIT SALAD

1 cup sliced peaches
1 cup pineapple chunks
1 cup sliced bananas
1 cup orange sections
½ cup fresh grapefruit sections
½ cup seedless grapes
½ cup strawberries

½ cup diced apple
1 cup chopped pecans
1 cup sugar
1 teaspoon vanilla flavoring
1 teaspoon lemon flavoring
2 cups whipped cream

Combine fruits, pecans and ½ cup sugar. Stir remaining sugar and flavorings into whipped cream; fold in fruit mixture. Chill thoroughly. Garnish with maraschino cherries. Yield: 12 servings.

Reprinted by permission of Favorite Recipes Press, Nashville, Tennessee

FRESH PEACH AND CHEESE SALAD WITH HONEY DRESSING

3 oz. cream cheese, cut into 6
    parts
½ cup chopped pecans
3 large ripe peaches
Lemon juice

½ cup honey
½ cup lemon juice
Pinch of nutmeg
Lettuce

Roll cream cheese into balls, then in chopped pecans. Pare peaches and cut in half; remove seed. Dip in lemon juice to prevent discoloration. Arrange peaches on lettuce; place a cheese-pecan ball in center of each peach half. To make dressing, combine honey, lemon juice and nutmeg. Mix thoroughly. Top peach and cheese ball with dressing. Serves 6.

Reprinted by permission of The National Pecan Marketing Council, Inc.

COMFORT FRUIT SALAD

1 1-lb. can pineapple chunks
1 1-lb. can grapefruit sections
½ cup maraschino cherries,
    halved, or strawberries,
    halved

1 cup mandarin orange sections
1 cup peaches, cut up
½ cup shredded coconut
¾ cup sweet orange marmalade
¼ cup Southern Comfort

Drain pineapple chunks and grapefruit sections. Combine with cherries or strawberries; mandarin orange sections; peaches and shredded coconut. Warm sweet orange marmalade slightly, remove from heat and mix with Southern Comfort. Pour over fruit and mix well. Serves 6-8.

Fresh pineapple may be substituted for pineapple chunks. Cut pineapple in half lengthwise leaving leaves intact. Cut the pineapple from the shell. Trim away heart and cut into cubes. Mix as above, fill pineapple shell with salad. Beautiful!

Reprinted by permission of B-F Spirits Ltd.

COOL AND CREAMY FRUIT SALAD

1 8-oz. pkg. cream cheese,
   softened
2 tablespoons lemon juice
1 teaspoon grated lemon rind
½ cup whipping cream
¼ cup powdered sugar

2 cups peach slices
2 cups blueberries
2 cups strawberry slices
2 cups grapes
2 tablespoons chopped nuts

Combine cream cheese, juice and rind, mixing until well blended. Beat whipping cream until soft peaks form; gradually add sugar, beating until stiff peaks form. Fold into cream cheese mixture. Chill. Layer fruit in 2½-quart bowl. Spoon cream cheese mixture over fruit; sprinkle with nuts. Chill. 8 servings.

COOL SUMMER FRUIT KABOBS

1 cup mayonnaise
½ teaspoon sugar
½ teaspoon curry powder
Fresh plum slices
Fresh Bartlett pear slices

Fresh nectarine slices
Fresh peach slices
Ham cubes
Lettuce

Combine mayonnaise, sugar and curry powder; mix well. Chill. Alternate ham, peaches, nectarines, plums and pears on skewers. Arrange on lettuce-covered platter. Serve with dressing. Makes 1 cup dressing.
VARIATION: Substitute cooked turkey chunks for ham.

DRESSED PEACH SALAD

1 large can sliced peaches
2 tablespoons flour
¾ cup sugar
2 eggs, beaten

Juice of 1 lemon
½ lb. cheese, grated
Chopped nuts

Drain peaches; reserve juice. Chop peaches, combine flour and sugar, stir into eggs. Pour into top of double boiler; stir in lemon juice and reserved peach juice. Cook over hot water until thick, stirring constantly. Cool dressing thoroughly. Combine peaches, cheese and nuts; spread in shallow mold. Pour dressing over top; chill thoroughly. Cut into squares to serve. Yield: 8 servings.

PEACH SPINACH SALAD

½ pound spinach, stems removed, and leaves torn up
½ cucumber, scored and sliced (½ cup)
1 fresh California peach, sliced (1 cup)
2 fresh California plums, sliced (1 cup)
¼ cup sliced green onion
Yogurt Dressing (recipe follows)

Wash and drain spinach thoroughly. Combine spinach, cucumber, peaches, plums and green onion in a large bowl or in individual salad bowls. Serve with Yogurt Dressing. 4 to 6 servings.

Yogurt Dressing: Stir 1 cup plain yogurt with 1 tablespoon fresh lemon juice, 1 tablespoon water and ¼ teaspoon dill weed until smooth. Makes about 1 cup.

Reprinted by permission of California Tree Fruit Agreement

SUMMER SALAD

Leaf lettuce
1 29-oz. can peach halves, drained
1 16-oz. can pear halves, drained
1 15¼-oz. can sliced pineapple, drained

1 1-lb. Golden Star Ham by Armour, thinly sliced
Cream cheese
Chopped walnuts
Canned blueberries
Whole strawberries

DRESSING:

¾ cup dairy sour cream
1 tablespoon horseradish mustard

2 teaspoons sugar
1 teaspoon lemon juice

Line platter with lettuce; arrange peaches, pears, pineapple and ham on lettuce. Roll cream cheese into balls; roll in walnuts. Arrange cream cheese balls with pineapple. Fill each peach half with blueberries; garnish each pear half with a strawberry. Combine sour cream, mustard, sugar and lemon juice; chill. Serve with salad. Serves 4.

Reprinted by permission of Armour Food Companies

FROSTY FRUIT SALAD

½ cup Miracle Whip Salad Dressing
1 8-oz. pkg. cream cheese
2 cups vanilla ice cream, softened

1 10-oz. pkg. frozen raspberries, drained or 1 cup fresh raspberries
1 17-oz. can peach slices, drained
Lettuce

Gradually add salad dressing to softened cream cheese, mixing until well blended. Stir in ice cream. Fold in fruit; pour into 6-cup

72

ring mold or eight ¾-cup molds. Freeze until firm. Unmold; surround with lettuce. Garnish with additional raspberries and mint, if desired. 6 to 8 servings.

MACEDOINE OF FRESH FRUITS

3 tablespoons Hiram Walker
    Apricot Flavored Brandy
3 tablespoons Hiram Walker
    Triple Sec
1 tablespoon Hiram Walker
    Amaretto
¼ cup powdered sugar
2 cups seedless green grapes

2 medium oranges, peeled, sliced
    and quartered
4 medium peaches (or plums),
    sliced
1 pint strawberries, hulled and
    sliced
1 pint blueberries
2 kiwi peeled, sliced and
    quartered (optional)

Mix liqueurs and powdered sugar until dissolved: pour over fruit mixture. Chill several hours. Serve in sugar-rimmed wine glasses. About 16 servings.

Sugar-Rimmed Wine Glasses

Beat 1 egg white with 1 teaspoon water in shallow bowl. Dip rim of wine glass in egg white, then in shallow dish of sugar. Let stand several minutes to dry before filling.

Reprinted by permission of Hiram Walker Inc.

PACIFIC COAST FRUIT SALAD

1 16-oz. can cling peach slices,
    packed in syrup or juice
1 8-oz. can pineapple chunks
1 orange
1 banana
2 – 3 tablespoons flaked coconut
3 tablespoons dry roasted
    peanuts, coarsely chopped

1 tablespoon lime juice
1 teaspoon soy sauce
¼ teaspoon dried hot red pepper
    flakes (optional)
⅛ teaspoon salt
3 tablespoons peanut or
    vegetable oil

Drain canned fruits. Peel and slice orange and banana. Arrange fruits on serving plate. Sprinkle with coconut and chopped peanuts. Combine lime juice, soy sauce, red pepper flakes and salt. Beat in oil and drizzle over salad. Serves 5 – 6.

Reprinted by permission of Cling Peach Advisory Board

PEACH AMBROSIA

2 cups sliced fresh peaches
½ cup sliced bananas
½ cup blueberries or sliced
   strawberries

1 tablespoon fresh lemon juice
3 tablespoons sugar
¼ cup shredded coconut

Combine fruits, lemon juice and sugar; chill. Stir in coconut and spoon into serving dishes. Top with a fresh cherry, if desired. Serves 4.

Reprinted by permission of June Towers, Imperial Sugar Company

STUFFED PEACHES

12 canned peach halves
1 cup creamed cottage cheese
2 cups frozen whipped topping,
   thawed
¼ cup lemon-flavored gelatin

½ cup chopped, drained
   maraschino cherries
¼ cup chopped pecans
Red-leaf or salad bowl lettuce

Drain peach halves. In a medium bowl, combine cottage cheese and whipped topping. Sprinkle dry gelatin over top; stir in. Stir in cherries and pecans. Arrange peach halves, cut side up, in a 9-inch square pan. Mound cottage cheese mixture on top of each. Refrigerate until ready to serve. Shape lettuce leaves in bowls; place 2 stuffed peaches onto lettuce. 6 servings.

SUMMER FRUIT MEDLEY

2 Sunkist oranges, peeled, sliced
   into cartwheels
2 fresh peaches, peeled, sliced
3 fresh plums, quartered
1 cup seedless green grapes
1 cup whole strawberries

1 cup Cointreau, white wine, or
   ginger ale
½ cup firmly packed brown
   sugar
½ cup dairy sour cream

Arrange fruits in a shallow dish. Pour Cointreau over all. Cover and refrigerate at least 4 hours, turning and basting several times. Spoon fruit and juice into dessert dishes. Sprinkle each serving with 1 tablespoon brown sugar and top with a dollop of sour cream. 8 servings.

Reprinted by permission of Sunkist Growers, Inc.

BURGUNDY FRUIT DELIGHT

1 16-oz. can Del Monte Yellow
    Cling Sliced Peaches
1 3-oz. pkg. cherry-flavored
    gelatin
1 3-oz. pkg. raspberry-flavored
    gelatin
1½ cups boiling water

1½ cups Burgundy wine
1 16-oz. can Del Monte Bartlett
    Sliced Pears, drained
Lettuce
½ cup sour cream
½ cup mayonnaise

Drain peaches, reserving syrup. Dissolve gelatins in boiling water. Add reserved peach syrup and wine. Chill until partially set. Fold in drained pears and peaches. Pour into 6-cup mold. Chill until firm. Unmold on lettuce-lined plate. Combine sour cream and mayonnaise. Serve with gelatin. 10 to 12 servings.

Reprinted by permission of Del Monte Kitchens, Del Monte Corporation

CLING-A-LING SALAD

1 3-oz. pkg. orange-flavored
    gelatin
1 cup boiling water
2 cups (1-lb. can) cling peach
    slices
2 envelopes unflavored gelatin

½ cup lemon juice
1 3¾-oz. package instant lemon
    pudding mix
1 cup Miracle Whip Salad Dressing
½ cup milk

Dissolve orange gelatin in boiling water. Drain peach slices, reserving ¾ cup syrup. Add syrup to gelatin; chill until thickened. Pour into 1½-quart mold. Arrange peach slices in gelatin; chill until firm. Soften unflavored gelatin in lemon juice; stir over low heat until dissolved. Cool. Prepare pudding as directed on package; fold in salad dressing, milk and gelatin. Pour over molded peach layer. Chill until firm; unmold. Serve with additional salad dressing. 6 to 8 servings.

GOLDEN PEACH MOLDS

2 large cans peach halves
    (drained, reserve juice)
½ cup vinegar
2 tsp. whole cloves

2 4-inch sticks cinnamon
1 6-oz. package peach gelatin
2 16-oz. cans jellied cranberry
    sauce

In a saucepan, simmer peach syrup, vinegar, cloves and cinnamon uncovered for 10 minutes. Strain. Measure syrup mixture; add enough water to make 2 cups. Pour gelatin into bowl, pour syrup mixture over gelatin in bowl to dissolve. Stir until completely dissolved. Divide peach halves into 16 molds. Pour gelatin mixture over peach halves. Chill 8 hours. Unmold onto slices of cranberry sauce. Yield: 16 servings.

Adapted by Barbara Sisk, Hempstead, Texas, from Golden Apricot Molds.
From Betty Crocker's Recipe Card Library, by permission of General Mills, Inc.

GOLDEN PEACH SALAD

2 cups boiling water	¾ cup miniature marshmallows
1 6-oz. package peach-flavored gelatin	¼ cup sugar
	1 tablespoon flour
1 39-oz. can peach halves (drain, reserve syrup)	1 egg, beaten
	1 cup chilled whipping cream
1 20-oz. can crushed pineapple (drain, reserve syrup)	Toasted coconut

Pour boiling water on gelatin in large bowl; stir until gelatin is dissolved. Mix peach and pineapple syrups; reserve 1 cup for later. Measure remaining syrup; add enough water to measure 1 cup. Stir syrup-water mixture into gelatin mixture. Refrigerate until slightly thickened, about 1 hour. Stir peaches, pineapples and marshmallows into gelatin mixture; pour into baking dish, 11¾ × 7½ × 1¾ inches. Refrigerate until firm, about 3 hours. Mix sugar and flour in 1-qt. saucepan. Stir in reserved syrups and the egg. Heat to boiling over low heat, stirring constantly. Boil and stir 1 minute; cool. Beat whipping cream in chilled small mixer bowl until soft peaks form. Fold in fruit syrup mixture. Spread evenly over gelatin layer. Sprinkle coconut over top. 10–12 servings.

Adapted by Barbara Sisk, Hempstead, Texas, from Golden Apricot Salad.
Reprinted from Betty Crocker's Recipe Card Library, by permission of General Mills, Inc.

HIDDEN PEACH SURPRISE RING

1 tablespoon mayonnaise	¼ cup chopped pecans
Juice from peaches	2 tablespoons sour cream
2 small packages orange gelatin	2 29-oz. jars spiced peaches,
1 8-oz. package cream cheese	reserve juice

Grease bundt pan or ring mold with 1 tablespoon mayonnaise. Bring peach juice to full boil and add gelatin. Stir until gelatin dissolves. Cool. Mix cream cheese, pecans and sour cream together. Remove pits from peaches very carefully and stuff each peach half with 1 tablespoon of cheese mixture. Press peach halves back together. Place stuffed peaches in pan or mold and pour gelatin mixture over them. Chill until completely set. 12 servings.

Reprinted by permission of The National Pecan Marketing Council, Inc.

IMPERIAL PEACH SALAD

1 17-oz. can peach slices
1 3-oz. package cherry-flavored
  gelatin
1 cup boiling water

1 3-oz. package lemon-flavored
  gelatin
1 cup boiling water
¾ cup cold water
1 8-oz. pkg. cream cheese

Drain peaches, reserving 1 cup syrup. Dissolve cherry gelatin in boiling water; add reserved syrup. Chill until partially set. Arrange peach slices in bottom of an oiled 1½-quart ring mold; cover with gelatin. Chill until almost set. Dissolve lemon gelatin in boiling water; add cold water. Gradually add to softened cream cheese, mixing until blended. Pour over molded layer; chill until firm. 6 to 8 servings.

MOLDED PEACH–MARSHMALLOW SALAD

1 pkg. lemon-flavored gelatin
1 cup boiling water
1 cup ginger ale
2 cups miniature marshmallows

1½ cups drained sliced peaches
Lettuce
Mayonnaise or Miracle Whip Salad
  Dressing

Dissolve lemon gelatin in boiling water. Add ginger ale; chill until slightly thickened. Fold in marshmallows. Arrange half of peaches in a l-quart mold. Cover with half of gelatin mixture. Arrange remaining peaches on gelatin; cover with remaining gelatin. Chill until firm. Unmold on lettuce. Serve with mayonnaise or salad dressing.

PEACH ALMOND SOUFFLE SALAD

1 cup boiling water
1 3-oz. package orange-flavor
  gelatin
½ cup cold water
2 tablespoons lemon juice
½ cup Hellmann's or Best Foods
  Real Mayonnaise

¼ teaspoon salt
1 1-lb. can sliced cling peaches,
  drained and diced
1 3-oz. package cream cheese,
  softened
¼ cup toasted slivered almonds

Pour boiling water over gelatin; stir until dissolved. Add cold water, lemon juice, real mayonnaise and salt; blend with rotary beater. Pour into 9 × 5 × 3-inch metal loaf pan. Chill in freezing unit 20 – 25 minutes or until firm about 1 inch from edges of pan but soft in center. Meanwhile mix peaches, cream cheese and almonds together. Turn chilled gelatin mixture into bowl and whip with rotary beater until thick and slightly fluffy. DO NOT OVERBEAT. Fold in peach mixture. Pour into 1-quart mold or individual molds. Chill in refrigerator (not freezing unit) at least 1½ hours or until firm. Unmold. If desired serve on salad greens and garnish with mint, peach slices, almonds or real mayonnaise. Makes 4 to 6 servings.

Reprinted by permission of Best Foods Division Corn Products Company

PEACH PARFAIT SALAD

1 11-oz. can mandarin oranges
1 1-lb. can peach slices
1 3-oz. package peach gelatin
1 pint vanilla ice cream
1 cup halved, seeded grapes
¼ cup broken walnuts

Drain oranges and peaches; reserve juices. Chop peaches. Add enough water to juices to measure 1½ cups liquid; pour into saucepan. Bring to a boil. Add gelatin; stir until dissolved. Add spoonfuls of ice cream; stir until melted. Chill until partially congealed. Stir in fruits and walnuts; pour into 9-inch square pan. Chill until firm. Yield: 9 servings.

PEACHES AND CREAM SALAD

1 3-oz. package peach-flavored
  gelatin
1 cup boiling water
¾ cup cold water
3 cups sliced peaches
1 small banana, sliced
1 envelope unflavored gelatin
3 tablespoons cold water
½ cup half-and-half
1 8-oz. package cream cheese,
  softened
1 cup whipping cream
½ cup plus 2 tablespoons sugar
1 cup pureed peaches

Dissolve peach gelatin in 1 cup boiling water; stir until dissolved. Add cold water and mix well. Chill until the consistency of unbeaten egg white. Stir in sliced peaches and banana. Pour into a lightly oiled 8-cup mold. Chill until set. Soften unflavored gelatin in 3 tablespoons cold water. Scald half-and-half, and stir into gelatin mixture. Beat cream cheese with electric mixer. Add whipping cream, sugar, and pureed peaches; mix well. Add to gelatin mixture, and stir well. Pour over peach and banana layer; chill at least 8 hours or until firm. Yield: 10 to 12 servings.

Reprinted by permission of Oxmoor House, Inc., publisher of *Southern Living Annual Recipes* 1983, Copyright 1983. This book may be purchased at all bookstores or from: Southern Living Books, P.O. Box 2463, Birmingham, Alabama 35280

SPARKLING FRUIT

¾ cup boiling water
1 3-oz. package peach- or orange-
    flavored gelatin
1¼ cups sweet white wine
    (sauterne, muscatel, Tokay)
1 medium banana, sliced

4 medium peaches, cut into
    eighths
1 pint strawberries or raspberries
1½ cups seedless green grapes
Whipped topping
Ground nutmeg

Pour boiling water on gelatin in bowl; stir until gelatin is dissolved. Stir in wine. Refrigerate until slightly thickened, about 1¼ hours. Mound fruit in attractive arrangement in compote, shallow glass bowl or 9-inch pie plate. Pour gelatin mixture on fruit. Refrigerate until chilled. Spoon ring of whipped topping around edge; sprinkle topping with nutmeg. Serves 8.

Reprinted from Betty Crocker's Recipe Card Library, by permission of General Mills

PEACHY SURPRISE SALAD

¾ cup butter, melted
2¼ cups crushed pretzels
1¾ cups sugar
2 8-oz. packages cream cheese,
    softened

1 large carton whipped topping
3 cups sliced peaches
1 15-½ oz. can pineapple chunks
1 6-oz. package peach gelatin

Combine butter, pretzels and ¼ cup sugar in 13″ × 9″ pan, mixing and spreading over bottom of pan. Blend cream cheese, whipped topping and 1½ cups sugar in a bowl. Spread over pretzel layer. Drain juices from peaches and pineapples, reserving juices. Combine juices with enough water to measure 2 cups. Dissolve gelatin in hot juice mixture. Stir in 2 cups ice, chill until thickened. Fold in fruit. Spread over cream cheese mixture. Garnish with pecans.

Barbara Sisk, Hempstead Texas

PRETTY AND EASY SALAD

1 small box diet strawberry
    gelatin
1 16-oz. can sliced diet apricots,
    drained
1 16-oz. can sliced diet peaches,
    drained

1 small can mandarin oranges,
    drained
1 small can unsweetened
    crushed pineapple, drained
1 9-oz. carton Cool Whip
1 8-oz. carton cottage cheese

Sprinkle gelatin over drained fruits. Combine Cool Whip and cottage cheese; fold into fruit mixture. Refrigerate for several hours.

Reprinted by permission of Favorite Recipes Press, Nashville, Tennessee

SPICED PEACH MOLD

2 large jars spiced peaches
2 packages orange or lemon
  gelatin
2 cans white seedless grapes,
  drained

1 No. 2 can pineapple tidbits,
  drained
1 cup chopped almonds or
  pecans

Drain peaches; reserve juice. Dice peaches. Bring 2½ cups reserved peach juice to a boil. Pour into gelatin; stir until gelatin is dissolved. Chill until partially congealed. Combine peaches, grapes and pineapple; stir into gelatin. Add almonds; pour into mold. Chill until firm. Yield: 10 – 12 servings.

Reprinted by permission of Favorite Recipes Press, Nashville, Tennessee

HOT FRUIT COMPOTE

2 16-oz. cans sliced peaches in
  heavy syrup, well drained
2 29-oz. cans pear halves in
  heavy syrup, well drained
1 20-oz. can chunk pineapple in
  heavy syrup, well drained
1 16-½ oz. can pitted dark sweet
  cherries, well drained

3 medium-size bananas, sliced
¾ cup plus 3 tablespoons packed
  light brown sugar
1 16-oz. jar applesauce (about 2
  cups)
½ cup butter or margarine
1 4-oz. can pecan halves (1 cup)

Arrange peaches, pears, pineapple, cherries and bananas in attractive design in 13 × 9 × 2-inch baking dish. Heat ¾ cup brown sugar with applesauce and butter in small saucepan over medium heat, stirring until blended. Pour evenly over fruit. Arrange pecan halves on top and sprinkle with the 3 tablespoons brown sugar. If desired, refrigerate overnight. Heat oven to 300°F. Bake fruit 1 hour until hot and bubbly. Makes about 8 to 10 servings.

Reprinted by permission of National Food Processors Association

SWEDISH CHERRY SOUP

1 No. 303 can red cherries, water
  packed
½ cup sugar
1 medium orange, sliced
1 2-inch cinnamon stick

6 – 8 whole cloves
½ teaspoon lemon juice
1 No. 2 can peaches, sliced
½ teaspoon cornstarch

Heat cherries, sugar, orange, cinnamon stick, cloves and lemon juice to boiling. Drain peaches. Combine cornstarch and a small amount of peach juice. Add remaining juice to cherries; heat. Slowly add cornstarch mixture, stirring constantly, and cook until thickened. Add peaches. Serve warm or cold as a first course or dessert.

Reprinted by permission of National Red Cherry Institute, Box 30285, Lansing, Michigan 48909

CREAMY FRESH PEACH SOUP

2 tablespoons butter
1½ tablespoons flour
¼ teaspoon salt
1 cup half-and-half

1¼ cups peach puree (about 2 large peaches)
1 tablespoon sugar

Melt butter in medium-size saucepan. Mix in flour and salt and heat until bubbly. Add the half-and-half and the peach puree that has been sweetened with the tablespoon of sugar. Cook over low to moderate heat, stirring constantly, until thick. Serve warm or cold. (A garnish might be a dollop of whipped cream or sour cream.) Soup can be made a day ahead of time and stored in the refrigerator. Serves approximately 4.

Carol Coles, Houston, Texas

CATAWBA CORN AND PEACH SOUP

12 fresh white peaches, halved and peeled
2 tablespoons maple syrup
1 quart hot water
1 teaspoon ground ginger

1½ cups fresh corn kernels (about 3 ears)
2 tablespoons sunflower seeds
1 lb. whole kernel corn
¼ teaspoon fresh mint, diced

Put fresh corn kernels with about 1 cup of the water into the blender or food processor until smooth corn milk (about 20 seconds). Add sunflower seeds and mint leaves; process another 20 seconds. Add to remaining ingredients in a large enamel pot and simmer, stirring gently, about 30 minutes until flavors blend and develop. Serve hot or cool, sprinkle with favorite garnishes and serve with fresh nasturtium blossoms (in season) for a peppery accent.

Reprinted by permission of Co-Op Power

PEACH FESTIVAL SOUP

3 cups chopped fresh peaches (6 to 8 peaches)
1½ cups milk
1 10¾-ounce can Campbell's Condensed Cream of Chicken Soup

2 – 3 tablespoons honey
1 teaspoon grated, fresh, peeled ginger root (or ½ teaspoon ground ginger)

In 1½-quart saucepan over medium heat, cook peaches, milk, soup, honey and ginger about 10 minutes, stirring occasionally until peaches are tender.

In covered blender container or food processor, at high speed, blend soup mixture until smooth. Chill at least 4 hours or overnight. Serve cold in chilled bowls. Makes 4½ cups or 6 servings.

Reprinted by permission of Campbell Soup Company

Breads, Pastries & Cobblers

PEACHES PEACHES PEACHES

There are more peach varieties than I can say,
That are located in the peach orchards of today.
A beautiful kind to behold,
Is the one titled as Maygold.
This peach is grown in the Lone Star State,
Which between other varieties can cause debate.
One type that can be a big demander,
Is a favorite peach — the Early Amber.
A kind which can be grown in sand,
Is a huge peach named the Rio Grande.
One peach's popularity is slowly soaring,
And is widely known as the Loring.
These are only a few, but I must close,
Because these are the ones which everyone knows.

By Michael Freeman, Ennis Texas, June 10, 1985

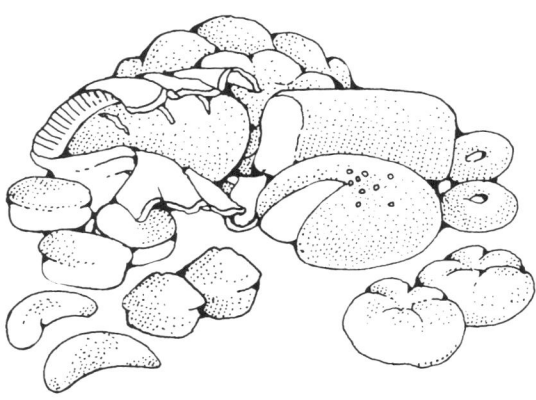

BABY BLINTZE STACKS

Peach Filling (recipe follows)
1½ cups all-purpose flour*
1 tablespoon granulated sugar
½ teaspoon baking powder
½ teaspoon salt
½ teaspoon ground nutmeg
2 cups milk
2 eggs

2 tablespoons butter or
   margarine, melted
½ teaspoon vanilla
½ cup dairy sour cream
2 tablespoons packed brown
   sugar
Peach slices

Prepare Peach Filling; refrigerate. Mix flour, granulated sugar, baking powder, salt and nutmeg in large bowl. Beat in milk, eggs, butter and vanilla. Lightly butter griddle; heat until bubbly. Pour batter onto griddle, bake only on 1 side until bottoms are brown. Place blintzes on towel; cover. For each serving, stack 5 blintzes, spreading 1 tablespoon Peach Filling between each blintze. Mix sour cream and brown sugar; spoon onto blintze stacks. Garnish with peach slices. 10 servings.

*If using self-rising flour, omit baking powder and salt.

Peach Filling

1 24-oz. carton creamed cottage
   cheese
2 medium peaches, peeled and
   chopped

3 tablespoons sugar
½ teaspoon ground nutmeg
¼ teaspoon salt
¼ teaspoon almond extract

Mix all ingredients thoroughly.

Reprinted from Betty Crocker's Recipe Card Library, by permission of General Mills

DUTCH BOY PANCAKE

1 7-oz. jar marshmallow creme
1 8-oz. pkg. cream cheese
2 eggs
½ cup flour
¼ teaspoon salt

½ cup milk
1 tablespoon margarine
1 qt. sliced strawberries, sliced
   peaches or blueberries

Gradually add marshmallow creme to softened cream cheese, mixing until well blended. Combine eggs, flour, salt and milk; beat until smooth. Heat heavy oven-proof 9-inch skillet in 450-degree oven until very hot. Coat skillet with margarine; immediately add batter. Bake on lowest shelf in oven at 450 degrees, 10 minutes. Reduce heat to 350 degrees; continue baking 10 minutes or until golden brown. Fill with fruit; top with cream cheese mixture. Serve immediately. 6 to 8 servings.

FRESH PEACH CREPES

2 8-oz. packages cream cheese, softened
½ cup sugar
2 teaspoons vanilla extract
8 crepes (recipe follows)
6 large ripe peaches, peeled, seeded and sliced

½ cup butter or margarine, softened
½ cup firmly packed light brown sugar
1 cup whipping cream
1 tablespoon powdered sugar

Combine cream cheese, ½ cup sugar, and vanilla; beat until smooth. Spread about 3 tablespoons of cream cheese mixture over each crepe. Place a row of peach slices down the center of each crepe, reserving enough slices for garnish. Dot peaches in each crepe with 1 tablespoon butter, and sprinkle with 1 tablespoon brown sugar. Roll up crepes, and place in a 13 × 9 × 2-inch baking dish; bake at 325 degrees for 8 to 10 minutes.

Combine whipping cream and powdered sugar; beat until stiff peaks form. Place crepes on serving dishes; garnish with whipped cream and peach slices. Serve immediately. Yield: 8 servings.

Crepes:

¾ cup all-purpose flour
¾ cup milk
2 eggs
1 tablespoon light brown sugar
1 tablespoon vegetable oil

Dash of ground cinnamon
Dash of ground nutmeg
Dash of ground ginger
Vegetable oil

Combine first 8 ingredients in container of electric blender; process 1 minute. Scrape down sides of blender with rubber spatula; process an additional 15 seconds. Refrigerate 1 hour. (This allows flour particles to swell and soften so crepes are light in texture.) Brush the bottom of a 6-inch crepe pan or nonstick skillet with vegetable oil; place pan over medium heat until oil is just hot, not smoking. Pour about 3 tablespoons batter into the hot pan; quickly tilt pan in all directions so that batter covers the pan in a thin film. Cook crepe 1 minute. Lift the edge of crepe to test for doneness. Crepe is ready for flipping when it can be shaken loose from pan. Flip crepe, and cook about 30 seconds on other side. (This side is rarely more than spotty brown and is the side on which the filling is placed.) Place crepes on a towel to cool. Stack crepes between layers of waxed paper. Yield: 8 crepes.

Reprinted by permission of *Southern Living Annual Recipes*, 1984.

CHEESY PEACH LATTICE

1 pkg. dry active yeast
¼ cup warm water
1 cup milk
⅓ cup butter or margarine
¼ cup granulated sugar
1 teaspoon salt
1 egg, beaten

3½ to 4 cups all-purpose flour
1 3-oz. pkg. cream cheese,
  softened
½ cup powdered sugar
1 pint peach jam
1 cup powdered sugar
3 tablespoons milk

Preheat oven to 350 degrees. In large bowl, dissolve yeast in warm water. Set aside until foamy. Heat 1 cup milk to almost boiling. Stir in butter, granulated sugar and salt. Cool to lukewarm. Stir cooled milk mixture and egg into yeast. Stir in enough flour to make soft dough. Turn dough out onto lightly floured board; knead until smooth. Grease large bowl; place dough into bowl, turn to grease all sides. Cover with clean dry towel; let rise in warm place until double in size (approx. 1 to 1½ hours). In small mixing bowl mix cream cheese and ½ cup powdered sugar until smooth; set aside. Punch down dough. Divide into 3 equal portions. On lightly floured board roll each portion to 12 × 7 inches. With kitchen scissors cut 3-inch slits 1 inch apart on both 7-inch sides. Spread one-third of cheese filling onto center of dough and one-third of jam on top of cheese. Bring 1-inch strips across jam to form lattice. Place on greased baking sheet. Repeat with others. When all three are on baking sheet, cover with clean dry towel and let rise for 45 minutes. Bake for 30 minutes or until lightly brown. In small mixing bowl beat 1 cup powdered sugar with milk until smooth. Drizzle over coffee cake.

Reprinted by permission of Barbara Sisk, Hempstead, Texas

PEACH MUFFINS IMPERIAL

1½ cups all-purpose flour
¾ teaspoon salt
½ teaspoon soda
1 cup Imperial Granulated Sugar
2 eggs, well beaten
½ cup salad oil

1¼ cups fresh or drained canned
  peaches, coarsely chopped
½ teaspoon vanilla
⅛ teaspoon almond extract
½ cup almonds, chopped

Combine flour, salt, soda and Imperial Granulated Sugar. Make a well in center of dry ingredients. Add eggs and oil. Stir only until dry ingredients are moistened. Stir in peaches, vanilla, almond extract and nuts. Measure ⅓ cup batter into each cavity of muffin tin. Bake at 350 degrees for 20–25 minutes, or until muffins test done. Yield: 12 muffins.

COOKING TIP: For Peach Bread, spoon batter into one 9-inch loaf pan. Bake at 350 degrees for 1 hour, or until bread tests done.

Reprinted by permission of June Towers, Imperial Sugar Co., Sugar Land, Texas

PEACHY WAFFLES

3 eggs	½ cup shortening
1½ cups buttermilk	1 teaspoon almond extract
1¾ cups Gold Medal flour	½ cup diced, roasted almonds
2 teaspoons baking powder	1 cup dairy sour cream
1 teaspoon soda	¼ cup brown sugar, packed
½ teaspoon salt	4 cups sweetened, sliced peaches

Beat eggs; beat in buttermilk, flour, baking powder, soda, salt and shortening with rotary beater until smooth. Stir in extract and almonds. Pour batter from cup or pitcher onto center of hot waffle iron. Bake until steaming stops. Lift off waffle carefully with fork. Mix sour cream and sugar. Serve waffles topped with peaches and sweetened sour cream. Three 9-inch waffles.

Reprinted from Betty Crocker's Recipe Card Library, by permission of General Mills

GEORGIA "PEACH" BREAD

3 cups sliced FRESH peaches	1 teaspoon ground cinnamon
6 tablespoons sugar	1½ cups sugar
2 cups all-purpose flour	½ cup shortening
1 teaspoon baking powder	2 eggs
1 teaspoon soda	1 cup finely chopped pecans
¼ teaspoon salt	1 teaspoon vanilla extract

Place peaches and 6 tablespoons sugar in container of electric blender; process until pureed. (Mixture should yield about 2¼ cups.) Combine flour, baking powder, soda, salt and cinnamon; set aside. Combine 1½ cups sugar and shortening; cream well. Add eggs, mix well. Add peach puree and dry ingredients, mixing until all dry ingredients are moistened. Stir in nuts and vanilla. Spoon batter into 2 well-greased and floured 9 × 5 × 3-inch loaf pans. Bake at 325 degrees for 55 – 60 minutes or until well done. Cool 10 minutes in pan, turn out on rack and let cool completely. 2 loaves.

Jean Pryor, Houston, Texas

PEACH WHEAT BREAD

2 cups unsifted Robin Hood All Purpose Flour
¾ cup Kretschmer Wheat Germ, Regular or Brown Sugar & Honey
⅔ cup sugar
1 teaspoon baking powder
¾ teaspoon salt
½ teaspoon soda
¼ teaspoon nutmeg
2 eggs
1 16-oz. CAN sliced peaches with syrup, pureed
¼ cup buttermilk or sour milk
2 tablespoons softened butter or margarine
½ cup chopped walnuts

Combine flour, wheat germ, sugar, baking powder, salt, soda and nutmeg on wax paper. Stir well to blend. Beat eggs slightly in large bowl. Add dry ingredients, peaches, buttermilk and butter. Blend about 30 seconds. Beat at low speed about 1 minute until well-blended. Stir in walnuts. Spread batter in greased 9 × 5 × 3-inch loaf pan. Bake at 350 degrees for 60–65 minutes until wooden pick inserted in center comes out clean. Cool in pan 5–10 minutes. Remove from pan. Cool on rack. Wrap in foil or plastic wrap and store overnight for easier slicing. Makes 1 loaf.

Reprinted by permission of International Multifoods/Kretschmer Wheat Germ

PINEAPPLE-PEACH BREAD

Butter
¼ cup toasted sliced almonds
¾ cup milk
½ cup (1 stick) butter, melted and cooled
1 8-oz. can crushed pineapple
1 cup chopped, dried peaches
1 egg, slightly beaten
3 cups all-purpose flour
¾ cup sugar
1 tablespoon baking powder
¾ teaspoon salt
¼ teaspoon baking soda

Preheat oven to 350 degrees F. Generously butter a 9 × 5-inch loaf pan. Sprinkle with sliced almonds; gently press almonds to sides and bottom of pan. Combine milk, butter, pineapple, peaches and egg in large mixing bowl. Combine dry ingredients. Stir dry ingredients into milk-fruit mixture just until all ingredients are combined. Spread batter evenly in pan. Bake until wooden pick inserted in center comes out clean, about 70–75 minutes. Cool in pan 15 minutes. Remove from pan and cool completely on wire rack. Wrap tightly in plastic wrap and store 24 hours before serving.

HOWIE'S MICROWAVE COBBLER

1 9-oz. package Jiffy yellow cake mix
1½ tablespoons brown sugar
½ teaspoon cinnamon
½ stick butter
1 can peach pie filling

Blend first three ingredients in bowl, spread pie filling on bottom of 9 × 9-inch glass baking dish. Pour cake batter on top, melt butter and drizzle on top of cake batter. Microwave on HIGH 12 – 14 minutes. Great with vanilla ice cream.

Reprinted by permission of Howard L. Rappaport, Amesbury, Massachusetts

EASY PEACH COBBLER

5 cups peeled, sliced peaches
¾ cup sugar
2 tablespoons all-purpose flour
½ teaspoon ground cinnamon
¼ teaspoon salt
¼ cup water
1 teaspoon vanilla extract
1 tablespoon butter or margarine, softened
½ cup all-purpose flour
½ cup sugar
½ teaspoon baking powder
¼ teaspoon salt
2 tablespoons butter or margarine, softened
1 egg, slightly beaten

Combine the first 7 ingredients; mix gently. Spoon into a lightly greased 9-inch square baking pan; dot with 1 tablespoon butter. Set aside. Combine remaining ingredients; mix well. Spoon over peach mixture in 9 equal portions (batter will spread during baking). Bake at 375 degrees for 35 to 40 minutes. Yield: 6 servings.

Reprinted by permission of North Carolina Department of Agriculture

OLD-FASHIONED FRESH PEACH COBBLER

1½ cups Rice Chex cereal crushed to ½ cup
2½ tablespoons and 1 tablespoon butter or margarine, softened
½ cup milk
1 egg, slightly beaten
⅛ teaspoon almond extract
¾ cup sifted all-purpose flour
¼ cup sugar
1½ teaspoons baking powder
¼ teaspoon salt
⅓ cup packed brown sugar
1½ tablespoons cornstarch
⅓ cup cold water or ½ cup reserved peach syrup
4 cups peeled, sliced, fresh peaches or 1 29-oz. can peaches in heavy syrup, drained (reserve syrup)

Preheat oven to 400 degrees. Have ready a 1½-quart shallow baking dish. Combine Rice Chex and 2½ tablespoons butter until well blended. Beat in milk, egg and extract. Sift together flour, sugar, baking powder and salt. Add to liquid ingredients. Stir just until dry ingredients are moistened. In saucepan combine brown sugar and cornstarch. Stir in water or peach syrup. Add peaches*. Cook and stir over medium heat until sauce comes to a boil and is thickened. Stir in 1 tablespoon butter. Turn into dish. Drop dough by spoonfuls over top. Bake 20–25 minutes or until top is browned. Serve warm. Makes 6 servings.

*When using canned peaches, add after sauce is thickened.

Reprinted by permission of Ralston Purina Company

PEACH RICE COBBLER

3 cups hot, cooked Carolina Rice	⅓ cup brown sugar
1 1-lb. can sliced cling peaches, drained (reserve liquid)	⅓ cup chopped nuts
	2 tablespoons flour
¾ cup milk	3 tablespoons butter or
½ cup sugar	margarine
½ teaspoon grated lemon rind	

Mix rice with ¾ cup liquid from peaches, the milk, sugar and lemon rind. Pour into buttered 1-quart casserole. Arrange sliced peaches on top. Combine brown sugar, nuts and flour. Cut in butter until mixture is crumbly. Sprinkle over peaches and bake at 375 degrees F. for 45 minutes. Makes 8 servings (about ½ cup each).

Reprinted by permission of Riviana Foods, Inc.

PEACH SKILLET COBBLER

1 cup brown sugar	½ cup granulated sugar
1 16-oz. can S&W Natural Style Sliced Cling Peaches, drained (reserve juice)	1 cup flour
	1 tablespoon baking powder
	½ teaspoon cinnamon
½ cup butter	1 cup milk
½ cup chopped nuts	

Mix brown sugar, reserved juice and butter in an 8 or 9-inch roof skillet. Bring to a boil and simmer uncovered for 5 minutes, stirring occasionally. Stir in peaches and nuts. In a small bowl, sift together granulated sugar, flour, baking powder and cinnamon. Add milk and stir just to mix (some lumps will remain). Spoon dough over hot fruit mixture in skillet. Place skillet in oven and bake at 350 degrees for 30–35 minutes. Spoon out of skillet and serve with ice cream if desired. Serves 6.

Reprinted by permission of S.& W. Fine Foods Incorporated

PEACHY PLUM COBBLER

1 cup sugar
3 tablespoons cornstarch
½ teaspoon ground cinnamon
3 cups sliced fresh red plums
  (about 10 to 12 large)
4 medium peaches or nectarines,
  peeled and sliced (about 3
  cups)
1 cup all-purpose flour*

⅓ cup shortening
2 tablespoons sugar
1½ teaspoons baking powder
½ teaspoon salt
¼ cup milk
1 egg, slightly beaten
1 tablespoon sugar
Ice cream or light cream
  (optional)

Heat oven to 375 degrees. Mix 1 cup sugar, the cornstarch and cinnamon in 3-quart saucepan. Stir in plums and peaches. Cook, stirring constantly, until mixture thickens and boils. Boil and stir 1 minute. Pour into ungreased baking dish, 8 × 8 × 2-inches, or 1½-quart casserole. Mix flour, shortening, 2 tablespoons sugar, the baking powder and salt with pastry blender or fork until crumbly. Stir in milk and egg. Drop dough by spoonfuls onto hot fruit mixture; sprinkle with 1 tablespoon sugar. Bake until topping is golden brown, 25 to 30 minutes. Serve warm with ice cream. 9 servings.

*If using self-rising flour, omit baking powder and salt.

Reprinted from Betty Crocker's Recipe Card Library, by permission of General Mills

RHUBARB AND PEACH COBBLER

1 29- or 30-oz. can cling peaches
1 lb. rhubarb, cut into 1-inch
  chunks (about 4 cups)

¼ cup sugar
2 cups buttermilk baking mix
⅔ cup milk

Preheat oven to 425 degrees F. Drain peaches, reserving ½ cup syrup. In 2-quart saucepan over medium heat, heat rhubarb, sugar and reserved peach syrup to boiling. Reduce heat to low, cover and simmer 7 minutes or until rhubarb is tender, stirring occasionally. Stir in peaches. Spoon mixture into eight 8-ounce oven-safe dessert bowls.

In medium bowl, stir buttermilk mix and milk until soft dough forms. Drop mixture by scant ¼ cupfuls onto fruit mixture in each bowl. Bake 10 minutes or until biscuits are golden brown. Makes 8 servings.

Jean Pryor, Houston, Texas

PEACH CREAM PUFF RING

1 cup water
½ cup butter or margarine
1 cup all-purpose flour
4 eggs
1 cup milk

¾ cup dairy sour cream
1 3¾-oz. pkg. instant vanilla
  pudding
¼ teaspoon almond extract
1 Can peach pie filling

Heat oven to 400 degrees. Heat water and butter to boiling in 1-qt. saucepan; stir in flour. Stir vigorously until mixture forms ball, about 1 minute. Remove from heat. Add eggs; beat until smooth. (or place dough in small mixer bowl, add eggs and beat on low speed for 2 minutes). Drop dough by tablespoons onto greased baking sheet to form an 8-inch ring. Smooth with spatula. Bake until puffed and golden, 50–60 minutes. Cool. Cut off top with a sharp knife; pull out any soft dough. Beat milk and sour cream and pudding (dry), add extract, in small mixing bowl at low speed, about 1 minute or until well blended. Fill cream puff with pudding mixture and ½ cup pie filling. Replace top of cream puff ring and spoon remaining peach filling on top. 10–12 servings.

Adapted by Barbara Sisk

BAKED PEACH DUMPLINGS

2 cups sifted flour
1 teaspoon salt
¼ cup shortening
1 egg yolk
¾ cup Milnot*
¼ cup water
1 tablespoon lemon juice

¼ cup sugar
½ teaspoon cinnamon
6 peach halves
¾ cup sugar
⅔ cup water
⅛ teaspoon salt

Sift flour and salt together. Cut in shortening. Blend egg yolk and Milnot; add to flour mixture, blend in water and lemon juice. Form dough into a ball. Roll out to ⅛-inch thickness, cut in 6-inch squares. Mix sugar and cinnamon; roll each peach half in sugar mixture and place cut side down in center of each pastry. Bring opposite points together, overlap, moisten, and seal. Place in greased shallow pan leaving space between each dumpling. Heat sugar, salt, and water to boiling, pour over dumplings. Bake at 425 degrees for 40 min.

*Milnot Brand Dairy Vegetable Blend (no butterfat, virtually no cholesterol)

EASY PEACH FRIED PIES

Filling:

3 tablespoons cornstarch	¼ teaspoon almond flavoring
¾ cup sugar	(optional)
¾ cup water	3 fresh peaches, peeled and diced
Pinch salt	fine (about 2 cups)

Mix cornstarch, sugar, salt and water in a small saucepan until thoroughly dissolved. Cook over low heat, stirring constantly until thick and clear. Add diced peaches and flavoring and set aside while preparing pastry.

PASTRY

2 cans refrigerated biscuits   Vegetable cooking oil

On lightly floured board roll out each biscuit until very thin. Set aside and let rise approximately 10 minutes. After dough has risen, roll each biscuit very thin again. Spread filling of thickened fresh peaches over half of each biscuit. Crimp edges together with a fork. Heat oil in an electric skillet or on top of range to 360 degrees. Place pies in hot oil and fry to desired brownness. Turn only once. Drain on paper towel. Serve warm. Makes approximately 20 pies.

Reprinted by permission of Texas Department of Agriculture

BLUSHING PEACH FRIED PIES

2 sticks or 1 packet of Betty	2 tablespoons granulated sugar
Crocker pie crust mix	1½ tablespoons cornstarch
1 29-oz. can peach slices, drained	Confectioners' sugar
1 tablespoon red cinnamon	
candies	

In deep fat fryer or heavy kettle, heat salad oil (3 to 4 inches) to 375 degrees. Prepare pastry for Two-crust Pie as directed on package except — after rolling pastry, cut into sixteen 4½-inch rounds. Stir together peach slices, candies, granulated sugar and cornstarch. Place about 1 tablespoon fruit mixture on half of each round. Moisten edge of pastry; fold over fruit and press edges with fork to seal. Fry in hot oil, turning once, until golden brown, about 5 minutes. Drain pies on paper towels. Sprinkle with confectioners' sugar. Serve hot or cool. 16 fried pies.

These tender, crusty little pies can be fried in an electric skillet in 1 inch oil.

Reprinted from Betty Crocker's Recipe Card Library, by permission of General Mills

BAKED PEACH TURNOVERS

2 cups all-purpose flour
2 tablespoons sugar
4 teaspoons baking powder
½ teaspoon salt
½ cup shortening
⅔ cup milk
3 cups sliced, drained fresh or
   frozen peaches

¼ cup sugar
½ teaspoon nutmeg
6 tablespoons margarine or
   butter
1 egg
10X powdered sugar

PASTRY: Measure flour, sugar, baking powder and salt into mixing bowl. Cut in shortening until particles are fine. Add milk, stirring lightly until dough clings together into a ball. Knead lightly on floured surface a few times. Divide into 6 to 8 pieces and roll each into a circle.

FILLING: Combine peaches, sugar, nutmeg, margarine and 1 to 2 tablespoons flour if peaches are very juicy. Divide filling among circles of pastry; fold to make half-circle shaped pies; crimp edges of pastry with fork dipped in flour to seal. Brush each pie with an egg wash made by beating an egg with 1 tablespoon of water. Place pies on baking sheet in 450-degree oven 8 to 10 minutes, or until golden. Combine some peach juice with powdered sugar to make a glaze for brushing on warm pastries. Sprinkle with sugar. Makes 6 to 8 pastries.

Note: The dough is an excellent all-purpose recipe; when making meat pies, omit sugar. These pies are like the old-fashioned fried pies and can be cooked in a heavy skillet in butter or margarine, if desired.

Reprinted by permission of June Towers, Imperial Sugar Company

GRILLED TURNOVERS

2 Betty Crocker pie crust sticks,
   crumbled
1 tablespoon plus 1 teaspoon
   nonfat dry milk

¼ cup water
1 21-oz. can cherry, peach,
   blueberry or apple pie filling

Mix pie crust sticks, dry milk and water until dough loses stickiness and cleans bowl. Remove label from unopened can of pie filling; lightly flour side of can. Divide dough into 6 equal parts; roll each part on aluminum foil into 6-inch circle, using floured can as rolling pin. Place scant 2 tablespoons pie filling on each pastry circle; fold pastry over filling and press edges with fork to seal. Place on grill over medium coals. Cook 10 minutes on each side or until pastry is delicate brown. 6 servings

Reprinted from Betty Crocker's Recipe Card Library, by permission of General Mills

AUSTRIAN PEACH FRITTERS

2 egg yolks
⅓ cup milk
3 tablespoons wine or brandy
1 tablespoon melted butter or
    margarine
1 cup unsifted all-purpose flour
1 6-oz. pkg. Mont Austria Cheese,
    finely grated

2 egg whites, stiffly beaten
4 fresh peaches, peeled and
    quartered, or well drained,
    canned
Fat or oil for deep frying
Confectioners' sugar

In a bowl, mix egg yolks, milk, wine or brandy, butter or margarine and flour. Fold in Mont Austria Cheese and egg whites. Dip peaches in batter, covering them completely, and drop them into hot fat or oil, at least 2 inches deep, heated to 375 degrees F. Fry until brown on both sides, about 5 – 6 minutes on each side. Place fritters on a plate and sprinkle with confectioners' sugar. Serve with Creamy Nutmeg Sauce. Makes 18 fritters.

Creamy Nutmeg Sauce

1 cup (½ pint) heavy cream
½ cup (2 oz.) grated Mont
    Austria Cheese

2 tablespoons confectioners'
    sugar
½ teaspoon nutmeg

Whip cream in a bowl and fold in remaining ingredients. Chill until ready to serve. Serve cold with hot peach fritters. Makes about 2½ cups.

Reprinted by permission of N. Dorman & Company, Inc.

JELLY ROLL

1 cup sifted cake flour
1 teaspoon baking powder
¼ teaspoon salt
3 eggs
1 cup sugar

⅓ cup water
1 teaspoon vanilla extract
Confectioners' sugar
1 8½-oz. jar peach jelly, jam or
    preserves

Grease a 15 × 10 × 1-inch jelly roll pan. Line the bottom with waxed paper and grease again. Sift together flour, baking powder and salt. In a medium bowl, beat eggs until thick and pale in color. Gradually beat in sugar and continue beating until mixture is stiff. Beat in water and vanilla. Mix in dry ingredients and beat just until batter is smooth. Pour into prepared pan. Bake in preheated 375-degree oven 12 to 15 minutes or until lightly browned. Loosen edges and immediately turn cake upside down on a tea towel that has been generously sprinkled with confectioners' sugar. Carefully peel off waxed paper. Cut away crisp edges of cake. While it is still hot, roll up cake and towel from the narrow end. Cool on cake rack. Unroll cake and remove towel. Spread cake with jelly and roll up again. Sprinkle with additional confectioners' sugar before serving. Serves 10.

PEACHY RUM PIE

Filling:

1 tablespoon gelatin	1½ cups whipping cream
2 tablespoons cold water	1½ cups fresh California
6 large egg yolks	peaches, peeled and diced
⅔ cup sugar	(about 2 medium), drained of
Pinch of salt	all excess liquid
¼ cup dark rum	9-inch pie shell, baked

Topping:

3 cups fresh California peaches, peeled and sliced (about 3 to 4 medium)	2 tablespoons lemon juice
	½ cup slivered almonds, toasted
2 tablespoons sugar (to taste)	Sprig of mint (optional)

Sprinkle gelatin over cold water. Beat egg yolks until light. Add sugar and salt, beating until lemon colored and fluffy. Add gelatin and heat mix in top of double boiler, beating constantly, until gelatin has melted and mix is light and fluffy. Add rum. Cool. Beat cream until nearly stiff; fold into cooled rum mixture. Refrigerate until mix *starts* to set, about 15 minutes. Do not allow to completely set! Peel, dice and drain peaches. Fold into filling. Turn mixture into prepared pie shell. Refrigerate until completely set, about 4 hours.

Peach Topping: Peel and slice peaches. Sauté with sugar and lemon juice. Cook over medium heat until peaches are very soft and thick-like jam — about 1 hour. Turn up heat if necessary to reduce liquid. Cool, strain and refrigerate. Drizzle peach topping in spiral pattern over top of pie. Sprinkle with toasted almonds. Add mint, if desired. 10 servings.

Reprinted by permission of *The Houston Post*

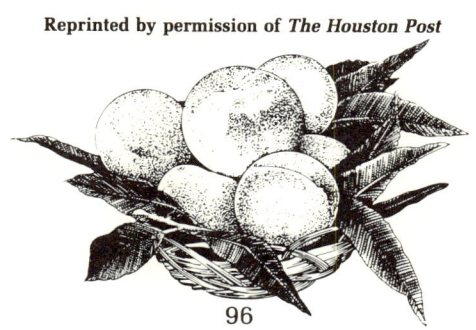

FROZEN FLUFFY PEACH PIE

2½ cups lightly toasted coconut
⅓ cup margarine or butter
1 3-oz pkg. cream cheese, softened
1 14-oz. can Eagle Brand sweetened condensed milk (NOT EVAPORATED MILK)

2½ cups fresh or frozen unsweetened thawed peaches, mashed or pureed (about 1½ cups)
3 tablespoons lemon juice
1 cup (½ pint) whipping cream, whipped
Additional fresh peaches, optional

In large saucepan, melt margarine; stir in toasted coconut. Mix well. Press into bottom and up sides of 9-inch pie plate; chill. In large bowl, beat cheese until fluffy; beat in Eagle Brand. Stir in pureed peaches and lemon juice. Fold in whipped cream. Pour into coconut crust (mixture should mound slightly). Freeze 4 hours or until firm. Before serving, garnish with additional fresh peaches if desired. Return leftovers to freezer.

TIP: One 9-inch baked pastry shell or graham cracker crust can be substituted for the coconut crust.

BLUEBERRY PEACH PIE

1 cup sugar
3 tablespoons Argo or Kingsford's cornstarch
½ teaspoon ground cinnamon
4 medium peaches, peeled, sliced (3 cups)

2 cups blueberries
1 tablespoon lemon juice
Double crust pastry for 9-inch pie
1 tablespoon Nucoa or Mazola margarine

In large bowl stir together sugar, cornstarch and cinnamon. Add peaches, blueberries and lemon juice, tossing to coat fruit. Line 9-inch pie plate with ½ of the pastry rolled to ⅛-inch thickness, allowing 1-inch overhang. Fill with fruit mixture. Dot with margarine. Roll remaining pastry into 12-inch circle. Cut several slits to permit steam to escape. Cover pie with top crust; seal and flute edge. Bake in 425-degree oven 15 minutes. Reduce heat to 350 degrees and continue baking 40 minutes or until filling is bubbly. Makes 8 servings.

Reprinted by permission of Best Foods, a Division of CPC International, Inc.

CREAMY DUTCH PEACH PIE

10 or more ripe peaches (peeled and sliced)
1 unbaked 9-inch pie shell
1 cup sour cream
1 egg (slightly beaten)
3 tablespoons margarine (softened)

¾ cup sugar
5 tablespoons flour
1 teaspoon cinnamon
½ tsp. nutmeg
¼ cup packed brown sugar
½ cup chopped pecans

In a bowl combine margarine, sour cream, egg, sugar, 2 tablespoons flour, and spices. Mix well and set aside. Put peaches in pie shell. Pour sour cream mixture over peaches. Bake for 20 minutes at 350 degrees. Mix 3 tablespoons flour, brown sugar and pecans and sprinkle over pie. Bake 15 minutes more.

Barbara Sisk, Hempstead, Texas

DEEP-DISH PEACH PIE

Margarine Pastry No. 2

1⅓ cups sifted flour
⅛ teaspoon Morton Lite salt mixture

½ cup unsalted polyunsaturated margarine
3 tablespoons cold water

Mix flour and salt. With pastry blender or 2 knives, cut in margarine until mixture is well blended and fine crumbs form. Sprinkle water over mixture while tossing to blend well. Press dough firmly into ball. Flatten slightly.

Nutritional information per recipe:
Calories — 550, Carbohydrates — 111 gm. Fat — 4 gm. Protein — 15 gm. Sodium — 135 mg. Potassium — 400 mg. Cholesterol — 0.

Filling

3 lbs. peaches (12 medium) or nectarines
½ cup light brown sugar
3 tablespoons cornstarch

¼ teaspoon Morton Lite salt mixture
½ cup light corn syrup
2 tablespoons unsalted polyunsaturated margarine

Prepare pastry as directed above. Roll it out ¼-inch wider than a baking dish 10 × 6 × 2-inches, or a 1½-quart casserole. Pare and slice peaches. Combine brown sugar, cornstarch and salt; stir in corn syrup. Lightly toss with peaches. Turn into baking dish and dot with margarine. Place dough over peaches, letting it extend up the sides of the dish. Bake at 425 degrees for 40 minutes, or until peaches are tender and crust is lightly browned. Makes 8 servings.

Nutritional information per recipe:
Calories — 306. Carbohydrate — 66 gm. Fat — 4 gm. Protein — 3 gm.
Sodium — 64 mg. Potassium — 614 mg. Cholesterol — 0.

Reprinted by permission of Morton Salt Division of Morton Thiokol, Inc.

FRESH PEACH PARFAIT PIE

1 Keebler Ready-Crust Butter
 Flavored Pie Crust
1 3-oz. package peach-flavored
 gelatin

½ cup boiling water
1 pint vanilla ice cream, softened
2 cups fresh peaches, sliced

In medium bowl, pour hot water over peach gelatin; stir until dissolved. Add ice cream; stir until smooth. Fold in peaches. Pour into crust. Freeze until set, about 3 hours.

Reprinted by permission of Keebler Company

FROZEN PEACH MELBA PIE

2 cups peeled, sliced peaches
 (about 1 lb.)
¾ cup Karo light corn syrup
1 tablespoon lemon juice
2 drops red food color (optional)
1 pint raspberry sherbet, softened

1 9-inch graham cracker crust
2 drops yellow food color
 (optional)
1 cup vanilla ice cream, softened
Peach slices

In blender container place peaches, corn syrup and lemon juice. Cover and blend 30 seconds or until pureed. Fold 1 cup of the pureed peaches and red food color into raspberry sherbet. Pour into crust. Freeze about 1 hour or until firm. Fold remaining 1 cup pureed peaches and yellow food color into vanilla ice cream. Pour over raspberry layer. Freeze until firm. If desired, garnish.with peach slices. Makes 8 servings.

Reprinted by permission of Best Foods, a Division of CPC International, Inc.

GOLDEN COCONUT PEACH PIE

4 to 4½ cups sliced, fresh peaches
½ cup sugar
3 tablespoons flour
¼ teaspoon nutmeg
⅛ teaspoon salt
¼ cup orange juice

1 9-inch unbaked pie shell
2 tablespoons butter
2 cups flaked coconut
½ cup evaporated milk
1 egg beaten
¼ to ½ cup sugar
¼ teaspoon almond extract

Mix together peaches, sugar, flour, nutmeg, salt and orange juice in medium bowl. Pour mixture into pie shell. Dot with butter; bake at 450 degrees for 15 minutes. Meanwhile, combine coconut, milk, egg, sugar and almond. Pour over hot peach mixture. Reduce heat to 350 degrees and bake until coconut is toasted, about 30 minutes. Chill pie unless eaten at once.

Gloria Kratz, Des Moines, Iowa

PEACH CHEESE PIE

1 9-inch graham cracker crumb crust
1 8-oz. package cream cheese, softened
1 14-oz. can Eagle Brand Sweetened Condensed Milk

⅓ cup Realemon Juice Concentrate
1 teaspoon vanilla extract
1 can peach pie filling, chilled

In large mixing bowl, beat cheese until fluffy. Beat in Eagle Brand until smooth. Stir in Realemon and vanilla. Pour into crust. Chill 3 hours or until set. Top with pie filling before serving. Refrigerate leftovers.

Juanita Grant, Houston, Texas

PEACH CHEESE PIE

2 3-oz. packages cream cheese, softened
½ cup Karo light corn syrup
1 tablespoon Argo or Kingsford's cornstarch
¼ cup milk

1 egg, slightly beaten
1 teaspoon vanilla
1 8-inch unbaked pastry shell
3 peaches
1 tablespoon lemon juice
Glaze (recipe follows)

In small bowl, with mixer at medium speed, beat together cream cheese and corn syrup until smooth. In small bowl, stir together cornstarch and milk until smooth. Add to cream cheese mixture. Beat in egg and vanilla until well mixed. Pour into pastry shell. Bake in 350-degree oven 45 to 50 minutes or until knife inserted in center comes out clean. Cool on wire rack about 1 hour or until warm but not hot. Peel, pit and slice peaches; toss gently with lemon juice. Arrange peach slices over cheese filling. Prepare glaze; cool 1 minute. Spoon glaze over peaches. Refrigerate about 2 hours or until thoroughly chilled. Makes 1 (8-inch) pie.

Glaze

In 1-quart saucepan, stir together 2 tablespoons sugar and 1 tablespoon Argo or Kingsford's cornstarch. Gradually stir in ⅔ cup water until smooth. Stirring constantly, bring to boil over medium heat and boil 1 minute. Remove from heat. Stir in 1 tablespoon lemon juice. Makes about ½ cup.

Blueberry Cheese Pie: Follow recipe for Peach Cheese Pie. Omit peaches and lemon juice. Toss 1 cup blueberries and glaze. Spread evenly over cheese filling.

Reprinted by permission of Best Foods, a unit of CPC North America

PEACH CUSTARD PIE

2 cups all-purpose flour
¾ cup granulated sugar
½ teaspoon salt
½ cup butter or margarine
White of 1 large egg, slightly
    beaten

5 medium-sized freestone
    peaches (about 1¾ lbs.),
    peeled (see note)
½ teaspoon ground cinnamon
⅛ teaspoon ground nutmeg
¾ cup heavy cream
Yolks of 3 large eggs

In a medium-sized bowl mix flour, 2 tablespoons of the sugar and the salt. Add butter and cut in with a pastry blender or two knives until mixture resembles coarse meal. Press evenly onto the bottom and sides of a 10-inch pie pan. Brush crust with beaten egg white. Chill about 15 minutes. Heat oven to 400 degrees F. Halve and pit peaches. Arrange fruit in pie crust, cut side up. In a small bowl mix cinnamon, nutmeg and the remaining sugar. Sprinkle evenly over fruit and crust. Bake 12 minutes, until most of the sugar is melted and the crust is just turning golden. In a small bowl mix heavy cream and yolks. Pour over fruit. Bake about 20 minutes, until custard is set and a knife inserted in the middle comes out clean. Serve warm or cold. Makes 12 servings.

Nutritional information (per serving): calories — 282, protein — 4 gm., fat — 15 gm, carbohydrate — 34 gm.

Note: To peel peaches, dip in boiling water 1 minute; pull off skins.

Reprinted by permission of *Redbook Magazine*

PEACH MELBA STREUSEL PIE

1 Keebler Ready-Crust Butter
    Flavored Pie Crust
1 egg yolk, beaten
¼ cup butter
¾ cup flour
½ cup brown sugar
1 10-oz. package frozen
    raspberries, thawed and
    drained

1 16-oz. package frozen sliced
    peaches, thawed
¼ cup sugar
3 tablespoons cornstarch
¼ teaspoon cinnamon
1 tablespoon lemon juice

Preheat oven to 375 degrees F. Brush bottom and sides of crust evenly with egg yolk; bake on baking sheet until light brown, about 5 minutes. Remove from oven. Cut butter with pastry blender or 2 knives into flour and brown sugar until crumbly. Sprinkle half onto bottom of crust. In medium bowl, combine thawed fruit with sugar, cornstarch and cinnamon. Add lemon juice and toss to mix well. Turn into crust. Sprinkle with remaining topping. Bake on baking sheet 35 to 40 minutes until bubbly and topping is browned. Cool. Serve with scoop of vanilla ice cream.

Reprinted by permission of Keebler Company

PEACH-MINCE PIE

1 Keebler Ready-Crust Graham
    Cracker Pie Crust
1 egg yolk, beaten
1¼ cups prepared mincemeat
1 21-oz. can peach pie filling

2 teaspoons grated orange peel
¼ cup brown sugar
¼ cup flour
3 tablespoons butter or
    margarine

Preheat oven to 375 degrees F. Brush bottom and sides of crust evenly with egg yolk; bake on baking sheet until light brown, about 5 minutes. Combine mincemeat, peach filling and orange peel. Pour into crust. Mix brown sugar and flour; cut in butter until crumbly. Sprinkle over filling. Bake on baking sheet 40 minutes or until top is brown and filling bubbling.

Reprinted by permission of Keebler Company

PEACH PIE

3 tablespoons Minute tapioca
¾ cup sugar
¼ teaspoon salt
4 cups sliced fresh peaches

1 tablespoon lemon juice
Pastry for two-crust 9-inch pie
1 tablespoon butter or margarine

Combine tapioca, sugar, salt, peaches and lemon juice. Let stand 15 minutes. Roll out half of pastry very thin (less than ⅛ inch thick).

Line a 9-inch pie pan. Trim pastry at edge. Roll out remaining pastry very thin; cut several small slits or a design near center. Fill bottom crust with peach mixture. Dot with butter. Moisten edge of bottom crust. Place top crust over filling. Open slits to permit escape of steam. Trim top crust, letting it extend ½ inch over rim. To seal, press top and bottom crusts together on rim; then fold edge of top crust under bottom crust and flute. Bake at 425 degrees for 55 minutes, or until syrup boils with heavy bubbles that do not burst immediately.

Reprinted by permission of General Foods

PEACHY PEANUT BUTTER PIE

½ cup Skippy creamy or super chunk peanut butter
⅓ cup sugar
⅓ cup unsifted flour
1 29-oz. can sliced peaches in heavy syrup
3 tablespoons Argo or Kingsford's cornstarch
¼ cup firmly packed brown sugar
¼ cup orange juice
½ teaspoon ground cinnamon
1 unbaked 9-inch pie shell

In small bowl with pastry blender or 2 knives cut peanut butter into sugar and flour until course crumbs form. Drain peaches; reserve 1⅓ cups syrup. In 2-quart saucepan stir together cornstarch and brown sugar. Stir in peach syrup, orange juice and cinnamon until smooth. Stirring constantly, bring to boil over medium heat and boil 1 minute. Remove from heat; stir in peach slices. Pour peach mixture into pie shell. Sprinkle peanut butter crumb mixture on pie. Bake in 400-degree oven 25 to 30 minutes or until golden. If desired, serve warm, with ice cream. Makes 8 servings.

Reprinted by permission of Best Foods, a unit of CPC North America

SPICED PEACH PAN PIE

Prepared Crust*
1 16-oz. can sliced peaches
3 tablespoons brown sugar
1½ teaspoons vinegar
¼ teaspoon ground cloves
1 3-oz. package cream cheese, softened
½ cup chopped pecans

Prepare dough and set aside. Drain peaches, reserving 1 tablespoon of juice and set aside. Combine brown sugar, peach juice, vinegar, and cloves. Add to cream cheese and mix until thoroughly blended. Spread evenly over pan dough. Sprinkle with pecans and arrange peaches over surface. Bake in 400-degree oven for about 10 to 12 minutes. Note: For a Make-Your-Own-Party, we suggest partially baking pan dough for 2 to 3 minutes in 400-degree oven to make for easier spreading of cream cheese mixture. Then set out all mixtures and toppings so that guests can do the fixing. Pan pies can then be returned to hot oven until heated through. Makes 6 to 8 servings.

*Use your favorite pizza dough, either dry mix or frozen, and prepare a standard 13-inch crust.

Reprinted by permission of The National Pecan Marketing Council, Inc.

TANGY PEACH PIE

2 cups fresh peaches, sliced
1 cup peaches, mashed
½ cup orange juice
1 cup sugar
2½ tablespoons cornstarch

Fill a 9-inch pastry shell with sliced peaches. Combine mashed peaches, orange juice, sugar and cornstarch in a saucepan and boil, stirring constantly, until mixture is clear and slightly thickened. Pour heated mixture over peaches in pie shell. Cool thoroughly before serving.

Reprinted by permission of Texas Department of Agriculture

PEACH PIE

2 cups plus 2 tablespoons all-purpose flour
1¼ teaspoons Sweet 'N Low granulated sugar substitute, divided
⅔ cup margarine
4 to 5 tablespoons cold water
4½ cups fresh, frozen or canned sliced peaches in juice, drained and divided
1 cup plain low-fat yogurt
¼ cup sugar
3 tablespoons quick-cooking tapioca
½ teaspoon ground cinnamon
¼ teaspoon ground ginger
⅛ teaspoon ground nutmeg
1 egg white, beaten

In bowl, mix 2 cups flour and ¼ teaspoon Sweet 'N Low granulated sugar substitute. With pastry blender, cut margarine into flour mixture. Gradually add water; mix well. On floured surface, roll three-quarters of dough and line 9-inch pie plate. Roll remaining dough into 11-inch circle; cut into six ½-inch strips of equal width. In food processor or blender, puree 1 cup peaches. In bowl, mix remaining flour and Sweet 'N Low granulated sugar substitute, pureed peaches, yogurt, sugar, tapioca, cinnamon, ginger and nutmeg; set aside about 10 minutes. Preheat oven to 425 degrees F. Fold remaining peaches into yogurt mixture; spoon into pie crust. Place pastry strips across pie; twist and fasten edges to pie crust. Seal; flute edges. Brush egg white over pastry. Bake 35 to 40 minutes. Makes 12 2-inch sector servings.

Calories per serving: 245.

Reprinted by permission of Cumberland Packing Corporation

FRENCH PEACH TART

1 cup Pioneer Baking Mix
¼ cup butter (softened)
2 tablespoons boiling water
2 peeled and sliced peaches
¼ cup sugar
1 teaspoon cinnamon

¼ cup evaporated milk
½ cup sugar
1 egg
1 teaspoon vanilla
¼ cup sour cream

Preheat oven to 400 degrees F. Grease 10-inch tart pan. Combine Pioneer Baking Mix and butter. Add boiling water, stirring until soft dough forms. Press dough into prepared pan. Lay peach slices in crust. Mix ¼ cup sugar and cinnamon together. Sprinkle over peaches. Blend milk, ½ cup sugar, eggs, vanilla and sour cream until smooth. Pour over peaches. Bake 40-45 minutes. Yield: 10 servings.

Reprinted by permission of Pioneer Flour Mills

FRESH PEACH TARTS

5 cups sliced ripe fresh peaches
1 cup sugar
1 tablespoon fresh lemon juice
4½ teaspoons cornstarch

6 baked 5-inch tart shells
Whipped cream
8 fresh peach slices

Combine peaches, sugar and lemon juice. Let stand 20 minutes. Drain juice into a measuring cup. There should be 1 cup of liquid. If not, finish filling cup with water. Blend in cornstarch and cook until transparent. Cool. Divide fruit equally among the 6 tarts. Spoon the cold sauce over each tart to form a glaze. Chill until the glaze is set. Garnish with whipping cream and peach slices. 6 servings.

PEACH AND GRAPE TARTS

½ cup sour cream
¾ cup seedless green grapes, halved
¾ cup diced fresh peaches
2 tablespoons almond liqueur*

1¾ cups (4 oz.) Birds Eye Cool Whip non-dairy whipped topping, thawed
6 or 7 commercial graham cracker crumb tart shells or pastry shells in aluminum foil cups

*Or use ½ teaspoon almond extract and 1 tablespoon milk.

Combine sour cream, grapes, peaches and liqueur; fold into whipped topping, blending well. Spoon into tart shells and chill 2 to 3 hours. Garnish with additional grapes or mint sprigs and peach slices, if desired.

Reprinted by permission of General Foods

PEACH TARTS

½ cup finely rolled Nabisco 100% Bran
¼ cup firmly packed light brown sugar
¼ cup Blue Bonnet Margarine, melted

1 8¾-ounce can sliced peaches, drained and coarsely chopped
⅓ cup Planters Walnuts, chopped
¼ teaspoon ground cinnamon
Ice cream, optional

In small bowl, combine 100% bran, 2 tablespoons light brown sugar and margarine; press onto bottom and sides of 2 (4½ × 1-inch) tart pans. Combine peaches, remaining brown sugar, walnuts and cinnamon; spoon into prepared crusts. Bake in a 350-degree toaster oven 20 to 25 minutes or until heated through. If desired, serve with ice cream. Makes 2 servings.

Reprinted by permission of Nabisco Brands, Inc.

CHOCOLATE AND AMARETTO PEACH TART

Pastry:

4 oz. blanched almonds
1 cup plus 2 tablespoons flour
⅓ cup sugar
4 oz. unsalted butter

1 large egg yolk
1 tablespoon Amaretto
¼ teaspoon vanilla extract
¼ teaspoon almond extract

Grind sugar, almonds and flour in food processor to a fine meal. Cut in butter; blend in remaining ingredients. Press into tart tin and freeze until firm, then bake 20 minutes at 350 degrees.

Peach Topping and Glaze:

2 lbs. California cling peach
   halves
2 cups sugar

6 cups water
1 split vanilla bean

Bring sugar, water and vanilla bean to boil; steep 15 minutes. Return liquid to boil, add peach halves, reduce heat, simmer slowly 10 minutes; remove peaches and drain. Reduce syrup to glaze consistency and flavor with Amaretto.

Chocolate Filling:

¾ cup sugar
⅓ cup water
⅓ cup Amaretto
1 oz. bitter chocolate

4 oz. unsalted butter
¼ cup all-purpose flour
2 large eggs, beaten
1 teaspoon vanilla

Dissolve sugar in water, then caramelize to golden brown; pour in liqueur and heat to re-dissolve; blend in chocolate and butter; stir in remaining ingredients and bake in tart shell 15 minutes at 350 degrees. Cool 15 minutes; cover surface with peach halves and brush with reserved glaze.

Reprinted by permission of Chef Loren Cross/Loren Cross Catering
California Canning Peach Association, California Cling Peach Advisory Board

DRAMBUIE PEACH BLUEBERRY SHORTCAKE

2 10-oz. packages frozen sliced
   peaches, thawed
1 pint fresh blueberries or 1 16-
   oz. bag frozen blueberries

⅔ cup Drambuie
1 pound cake

whipped cream or ice cream, optional

Thirty minutes before serving, add Drambuie to undrained peaches. Add fresh blueberries. If using frozen blueberries, drain thoroughly and add just before serving. To serve, spoon fruit over slices of pound cake, top with whipped cream or ice cream, if desired. 6 to 8 servings.

Reprinted by permission of W. A. Taylor and Company

PEACH SHORTCAKE DELUXE

2⅓ cups biscuit mix
3 tablespoons granulated sugar
4 tablespoons melted butter or
   margarine
½ cup milk
2 tablespoons brown sugar

2 tablespoons slivered almonds
¼ teaspoon French's nutmeg
1 16-oz. package frozen peaches
   (or sliced, sweetened fresh
   peaches)
Almond Cream, recipe below

Mix together with a fork biscuit mix, granulated sugar, 3 table-spoons of the butter and milk. Press dough into ungreased 8-inch round cake pan. Brush with remaining butter. Combine brown sugar, almonds and nutmeg; sprinkle over dough. Bake in 400-degree oven 15 to 20 minutes. Serve wedges of warm shortcake with peaches and top with Almond Cream. Serves 6.

Almond Cream: Beat ½ pint heavy cream until stiff peaks form. Stir in 3 tablespoons sugar and ½ teaspoon French's Almond Extract.

Reprinted by permission of The R. T. French Company

PEACHES 'N BUTTERMILK SHORTCAKE

2 cups sifted flour
2 teaspoons baking powder
1 teaspoon salt
½ cup butter
⅔ cup buttermilk

4 fresh California peaches,
   peeled, sliced and sugared
1 cup whipping cream, whipped
   and sweetened

Preheat oven to 450 degrees. Sift flour, baking powder and salt into a mixing bowl. Cut in 6 tablespoons butter with pastry blender until mixture is grainy. Stir in buttermilk. Shape dough into a ball and roll out to ½-inch thickness on lightly floured board. Cut dough into 4-inch rounds. Bake for 18 to 20 minutes. Split biscuits while warm. Butter with remaining butter. Serve in individual dishes with peaches between split layers. Top with remaining peaches and whipped cream. Makes 4 servings.

Reprinted by permission of Produce Marketing Association

Cakes, Cookies And Bars

PEACH IN TIME

In the New World, by the people of Spain,
A fruit was introduced and peach is its name.
The century was the 16th, I know not the year,
If it wasn't for them, it wouldn't be here.
Sometimes it's tart, but mostly mild,
It was first found growing wild.
Most are bought today shipped in crates,
In the popular country—the United States!
They can be grown as far as the reaches,
Of the Great Lakes and by the beaches.
The peach is only third to the apples and pears,
It makes trees beautiful when it bears.
Yes, the peach has lots of fame and glory,
But this is only the beginning of the peach's story.

By Michael Freeman, Ennis, Texas, June 11, 1985

COOL AND CREAMY CHEESECAKE

1 cup graham cracker crumbs
¼ cup sugar
¼ cup margarine, melted
1 envelope unflavored gelatin
¼ cup cold water
1 8-oz. pkg. cream cheese, softened

½ cup sugar
Dash of salt
¾ cup milk
¼ cup lemon juice
1 cup whipping cream, whipped
Peach slices, strawberries or blueberries

Combine crumbs, sugar and margarine; press onto bottom of 9-inch springform pan.

Soften gelatin in water; stir over low heat until dissolved. Combine cream cheese, sugar and salt, mixing at medium speed on electric mixer until well blended. Gradually add milk, juice and gelatin; chill until slightly thickened. Fold in whipped cream; pour over crust. Chill until firm. Top with fruit just before serving.

PEACH MELBA CHEESECAKE

9-inch unbaked pastry shell with high fluted edge (not frozen)
1½ cups (2 medium) peeled, sliced peaches*
1 8-oz. package softened cream cheese
2 eggs

½ cup sugar
1 tablespoon flour
⅔ cup *undiluted* Carnation Evaporated Milk
1 tablespoon lemon juice
½ teaspoon grated lemon rind
½ cup seedless raspberry jelly

Line bottom of pastry shell with peaches. Bake 10 minutes in hot oven (400 degrees F.). Beat cream cheese in small mixer bowl until smooth. Beat in eggs. Add sugar and flour. Beat until blended. Add evaporated milk, lemon juice, and lemon rind. Beat until well blended. Pour mixture over peaches. Reduce oven temperature to moderate (350 degrees F.). Bake additional 25 to 30 minutes or just until center is set. Cool to room temperature. Melt raspberry jelly; spread over cheesecake. Chill thoroughly before serving. Makes 9-inch cheesecake.

*1½ cups (16-ounce **can**) well-drained, sliced peaches may be substituted for fresh peaches.

Reprinted by permission of Carnation

NO-BAKE CHOCOLATE CHEESECAKE

Crumb-nut Crust (recipe below)
1½ cups Hershey's Semi-Sweet
  Chocolate Mini-chips
1 each 8-oz. and 3-oz. package
  cream cheese, softened
⅓ cup sugar

¼ cup butter, softened
1½ teaspoons vanilla
1 cup heavy cream
Peach Topping (recipe below)
Chocolate curls (optional)

Prepare Crumb-nut Crust; set aside. Melt mini-chips in top of double boiler over hot water, stirring until smooth. Or, place in micro-proof bowl and microwave on full power for 1 to 2 minutes or until very warm. Remove from microwave and stir occasionally until chips are melted. Combine cream cheese and sugar in large mixer bowl; add butter, beating until smooth. Beat in chocolate all at once, add vanilla. Whip cream until stiff; fold in. Spoon into crust; chill while preparing Peach Topping. Spoon topping onto chocolate layer and chill completely. Before serving, garnish with additional peach slices and chocolate shavings or curls, if desired.

Crumb-nut Crust

1 cup ground almonds or pecans
¾ cup vanilla wafer crumbs*

¼ cup confectioners' sugar
¼ cup butter, melted

If using almonds, toast in shallow baking pan at 350 degrees for 8 to 10 minutes, stirring frequently. Cool. Chop nuts finely in food processor or blender. Combine with crumbs and sugar in mixing bowl; drizzle in butter. Press on bottom and partly up sides of 9-inch springform pan.

*1¾ cups graham cracker crumbs can be substituted for the nuts and vanilla wafer crumbs.

Peach Topping

1 teaspoon unflavored gelatin
1 tablespoon cold water
2 tablespoons boiling water
1 cup heavy cream

2 tablespoons sugar
1 teaspoon vanilla
½ cup diced sweetened peaches,
  drained

Sprinkle gelatin onto cold water in small glass dish; allow to soften a few minutes. Add boiling water and stir until gelatin is dissolved. Whip cream with sugar until stiff peaks form; beat in gelatin and vanilla. Fold in diced peaches.

Reprinted by permission of Hershey's Kitchens and Hershey Foods Corporation

BUTTERY PEACH UPSIDE-DOWN CAKE

½ cup Land O' Lakes Sweet
    Cream Butter, melted
1 10-oz. jar peach preserves

¼ cup chopped pecans
½ cup coconut

CAKE

1¾ cups all-purpose flour
½ cup sugar
2 teaspoons baking powder
¼ teaspoon salt

½ cup Land O' Lakes Sweet
    Cream Butter, softened
½ cup milk
2 eggs

Preheat oven to 375 degrees. In small bowl combine butter and preserves. Mix well; set aside. In 9-inch square baking pan sprinkle nuts and coconut. Gently spoon butter-preserve mixture over nuts. In 3-quart mixer bowl combine all cake ingredients; beat at low speed, scraping sides of bowl often, until smooth and well blended (2 to 3 minutes). Spoon over butter-preserve layer spreading to sides of pan. Bake near center of 375-degree oven for 35 to 45 minutes or until dark golden brown and wooden pick inserted in center comes out clean. *Do not underbake.* Let stand 5 minutes in pan. Loosen edges of cake from pan and invert onto serving plate. Serve warm. TIP: Do not use 8-inch square pan. Yield: 9-inch square cake.

Reprinted by permission of Land O'Lakes, Inc.

PEACH UPSIDE-DOWN CAKE

1 cup cooked Sun-Maid or
    Sunsweet dried peaches
6 maraschino cherries, quartered
¼ cup butter or margarine
½ cup brown sugar, packed
1 tablespoon cooking liquid from
    peaches

1¾ cups buttermilk baking mix
½ cup granulated sugar
1 egg
⅔ cup milk
2 tablespoons butter or
    margarine, softened
1 teaspoon vanilla

Cut cooked peaches in ½-inch chunks: mix with cherries. Melt butter in 9-inch square or round baking pan, stir in brown sugar and cooking liquid from peaches. Spread evenly in pan. Arrange fruit over mixture in pan. In mixer bowl, combine baking mix and remaining ingredients. Mix at low speed until all of mix is moistened, then beat at medium speed 4 minutes. Turn batter into pan over fruit. Bake at 350 degrees F. about 45 minutes or until pick inserted in center comes out clean. Remove from oven; let stand a minute; loosen edges with a small spatula and invert over serving plate. Allow pan to rest over cake a minute so syrup will drain. Serve warm. Makes one 9-inch cake, about 6 servings.

Reprinted by permission of Sun-Diamond Growers of California

PEACH UPSIDE-DOWN PUDDING CAKE

¼ cup butter or margarine,
  melted
⅓ cup firmly packed light brown
  sugar
1 29-oz. can sliced peaches, well
  drained
1 package (2-layer size) yellow
  cake mix or pudding-
  included cake mix

1 package (4-serving size) Jell-O
  vanilla flavor instant
  pudding and pie filling
4 eggs
1 cup (½ pt.) sour cream
¼ cup oil
½ teaspoon almond extract
  (optional)

Combine butter and brown sugar; pour into a 13 × 9-inch pan. Arrange peaches in rows on sugar mixture. Combine remaining ingredients in large mixer bowl. Blend; then beat at medium speed of electric mixer for 4 minutes. Spoon carefully over peach slices in pan. Bake at 350 degrees for 50 to 55 minutes or until cake springs back when lightly touched. Do not underbake. Cool in pan for 5 minutes. Invert onto serving platter; remove pan. Serve warm or cool with prepared whipped topping, if desired.

Reprinted by permission of General Foods

PUMPKIN PEACH CAKE

Topping:
Preheat oven to 350 degrees F. Melt ½ cup butter or margarine in 13 × 9-inch pan in oven. Remove from oven; stir in 2 cups firmly packed brown sugar, mixing until well-blended. Arrange 1 20-oz. **can** drained peach slices and maraschino cherries over brown sugar mixture.

Cake:

½ cup butter or margarine,
  softened
1¾ cups firmly packed brown
  sugar
6 eggs, slightly beaten
1 cup wheat germ
½ cup plain yogurt
3 cups flour

2 teaspoons baking soda
½ teaspoon salt
2 teaspoons ground ginger
1 teaspoon ground cinnamon
1 teaspoon ground nutmeg
½ teaspoon ground cloves
1 16-oz. can Libby's Solid Pack
  Pumpkin

Cream butter and sugar until light and fluffy. Blend in eggs, wheat germ and yogurt. Mix together flour, baking soda, salt and spices; mix well. Alternate additions of dry ingredients and pumpkin, mixing well after each addition. Pour over prepared peach mixture. Bake 60 to 65 minutes or until wooden pick inserted in center comes out clean. Cool 5 minutes; invert on wire rack. Cool. Yields 12 servings.

Adapted from Libby's Pumpkin Pineapple Cake

DRAMBUIE STRAWBERRY AND PEACH CAKE

4 eggs
1 cup plus 3 tablespoons
   confectioners' sugar
1 cup all-purpose flour, sifted
3 tablespoons butter, melted

6 tablespoons (3 ounces)
   Drambuie
1½ cups fresh strawberries
3 peaches, peeled and pitted
1½ cups heavy cream

Grease two 8-inch round cake pans. Preheat oven to 350 degrees F. Place eggs and 1 cup sugar in large mixing bowl; stand in a pan of hot water. Whisk until mixture is thick and fluffy; gently fold in flour and butter. Pour into prepared pans; bake 20 to 25 minutes or until layers are golden and spring back when lightly touched. Cool on wire rack. Shortly before serving, sprinkle each cake layer with 2 tablespoons Drambuie. Slice half the strawberries and peaches. Whip cream until thickened. Add remaining 3 tablespoons sugar and the 2 tablespoons Drambuie; continue whipping just until cream holds its shape. Assemble cake, using half of the whipped cream and sliced strawberries and peaches placed alternately between the layers. Spread remaining whipped cream over top of cake, using a pastry tube, if desired. Garnish with remaining peaches and strawberries, placed in alternating pattern.

Reprinted by permission of W. A. Taylor and Company

FRESH PEACH OVENCAKE

3 tablespoons butter or
   margarine
3 eggs
¾ cup milk
¾ cup flour

4 cups sliced fresh California
   peaches (about 1⅓ pounds)
1 tablespoon brown sugar
¾ cup sour cream
2 tablespoons maple syrup or
   maple-flavored syrup

Put butter in 10- or 12-inch skillet with ovenproof handle. Place in 450-degree oven. Beat eggs with rotary beater or wire whisk until light and lemon colored; beat in milk. Gradually stir in flour; beat until smooth. Remove skillet from oven. Pour batter into skillet. Bake 15 minutes. Reduce oven heat to 350 degrees F. Continue to bake 10 to 15 minutes until pancake is puffed and browned. While ovencake bakes, toss peaches with sugar in serving bowl; set aside. In separate bowl, mix sour cream with syrup. Serve hot ovencake topped with peaches and sour cream mixture. Makes 4 to 6 servings.

Reprinted by permission of California Tree Fruit Agreement

PEACH DELIGHT

Use a white cake mix and make it special by adding this peach-custard filling.

1 white cake mix	¼ cup flour
½ cup sugar	2 egg yolks (use whites in cake)
⅛ teaspoon salt	1 cup diced peaches
1 cup milk	1 teaspoon vanilla
1 teaspoon butter	

Bake cake per package directions. Cook custard in a double boiler until very thick. Add peaches and cook 3 more minutes. Cool and spread between layers of white cake. Sprinkle top with powdered sugar. May be eaten warm or cool.

Reprinted by permission of Gay L. Paris
Market Investigator, Produce Marketing Association

PEACH GINGER CREAM CAKES

1 29-oz. can cling peach halves	2 tablespoons butter
½ cup brown sugar, firmly packed	1 14- to 14½-oz. package gingerbread mix
¼ cup chopped walnuts	1 cup sour cream

Drain peaches thoroughly, reserving syrup. Place peach halves, cut side down, on absorbent paper. Combine brown sugar, nuts and butter in a small saucepan and heat, stirring occasionally, until butter melts and mixture is smooth. Place an equal amount of brown sugar mixture in each of nine 6-ounce baking dishes (custard cups). Pat peach halves dry with absorbent paper and place each cut side down, in a cup.* Prepare gingerbread mix according to package directions except substitute sour cream for the water and add ¼ cup reserved peach syrup. Spoon batter over peaches in individual cups. Bake in a preheated moderate oven (375 degrees F.) for 30 minutes or until done. Let stand 5 minutes before inverting on dessert plates or serving platter. 9 servings.

*Since the number of peach halves in a can vary from 7 to 9, you may wish to use additional halves from another can or bake some of the cakes without a peach half.

Reprinted by permission of Consumer Services Department, National Live Stock and Meat Board

PEACH-GLAZED SPICE CAKE

1 16-oz. can sliced peaches,
   reserve syrup
1 9-oz. package yellow cake mix
½ teaspoon ground ginger

1 egg
3 Snickers bars, cut up
½ teaspoon ground cinnamon

Preheat oven to 325 degrees F. (165 degrees C.). Grease and flour a 9-inch, round cake pan. Drain peaches; reserve ¾ cup syrup. In a medium mixing bowl, combine cake mix and ginger. Add ½ cup of the reserved syrup and the egg. Beat with electric mixer on medium speed until smooth, about 2 minutes. Pour into prepared pan. Bake 30 to 35 minutes or until golden brown and wooden pick inserted near center comes out dry. Cool 5 minutes. Remove from pan and place on oven-proof plate. Meanwhile, in a medium saucepan, combine candy, remaining syrup and cinnamon. Melt over low heat, stirring until smooth. Arrange peach slices on top of cake in a circular fashion. Pour melted chocolate mixture over peaches. Broil 6 to 8 inches from heat until bubbly, 2 or 3 minutes. Serve warm. Makes 6 to 8 servings.

Reprinted by permission of M&M/Mars, A Division of Mars, Inc.

PEACH NECTAR CAKE

1 box Duncan Hines Yellow Cake
   Mix
¼ cup sugar
½ cup Wesson Oil

1 cup peach nectar
4 eggs
½ teaspoon vanilla

Beat together 2 – 3 minutes, until smooth. Bake in tube pan at 350 degrees for 35 – 45 minutes. Cool 15 minutes and glaze with 2 tablespoons lemon juice and enough powdered sugar to make a consistency which can be drizzled over the cake.

Zula McKnight, Henderson, Texas

PEACH PARTY CAKE IMPERIAL

¼ cup Imperial brown sugar
2 eggs
¼ cup water
¼ cup butter at room
   temperature
1 8-oz. bar cream cheese at room
   temperature

1 yellow cake mix
1 pint heavy cream, whipped to
   stiff peaks (or whipped
   cream substitute)
4 cups sliced fresh peaches that
   have been tossed in lemon
   juice and drained

Beat together the brown sugar, eggs and water; then beat in the softened butter and cream cheese. Last, beat in the yellow cake mix to make a medium stiff batter and transfer it to a well-greased and floured jelly roll pan (15 × 10 × 1″ deep). Bake in preheated 350-degree oven about 15 minutes, or until cake tests done and is a golden brown. Cool cake thoroughly on cake rack. At serving time, top with whipped cream, sweetened, and top with the peaches which have been tossed with lemon juice and sugar. For ease of serving, the cake may be cut in squares before adding whipped cream. Yield: Depends on size of servings, but will serve a crowd of 20 or more.

Reprinted by permission of June Towers, Imperial Sugar Company

PEACH PUDDING CAKE

1½ pounds fresh California
  peaches, cut in wedges (2 to
  3 large)
2 tablespoons lemon juice
¼ teaspoon *each* orange and
  lemon rind
1¾ cubes butter (1¾ stick)
1 cup sugar

3 eggs, separated
1 tablespoon maple syrup
1½ cups flour
¼ teaspoon baking powder
½ teaspoon cinnamon
¼ teaspoon allspice
Whipping cream (optional)

Butter and flour 8 × 10-inch rectangular dish or 9-inch round cake pan. Toss peach wedges with lemon juice and rinds; set aside. In mixer, cream butter; add sugar, beating until well combined. Add egg yolks, one at a time, beating well after each addition. Beat in syrup. Sift together dry ingredients. Add dry ingredients to sugar mixture, mixing only until combined. In small bowl, beat egg whites until soft peaks form. Stir whites into cake dough. Spread half the dough evenly on bottom of pan; then a layer of peach wedges. Spread remaining batter on top of peaches until smooth and even. Bake in preheated 350-degree oven 1 hour. Serve warm with sweetened whipped cream. 4 to 6 servings.

Reprinted by permission of *The Houston Post*

PEACHY KEEN CAKE

¾ cup plus 3 tablespoons sugar,
  divided
½ teaspoon ground ginger
5 medium-size fresh peaches,
  pitted, sliced (do not peel)

½ cup butter or margarine, at
  room temperature
2 eggs
½ teaspoon vanilla
1½ cups unsifted flour
1 teaspoon baking powder

Combine 3 tablespoons sugar and ginger. In small bowl combine peaches and sugar mixture. Let stand 30 minutes, stirring occasionally. In small mixer bowl cream butter and remaining ¾ cup sugar. Add eggs, one at a time, beating well after each addition. Beat in vanilla. Sift together flour and baking powder. Gradually stir into creamed mixture. Spread batter into a buttered 9 × 13-inch baking pan. Spoon peaches and liquid over batter. Bake in a 350-degree oven 45 minutes. Cool thoroughly in pan. Cut in squares to serve. Makes 12 servings.

Reprinted by permission of United Fresh Fruit and Vegetable Association

PEACHY YOGURT CAKE

2 cups flour
1½ cups firmly packed brown sugar
½ cup butter or margarine, softened
1 cup chopped walnuts
1 egg
1 cup plain yogurt

1 teaspoon salt
1 teaspoon baking soda
1 teaspoon grated orange peel
2 16-oz. cans Del Monte Yellow Cling Sliced Peaches, well drained
Plain yogurt or sour cream

Mix flour, sugar and butter; stir in nuts. Place 2⅓ cups of mixture into ungreased 13 × 9-inch pan. Add egg, yogurt, salt, soda and orange peel to remaining crumb mixture. Spoon mixture evenly over base; place peaches on top. Bake at 350 degrees for 40 minutes or until tests done. Cut into squares. Top with additional yogurt or sour cream, if desired. 12 to 15 servings.

Reprinted by permission of Del Monte Kitchens, Del Monte Corporation

ALMOND CAKE WITH FRESH PEACH COULIS

Fresh Peach Coulis:

4 cups fresh California peaches, peeled and sliced (about 4 medium)

1 tablespoon lemon juice
4 tablespoons sugar (to taste)

Cake:

8 ounces almond paste (recipe follows) *or* 1 tube (7 or 8 ounces) almond paste
½ cup butter
¾ cup sugar
3 large eggs

3 drops almond extract
⅓ cup flour
¼ teaspoon baking powder
¼ cup blanched whole almonds, finely ground

To prepare Peach Coulis, combine peaches, lemon juice and sugar in medium saucepan. Cook over medium heat until fruit is soft and in small chunks, about 15 minutes. Cool and refrigerate. In mixer, beat almond paste until smooth. Add butter, then sugar, beating until smooth after each addition. Add eggs, one at a time. Add almond extract. Mix flour and baking powder together and

118

gently add to batter. Fold in ground almonds. Pour into buttered and floured 8-inch springform pan. Bake in preheated 350-degree oven 35 to 40 minutes or until cake is lightly browned and has pulled away from sides of pan. Cool in pan on wire rack. To serve, sprinkle powdered sugar over top of cake. Spoon Peach Coulis all around outside edge. 8 servings.

Almond Paste: In a food processor, puree ⅔ cup blanched almonds until they become a paste. Add 1 tablespoon melted unsalted butter, ½ cup sugar, salt to taste, 2 drops almond extract, ¼ teaspoon EACH finely grated fresh lemon and orange rinds and 1 egg white. Continue blending until it produces a fine paste.

Reprinted by permission of California Tree Fruit Agreement

GUILT-FREE CHOCOLATE CAKE

1 ½ cups all-purpose flour
1 cup sugar
¼ cup unsweetened cocoa
1 teaspoon baking soda
½ teaspoon salt
1 cup water

¼ cup plus 1 tablespoon
   vegetable oil
1 teaspoon vinegar
1 teaspoon vanilla extract
2 cups fresh peach slices

Heat oven to 350 degrees. Grease and flour 2 round pans 8 × 1½ inches. In a large mixing bowl combine flour, sugar, cocoa, baking soda and salt. Add water, oil, vinegar and vanilla; stir until smooth and thoroughly blended. Pour into prepared pans. Bake 22 to 25 minutes or until wooden pick inserted in center comes out clean. Cool 10 minutes; remove from pan. Cool completely on wire rack. Just before serving place one layer on serving plate; arrange half peach slices on layer. Top with second layer and remaining peaches.

10 servings. 226 calories without peaches.

Reprinted by permission of Hershey's Kitchens, Hershey Foods Corporation

CALIFORNIA PEACH DELIGHT

Cake:
One 10-inch angel food cake

Custard:

1½ cups milk
5 large egg yolks

½ cup sugar
1 teaspoon vanilla extract

Filling:

4 cups fresh California peaches, peeled and sliced (about 4 medium)

Syrup:

⅔ cup water

½ cup sugar

3 tablespoons Grand Marnier

Topping:

2 cups (1 pint) whipping cream

½ cup powdered sugar

1 teaspoon vanilla extract

1 cup sliced almonds, toasted

2 fresh California peaches,
 peeled and sliced

Custard: Bring milk to boil in a heavy saucepan. Remove from heat. Beat egg yolks and sugar together until lemon-colored, fluffy and very thick. Slowly stir milk into egg mixture. Return mix back into saucepan and cook over low heat, stirring constantly, until custard thickly coats back of a spoon. Take off heat immediately and set pan in large bowl of ice water to stop cooking. Add vanilla; let mix cool completely. (This may be prepared ahead of time and refrigerated in closed container.)

Syrup: Bring water and sugar to a boil, stirring until sugar is dissolved. Remove from heat and cool completely before adding Grand Marnier.

Topping: Whip cream until it begins to stiffen. Add powdered sugar and vanilla and continue beating until stiff. Split angel food cake into three horizontal layers. Place the bottom slice in a shallow glass bowl and sprinkle with ⅓ cup sugar syrup, ⅓ cup custard, some of the almonds and two cups of the Peach Filling. Repeat with second layer. Add the third layer and sprinkle with the last ⅓ cup sugar syrup. Spread whipped cream over sides and top covering completely. Place large dollops of cream on top of the cake. Sprinkle remaining almonds around sides and over top. Pour remaining custard all around outside of finished cake. Refrigerate. When ready to serve, garnish with remaining fresh peach slices. 10 to 12 servings.

120

PEACHY PECAN TORTE

⅔ cup firmly packed brown
    sugar
½ cup chopped pecans
1 cup all-purpose flour, divided
⅓ cup butter, softened
4 medium peaches (1 lb.), peeled
    and diced or 1 12-oz. pkg.
    frozen sliced peaches,
    thawed, drained and diced

6 eggs, separated
¾ teaspoon cream of tartar
⅔ cup sugar, divided
½ teaspoon vanilla
½ teaspoon almond extract
½ teaspoon salt
Pecan halves
Optional Whipped Cream
    Frosting (recipe follows)

Stir together brown sugar, pecans and ¼ cup of the flour. Cut in butter until mixture resembles coarse crumbs. Sprinkle half of the nut mixture (about ½ cup) evenly into each of 2 greased 9-inch round cake pans. Spoon half of the peaches (about 1 cup) evenly over nut mixture in each pan. Set aside. In large mixing bowl, beat egg whites with cream of tartar at high speed until foamy. Add ⅓ cup of granulated sugar, 1 tablespoon at a time, beating constantly until sugar is dissolved* and whites are glossy and stand in soft peaks. Set aside. In small mixing bowl, beat egg yolks with remaining granulated sugar and flavorings at high speed until thick and lemon-colored, about 5 minutes. Gently pour yolks over reserved whites. Stir salt into remaining flour and sprinkle over yolks. Gently fold yolks and flour into whites. Evenly spread half of the batter over peaches in each pan. Bake on bottom rack of preheated 375-degree oven until tops spring back when lightly touched with finger, 30 to 35 minutes. Loosen from pans with narrow spatula or knife. Invert onto wire racks and allow to stand 3 minutes. Gently shake from pans. Cool completely. Frost with Whipped Cream Frosting just before serving, or frost and refrigerate until serving. Garnish with pecan halves, if desired.

*Rub just a bit of meringue between thumb and forefinger to feel if sugar has dissolved.

Whipped Cream Frosting

1 tablespoon sugar
⅔ envelope unflavored gelatin
¼ cup water

1 pint whipping cream
½ teaspoon vanilla
½ teaspoon almond extract

In small saucepan, stir together sugar and gelatin. Add water. Cook and stir over medium heat until gelatin is dissolved, about 2 minutes. Remove from heat and cool to room temperature, about 5 minutes. In small mixing bowl, beat whipping cream with flavorings and cooled gelatin mixture at high speed until cream holds stiff peaks.

Reprinted by permission of American Egg Board, Park Ridge, Illinois

PEACH-RASPBERRY CHEESE TORTE

¾ cup Kretschmer Regular
   Wheat Germ
¾ cup fine coconut bar cookie
   crumbs

2 tablespoons sugar
¼ cup butter or margarine,
   melted

Combine all ingredients in bowl. Stir well to blend. Press evenly on bottom and 1 inch up sides of 9-inch springform pan. Fill with Cheese Filling (below). Bake at 350 degrees for 20 – 25 minutes until set. Arrange peach slices over hot cake. Heat preserves and spoon over peach slices. Refrigerate before serving. Remove sides of springform pan. Yield: 8 servings.

Cheese Filling

1 8-oz. pkg. softened cream
   cheese
2 eggs
1 teaspoon vanilla

¼ cup sugar
1 tablespoon unsifted Robin
   Hood All-Purpose Flour
⅛ teaspoon salt

Beat cream cheese until smooth. Add eggs, one at a time. Beat until smooth after each addition. Stir in vanilla. Combine sugar, flour and salt. Blend into cheese mixture.

Topping

1 16-oz. can sliced peaches,
   drained

½ cup raspberry preserves

Reprinted by permission of International Multifoods/Kretschmer Wheat Germ

STRAWBERRY-PEACH DREAMCAKE

1 envelope Knox Unflavored
   Gelatin
2 tablespoons sugar
1 cup boiling water
1 10-oz. package frozen
   strawberries, thawed
¼ cup peach brandy

1 16-oz. can sliced peaches,
   drained and chopped
1 4½-oz. container frozen
   whipped topping, thawed
8-inch angel food cake, cut into
   1-inch cubes (about 2 quarts)

In large bowl, mix unflavored gelatin and sugar; add boiling water and stir until gelatin is completely dissolved. Stir in strawberries until melted and brandy. Chill, stirring occasionally, until mixture mounds slightly when dropped from spoon. Fold in peaches, whipped topping and cake. Turn into 8-cup bowl, mold or springform pan; chill until firm. Makes 8 to 10 servings.

Tested recipe from the Lipton Kitchens, reprinted by permission of Thomas J. Lipton, Inc.

GINGER PEACHY MUFFIN RING CAKE

4 Bays English Muffins, lightly toasted
¾ cup gingersnap cookie crumbs
⅔ cup shredded coconut
⅔ cup chopped pecan
1 16-ounce can peach slices, in light syrup
8 pecan halves

⅓ cup brown sugar, firmly packed
½ cup margarine
1 cup sugar
4 eggs
⅓ cup milk
⅓ cup reserved peach syrup

Grind muffins to make fine crumbs, using a blender or food processor. Place muffin crumbs in a large bowl with gingersnap crumbs, coconut and pecans. Stir well to combine and set aside. Drain peach slices, reserving syrup. Spray a micro-safe bundt pan with non-stick spray. Arrange peach slices and pecan halves along the bottom. Sprinkle with brown sugar. Set aside. Cream margarine and sugar together in a large bowl. Beat in eggs, one at a time. Blend in milk and peach juice. Stir in reserved crumb mixture. Pour into the prepared bundt pan. Micro-cook on medium for 11 minutes. Give the pan a quarter-turn halfway through the cooking. Set the oven on high and give the pan another quarter-turn. Micro-cook for an additional 6 minutes, giving the pan its final quarter-turn after 3 minutes. The cake should begin to pull away from the sides of the pan. Let the cake rest for 5 minutes before unmolding. Cake can be served with whipped cream or ice cream.

Reprinted by permission of Bays English Muffins, Shirley De Santis, Bethlehem, PA

PEACH COFFEE CAKE

½ cup shortening
1 cup sugar
2 eggs
1 teaspoon vanilla

2 cups Pioneer Baking Mix
8 oz. sour cream
1½ cups peaches, peeled and chopped

TOPPING:

½ cup pecans, chopped
½ cup brown sugar, firmly packed

1 teaspoon cinnamon
2 tablespoons butter, melted

Preheat oven to 350 degrees F. Grease 9″ × 13″ pan. Cream shortening in a medium mixing bowl; gradually add sugar, beat well.

Add eggs, one at a time, beat well after each addition. Add vanilla, stir well. Add Baking Mix to creamed mixture alternately with sour cream, beginning and ending with Baking Mix. Stir in peaches. Spoon batter into prepared baking pan. Combine topping ingredients in a small mixing bowl; stir until crumbly. Sprinkle topping over batter in baking pan. Bake 35 – 40 minutes. Cut into 2½" × 3" squares and serve warm. Yield: 15 servings.

Reprinted by permission of Pioneer Flour Mills

PERFECT PEACH COFFEE CAKE

¾ cup Sun-Maid or Sunsweet
   dried peaches
½ cup water
Crumb Topping
2 cups buttermilk baking mix
¼ cup granulated sugar

2 tablespoons butter or
   margarine, melted
1 egg, beaten
¾ cup milk
1 teaspoon vanilla

Into a saucepan, cut peaches into ½-inch pieces; add water, bring to a boil, cover, simmer 5 minutes. Cool. Prepare Crumb Topping (recipe follows). Combine remaining ingredients; beat well. Spread into greased 8-inch square baking pan. Drain peaches and arrange over batter. Sprinkle evenly with Crumb Topping. Bake at 400 degrees F. for 20 to 25 minutes or until cake tests done. Serve warm, cut into 9 squares.

CRUMB TOPPING: Combine ¼ cup all-purpose flour with 2 tablespoons each granulated sugar and butter or margarine, and ⅛ teaspoon mace. Mix until crumbly.

Reprinted by permission of Sun-Diamond Growers of California

PEACH UPSIDE-DOWN COFFEE CAKE

¼ cup (½ stick) Fleischmann's
   margarine
½ cup firmly packed light brown
   sugar
1 teaspoon ground cinnamon
1 teaspoon light corn syrup
1 29-oz. can cling peach slices,
   drained
½ cup Planters Southern Belle
   Pecan Halves

¼ cup water
¼ cup milk
1 package Fleischmann's Active
   Dry Yeast
½ cup (1 stick) Fleischmann's
   margarine, softened
½ cup sugar
½ teaspoon salt
3 eggs (at room temperature)
2¼ to 2½ cups unsifted flour

Melt ¼ cup margarine in saucepan. Stir in brown sugar, cinnamon and corn syrup; bring to a boil. Immediately pour into a 9-inch square pan. Arrange peach slices and pecan halves in pan. Combine water and milk in a saucepan. Heat over low heat until liquids are warm (105 degrees F. — 115 degrees F.). Stir in Fleischmann's Active Dry Yeast until dissolved. Cream ½ cup margarine in a large bowl of electric mixer. Gradually add sugar and salt; cream together. Add yeast mixture and eggs. Beat at medium speed until well blended. Gradually add flour and continue beating until smooth. Carefully spread batter over topping in pan. Cover; let rise in warm place, free from draft, until doubled in bulk, about 1 hour. Bake at 375 degrees F. for 40 minutes, or until done. Invert cake onto wire rack; set over wax paper. Serve warm. Makes 1 9-inch square cake.

Reprinted by permission of Nabisco Brands, Inc.

FRESH PEACH PLUM KUCHEN

1 cup unsifted all-purpose flour
6 tablespoons sugar, divided
1 teaspoon baking powder
¼ teaspoon salt
6 tablespoons butter or
    margarine, divided

1 egg, slightly beaten
¼ cup milk
½ teaspoon vanilla
4 medium-size fresh peaches,
    peeled, sliced (2 cups)
6 fresh plums, sliced (2 cups)
1 teaspoon ground cinnamon

Sift together flour, 2 tablespoons sugar, baking powder and salt. Cut in 3 tablespoons butter with a pastry blender or 2 knives. In a small bowl, beat egg, milk and vanilla; add to flour mixture; beat with a fork until smooth, about 1 minute. (Batter will be stiff.) Spread batter evenly in a well-greased 9-inch springform pan. Arrange fresh fruit slices over batter in a circular pattern, alternating peaches and plums. In a small saucepan, melt remaining 3 tablespoons butter. Stir in remaining 4 tablespoons sugar and cinnamon. Sprinkle mixture over top. Bake in a 400 degree F. oven 25 to 35 minutes or until cake is done and fruit is tender. Cool 15 minutes; remove sides of springform pan; cool completely on wire rack. Makes: 6 servings.

Recipe reprinted by permission of United Fresh Fruit and Vegetable Association

PEACH KUCHEN

½ cup butter or margarine
½ cup sugar
1 egg
1 teaspoon grated lemon rind
1⅓ cups all-purpose flour
1 tablespoon Minute tapioca
2 cups sliced peeled fresh
  peaches

1 tablespoon lemon juice
1 tablespoon butter or margarine,
  softened
½-cup peach or apricot jam or
  crab apple jelly
¾-cup fresh raspberries
  (optional)

Cream ½ cup butter. Gradually beat in sugar and continue beating until mixture is very smooth. Add egg and lemon rind and mix well. Blend in flour. Spread dough evenly in greased 9-inch layer, flan or springform pan. Chill 30 minutes. Then bake at 375 degrees for about 20 minutes, or until edges brown slightly and pull away from sides of pan. Remove from oven; sprinkle tapioca evenly over dough. Arrange peaches in pan, sprinkle with lemon juice and dot with 1 tablespoon butter. Return to oven and bake 10 minutes longer. Meanwhile, heat jam until melted; spread over peaches, reserving 1 tablespoon. Bake 10 minutes, or until peaches are glazed. Add raspberries and brush with reserved jam. Serve warm or cool, with whipped topping, if desired.

Note: The kuchen may be stored in refrigerator a few hours or overnight; reheat before serving.

Reprinted by permission of General Foods

PEACH 'N BERRY KUCHEN

2 cups buttermilk baking mix
2 tablespoons sugar
1 Land O' Lakes Egg

1 cup Land O' Lakes Sour Cream
1 cup fresh peaches, sliced
½ cup fresh blueberries

Topping

½ cup buttermilk baking mix
½ cup firmly packed brown
  sugar

2 tablespoons Land O' Lakes
  Sweet Cream Butter, melted

Preheat oven to 400 degrees. In l-qt. mixer bowl combine buttermilk baking mix, sugar, egg and sour cream. Beat on medium speed until well blended (1 minute). Spread in bottom of greased 9-inch square baking pan. Layer peach slices in rows over cake mixture. Place blueberries in rows between peach slices. In small bowl combine all topping ingredients. Stir to mix and sprinkle over fruit.

Bake near center of 400 degree oven for 28 to 35 minutes or until cake tests clean with a wooden pick. Yield: 9 servings.

Recipe reprinted by permission of Land O' Lakes, Inc.

PEACH KUCHEN

2 cups flour
½ cup sugar
4 teaspoons baking powder
¾ teaspoon salt, optional
¼ teaspoon nutmeg
1 cup milk
1 egg

¼ cup butter or margarine, melted
1 21-oz. can Thank You Peach Pie Filling
¼ teaspoon cinnamon
1 cup sour cream

Combine flour, sugar, baking powder, salt and nutmeg, mix thoroughly. Combine milk, egg and butter; stir into dry ingredients just until blended. Pour into buttered 2-quart casserole. Top with pie filling, sprinkle with cinnamon. Bake at 375 degrees for 35 minutes. Spread evenly with sour cream, bake 5 minutes more. Serve warm. Serves: 6–8.

Recipe reprinted by permission of Michigan Fruit Canners

PEACH CRUNCH KUCHEN

1 cup all-purpose flour
½ teaspoon salt
½ cup sugar
⅓ cup butter
½ teaspoon cinnamon

¼ teaspoon nutmeg
1 1-lb. 13 oz. can sliced peaches, drained
4 eggs
1 cup dairy sour cream

Sift together flour, salt and 2 tablespoons sugar. Cut in butter until mixture resembles coarse crumbs. Reserve ¼ cup of this mixture for topping. Press remaining flour mixture onto bottom of 9-inch square baking pan. Combine remaining sugar with cinnamon and nutmeg. Arrange peach slices in pan. Sprinkle with 2 tablespoons of the cinnamon-sugar mixture. Bake in a 400-degree (hot) oven for 15 minutes. Reduce heat to 350 degrees (moderate oven). Beat eggs until light. Add sour cream and beat just until blended. Pour over hot peaches. Combine reserved flour mixture with remaining cinnamon-sugar mixture. Sprinkle over custard. Bake in a 350 degree oven for 25 to 30 minutes or until knife inserted in center comes out clean. Serve warm. Makes 6 servings.

Recipe reprinted by permission American Egg Board

CALIFORNIA PEACH SHORTCAKE

Sauce:

1 cup (2 cubes) unsalted butter

⅔ cup sugar
2 cups whipping cream

Shortcake:

⅓ cup sugar
1 cup flour
2 teaspoons baking powder
Pinch of salt
¼ teaspoon ground nutmeg

2 tablespoons (¼ stick) unsalted
 butter, chilled, cut into
 pieces
⅓ cup (plus 1 tablespoon, if
 needed) milk

Fresh California Peach Sauté:

1 tablespoon unsalted butter
6 medium-size fresh California
 peaches

2 teaspoons lemon juice
¼ cup brown sugar

Sauce: Combine ingredients in a heavy saucepan and bring to a boil. Boil gently for 15 minutes. If not ready to use, cool, then refrigerate. To serve, bring sauce slowly back to a boil. Serve warm over shortcake.

Shortcake: Combine dry ingredients together. Using your fingers or two knives, blend the butter and flour together into very fine particles. Add milk and stir into dough, only enough to make particles barely cling together. Divide dough into 6 rough shortcakes and place on a greased baking sheet. Bake in preheated 450-degree oven for 12 to 15 minutes. Serve hot.

Peach Sauté: While shortcake is baking, heat butter in a heavy sauté pan. Add peaches and toss. Sprinkle lemon juice and brown sugar over peaches. Sauté about 5 minutes. Divide peaches among 6 warmed dessert plates. Place a shortcake on top and drizzle a little sauce over all. Pass remaining sauce separately. 6 servings.

Reprinted by permission of California Tree Fruit Agreement

DEEP IN THE HEART OF TEXAS COOKIES

4 cups flour
2 teaspoons baking powder
Dash of salt
2 eggs

1 teaspoon vanilla
1 cup sugar
½ pound butter or margarine
Peach preserves

Sift together flour, baking powder and salt on table. Make a hole in the center. Drop eggs into hole and add vanilla. Slowly add sugar. Slice butter on top. Work with hands until dough is nice and smooth (about 5 to 10 minutes). Heat oven to 375 degrees. Roll out dough about ⅛-inch thick and cut into Texas-shape cookies. Each cookie has a top and a bottom. In half of the cookies, cut a heart out with a small heart-shaped cookie cutter. On a lightly greased cookie sheet, bake at 375 degrees for about 10 minutes or until lightly golden. Cool cookies. Spread bottom cookies with peach preserves. Stick top cookies onto bottoms and sprinkle with powdered sugar.

Another hint from Mrs. Fuerst: Always have a little flour on the table and rolling pin when you roll out the dough.

Reprinted by permission of Mrs. J. K. Fuerst, Houston, Texas

PEACH CHEESECAKE COOKIES

1 8-ounce package cream cheese,
    softened
1 tablespoon sugar
1 teaspoon grated lemon peel
2 tablespoons lemon juice

1 tablespoon milk
½ teaspoon vanilla
Granola Crust (recipe follows)
1 large or 2 small fresh peaches
    sliced into 20 wedges

Combine all ingredients except crust and peaches in a mixing bowl; beat until smooth. Spread over baked Granola Crust. Arrange peach wedges in rows on cheese mixture. Bake in 350-degree oven 12 minutes or until cheese is set. Cool and cut into bars. Makes 20 bars.

GRANOLA CRUST: Beat ¾ cup softened butter with ⅓ cup sugar, 3 egg yolks and 1½ cups flour until smooth. Mix in ¾ cup granola. Pat gently into bottom of 13 × 9-inch baking pan. Bake in 350-degree oven 15 minutes.

PEACHES AND CREAM COOKIE SANDWICHES

1¼ cups pecans
10 tablespoons butter
6 tablespoons sugar

1½ cups flour
¼ teaspoon salt
Powdered sugar (optional)

129

Filling:

1 to 2 cups fresh peaches, or
    other fruit in season, sliced
1 cup heavy cream, whipped
1 teaspoon vanilla

2 teaspoons sugar
Additional whipped cream
    (optional)
Powdered sugar (optional)

Preheat the oven to 375 degrees. Brown the nuts in the oven for 5 to 10 minutes, watching closely so they do not burn. Cool, and chop them in a grater or food processor until they are fine, but not a powder. Beat the butter and sugar together until it is creamy and white. Sift the flour with salt, add the nuts and stir into the creamed mixture to make a smooth dough. Divide into 3 equal pieces and shape into flat rounds. Place each between 2 sheets of wax paper and chill 30 minutes until firm. Roll or pat out into ⅛-inch thick rounds. Refrigerate if hard to handle. Remove the top layer of the paper, and cut into small 2- or 3-inch rounds with a cookie cutter. Remove to a cookie sheet. Bake 10 minutes or until the edges begin to brown. Be careful not to overbake. They will be soft when done and will harden as they cool. Remove them from the cookie sheets to racks to cool. Store, covered, at room temperature or in the freezer. One hour before serving, whip the cream with vanilla and sugar. Sandwich the whipped cream and peaches between 2 cookie rounds. Immediately before serving, decorate the top with additional whipped cream or sprinkle with powdered sugar. Makes 10 to 15 cookie sandwiches.

Reprinted by permission of The National Pecan Marketing Council, Inc.

PEACH OATMEAL COOKIES

2 eggs
1½ teaspoons vanilla
¾ cup shortening or margarine
¾ cup sugar
¾ cup brown sugar (packed)
1½ cups whole wheat flour

1 teaspoon salt
2 teaspoons baking powder
2½ cups rolled oats
1½ cups diced fresh California
    peaches
1 cup raisins

Beat eggs with vanilla, shortening and sugars in a mixing bowl. Combine flour, salt and baking powder. Add to egg mixture and beat at low speed 2 or 3 minutes or until smooth. Stir in oats, peaches and raisins. Chill. Drop by heaping tablespoons onto greased baking sheet and bake in 350-degree oven 10 to 15 minutes or until golden. Makes 2 to 2½ dozen large cookies.

Reprinted by permission of *The Houston Post*

HI-ENERGY COOKIE BAR

½ cup honey
⅓ cup packed light brown sugar
¼ cup butter or margarine
5 cups bran flakes with raisins, slightly crushed
1 3½-oz. can flaked coconut

1 4-oz. can walnuts, chopped (1 cup)
1 cup dried peaches, chopped and mixed with ¼ cup all-purpose flour
2 large eggs, well beaten

Heat oven to 400 degrees. Grease a 13 × 9 × 2-inch baking pan. Stir honey, sugar and butter in medium-size saucepan over medium heat until sugar dissolves. In large bowl, toss bran flakes, coconut, walnuts and peach-flour mixture. Pour in warm honey mixture, stir in eggs and mix to coat evenly. Press firmly into prepared pan. Bake until golden brown, about 15 to 20 minutes. Cool 10 minutes; cut into 24 bars.

FRUIT PRESERVE SQUARES

2½ cups Pioneer Buttermilk Baking Mix
1 cup sugar
1 egg

3 tablespoons melted shortening or butter
¼ cup milk
1½ cups peach preserves

Heat oven to 375 degrees F. Combine ingredients, except preserves, and mix well. Hint: greased fingertips prevent dough sticking. Pat half into 9 × 13-inch pan to ¼-inch of edges. Spread with preserves. Pat other half of dough, on waxed paper, to same size. Turn over on preserves and pull off wax paper. Bake for 30 minutes. Frost with icing. Cut into bars. Yield: 3 dozen.

Reprinted by permission of Pioneer Flour Mills

PEACH CRUMBLE

4 large ripe peaches (4 cups sliced)
¼ cup sugar (and dash of cinnamon if desired)
1 tablespoon lemon juice

2 tablespoons butter or margarine
¼ cup sugar
1 tablespoon all-purpose flour
¼ teaspoon salt
1 cup soft white bread crumbs

Put peaches, ¼ cup sugar, lemon juice, and butter in buttered casserole. Combine remaining ingredients and sprinkle over peaches, allowing some crumbs to combine with peaches. Bake at 375 degrees F. about 30 minutes. Serves 6.

Reprinted by permission of June Towers, Imperial Sugar Company

NO-BAKE FRESH PEACH CRISP

3 to 4 cups sliced fresh Texas
    peaches
1 cup sugar
3 tablespoons cornstarch
Pinch of salt

½ cup water
2 tablespoons butter
⅛ teaspoon vanilla
2 cups "natural" cereal

Measure ¼ cup sugar, cornstarch, salt and water into medium-size saucepan; stir until dissolved, then cook over medium heat, stirring constantly, until mixture thickens. Add remaining sugar and butter and cook until sugar is dissolved. Stir vanilla and fresh peaches into sugar mixture. Pour into an 8-inch square pan, pie pan or individual serving dishes. Top with cereal. Serve with cream, whipped cream or ice cream. Yield: 4–6 servings.

Reprinted by permission of Texas Department of Agriculture

CRUNCHY PEACH CRISP

3 pounds fresh California
    peaches, peeled (6 large or
    9 medium)
2 tablespoons lemon juice
⅓ cup sugar
½ teaspoon cinnamon
¼ teaspoon ground ginger
⅛ teaspoon ground nutmeg

¾ cup oats
⅔ cup brown sugar (packed)
½ cup butter, cut in ½-inch
    chunks
½ cup flour
⅛ teaspoon salt
½ cup almonds, sliced
½ teaspoon cinnamon

Cut each peach into 6 wedges; cut each wedge in half crosswise. Place chunks in bowl and toss with lemon juice, sugar, cinnamon, ginger and nutmeg. Turn into 8 × 8 × 2-inch ovenproof pan. In bowl, combine remaining ingredients; mix with fork until crumbly. Sprinkle evenly over peaches and press lightly. Bake in preheated 375-degree oven 45 minutes, until golden. Cool slightly. Serve warm. 6 to 8 servings.

Courtesy of *The Houston Post*

FRUIT CRISP

Topping:

1 cup 3-Minute Brand Quick Oats	½ teaspoon salt
½ cup brown sugar	½ cup chopped nuts (optional)
⅓ cup flour	¼ cup vegetable oil

Filling:

1 21-ounce can peach pie filling

Combine first five ingredients and mix well. Stir in oil. Press half of mixture in the bottom of a greased 8- or 9-inch baking dish. Spread pie filling atop crust. Sprinkle with remaining oat mixture. Bake at 350 degrees F. for 45 minutes.

Reprinted by permission of The 3-Minute Brand Oats Company, Cedar Rapids, Iowa, Michele E. Gaffney, Home Economist

PEACH CRINKLE

1 29-oz. can sliced peaches, drained	¾ cup Domino Light Brown Sugar, firmly packed
1 teaspoon grated lemon rind (optional)	Butter or margarine
1¼ cups pie crust mix	Whipped dessert topping or light cream

Place peaches in medium-sized baking dish, add lemon rind, if used. Crumble pie crust mix and sugar together, mixing well. Dust onto peaches and dot liberally with butter or margarine. Bake 45 minutes in 325-degree oven. Serve warm with cream. Makes 6 servings.

Jean Pryor, Houston, Texas

FESTIVE FRUIT CRUNCH

1 1 lb.-5 oz. can peach pie filling	½ teaspoon cinnamon
½ cup Malt-O-Meal	¼ cup coconut
¼ cup brown sugar	¼ cup melted butter

Preheat oven to 400 degrees. Spread pie filling in 8-inch square baking dish. Combine remaining ingredients until crumbly; spoon over filling. Bake at 400 degrees for 20 minutes. Serve warm or cold topped with whipped cream or ice cream.

Reprinted by permission of Malt-O-Meal Company

Puddings and Frozen Desserts

THE HAPPY, HEALTHY PEACH

One fruit that's good for everyone's health!
Is the peach with all of its wealth.
The peach is a beautiful sight to see,
That's low in fat and calories.
It can kill your hunger and make your day,
And has a good source of Vitamin A.
This vitamin is good for the eyes and skin.
So pick a lot to give all of your kin.
Peaches are a healthy fruit, as you can see
With a healing source of Vitamin C.
Calcium and iron are included, too,
Eating peaches is good for you.

By Michael Freeman, Ennis, Texas, June 9, 1987

PEACH ICE

1 envelope unflavored gelatin
½ cup water
4 cups peeled, pitted, ripe
    peaches (about 2 pounds)

2 tablespoons lemon juice
1½ cups Karo light corn syrup

In small saucepan sprinkle gelatin over water. Stir constantly over low heat until gelatin dissolves. Place half of peaches and lemon juice in blender container; cover. Blend at high speed 1 minute or until liquefied. Add remaining peaches 1 at a time, continuously blending until all are liquefied. With blender at low speed gradually add gelatin mixture and corn syrup until blended. Pour into 9 × 5 × 3-inch loaf pan. Freeze 1 to 2 hours or until almost firm. Beat until smooth but still frozen. Cover and freeze 3 hours, or until firm. Makes 1½ quarts.

Reprinted by permission of Best Foods, A Division of CPC North America

HOMEMADE PEACH ICE CREAM

½ cup sugar
4 cups sliced, peeled fresh Texas
    peaches
6 eggs
1 cup sugar

1 13-oz. can evaporated milk
1 14-oz. can sweetened
    condensed milk
1 pint whipping cream
1 tablespoon vanilla

Sprinkle sugar on peaches and cover. Beat eggs well. Add sugar, milk and whipping cream and mix well. Stir in sugared peaches and vanilla. Pour into freezer container. Finish filling container with milk. Freeze. Makes 1 gallon.

Reprinted by permission of Texas Department of Agriculture

OLD-FASHIONED PEACH ICE CREAM

4 cups diced peaches (2½ – 3
    pounds)
2 cups sugar, divided
1 teaspoon almond flavor
¼ teaspoon salt
3 tablespoons cornstarch

4 eggs, beaten
3 cups diluted Milnot* (1½ cups
    Milnot and 1½ cups water)
1 teaspoon vanilla
3 cups Milnot

Combine peaches, 1 cup sugar and almond flavor; set aside. Combine other 1 cup sugar, cornstarch, and salt; stir in enough diluted Milnot to moisten. Blend in the eggs, stir in remaining diluted Milnot and cook over low heat until slightly thickened. Remove from heat. Cool. Pour into freezer container; add remaining ingredients, swish paddle to stir. Freeze with ice and salt according to manufacturer's suggestions. Makes 1 gallon.

*Milnot Brand Dairy Vegetable Blend (no butterfat, virtually no cholesterol)

PEACH ICE CREAM

3 cups North Carolina peach
   pulp
1 tablespoon lemon juice
2 cups sugar
¼ teaspoon salt

4 eggs, slightly beaten
2 quarts milk
1 pint whipping cream
¼ teaspoon almond flavoring
Ice and ice cream salt

To the peach pulp add the lemon juice and 1 cup of the sugar. Allow to stand 1 hour. Add the other cup of sugar and salt to the beaten eggs, then blend in half of the milk. Cook this sugar, egg and milk mixture in top of double boiler over hot water to make a thick custard. Cool. Add the remainder of milk, the cream that has been partially whipped, the flavoring and sweetened peach pulp. Freeze using 1 part salt to 6 parts ice. Makes 1 gallon.

Reprinted by permission of North Carolina Department of Agriculture

PEACH ICE CREAM

1 envelope Knox Unflavored
   Gelatin
½ cup cold milk
½ cup milk, heated to boiling
¾ cup sugar

3 cups chopped, unpeeled
   peaches
2 cups (1 pt.) whipping or heavy
   cream

In 5-cup blender, sprinkle Knox Unflavored Gelatin over cold milk; let stand 3 to 4 minutes. Add hot milk and process at low speed until gelatin dissolves, about 2 minutes. Gradually add sugar and peaches and process at high speed until smooth. Pour gelatin mixture and cream into cream can of at least 1½-quart capacity ice cream machine. Process and freeze according to manufacturer's directions. Makes about 1½ quarts.

Tested recipe for the Lipton Kitchens, reprinted by permission of Thomas J. Lipton, Inc.

PEACH SHERBET

1 cup milk
¾ cup light corn syrup
1 cup granulated sugar

3 cups fresh, peeled, sliced
   peaches
⅓ cup lemon juice
2 egg whites, stiffly beaten

Scald milk with corn syrup and sugar over low heat, stirring; cool. Blend peaches in blender to make 2 cups pulp and juice and add to first mixture. Freeze in refrigerator trays until firm. Remove sherbet to chilled bowl and break up with a wooden spoon; beat until free of hard lumps but still thick and mushy. Fold in stiffly beaten egg whites. Return to trays and freeze until firm. Yield: About 8 servings.

Reprinted by permission of June Towers, Imperial Sugar Company

PEACH AND LEMON SHERBET

1 3-oz. pkg. of lemon Jell-O
1 cup sugar
2 cups water

1 No. 2 can peaches
1 cup syrup from can peaches
1 cup whipping cream

Bring water to a boil, add the lemon Jell-O. Cool and add sugar, peach juice, peaches which have been put through a sieve and the cream. Mix and freeze in the refrigerator or in an ice cream freezer. If frozen in the refrigerator, when it becomes mushy, remove and beat with electric mixer then return to freezer. If possible, serve topped with a bit of fresh mint and a chocolate cookie. Serves 8.

Timothy Compton, Houston, Texas

PEACH SHERBET

1 envelope unflavored gelatin
¼ cup water
2 tablespoons lemon juice
1 cup orange juice

1½ cups sugar
1 17-oz. can Larsen Peach Puree
2 egg whites

Sprinkle gelatin over water and let stand 5 minutes. In a large bowl combine lemon juice, orange juice and sugar. Add gelatin and peach puree. Stir until gelatin and sugar dissolve. Pour into ice cube tray. Freeze just until mushy, about 1 hour. Then beat egg whites in a small bowl with an electric mixer at high speed until soft peaks form. Gently fold whites into peach mixture. Turn into 2 ice cube trays. Freeze until firm, about 2 hours. For extra smooth sherbet, return entire mixture to electric mixer, beat until thick and smooth and re-chill until firm. About 30 minutes. Serves 6 to 8.

Reprinted by permission of The Larsen Company

PEACH POPSICLES

½ teaspoon unflavored or peach
   gelatin
3 tablespoons cold water
¾ cup water

½ cup sugar
¾ lb. fresh peaches
½ teaspoon lime juice

Sprinkle gelatin over 3 tablespoons water; stir. Set aside to soften gelatin. Place sugar and water in small saucepan and bring to a boil; lower heat and keep at slow boil for 5 minutes without stirring. Remove from heat and pour into gelatin; stir until gelatin has melted. Set aside to cool. Peel and pit peaches; put in blender. Squeeze lime juice over peaches and blend until pureed. Add gelatin mix and blend until well mixed. Pour into molds, seal and freeze until firm.

Carol Ann McKnight, Houston, Texas

FRESH FRUIT PARFAIT

½ cup sugar
2 teaspoons lemon juice

1 cup fresh peaches
1 cup heavy cream, whipped

Combine sugar, lemon juice and finely chopped peaches; let stand about 10 minutes or until sugar dissolves. Fold in whipped cream. Turn into 8-inch square pan and freeze about 2 hours. Remove from freezer about 5 minutes before serving; pile lightly into parfait glasses and garnish with a mint leaf.

Reprinted by permission of June Towers, Imperial Sugar Company

GEORGIA SPECIAL (Frozen Dessert)

3 or 4 cups (as desired) mashed
   or pureed peaches
2 cups sugar
2 cups apricot nectar, divided

1 tablespoon unflavored gelatin
4⅓ cups Milnot*
Few grains salt, optional

Sprinkle sugar over peaches and 1 cup apricot nectar; toss to coat peaches. Soak gelatin in ⅓ cup nectar; dissolve over hot water; stir in remaining nectar and mix with peaches. Pour Milnot in freezer container, add peach mixture; swish paddle until well mixed. Freeze according to manufacturer's directions. Makes 1 gallon.

*Milnot Brand Dairy Vegetable Blend (no butterfat, virtually no cholesterol)

PEACHES CAFÉ

4 medium peaches, peeled and
   chopped (2⅔ cups)
2 tablespoons sugar
2 teaspoons instant or ground
   coffee

½ teaspoon ground nutmeg
1 4½-oz. carton frozen whipped
   topping, thawed
1 tablespoon instant or ground
   coffee

Sprinkle peaches with sugar. Fold peaches, 2 teaspoons coffee and the nutmeg into whipped topping. Divide among 6 dessert dishes. Freeze uncovered 1 hour. Sprinkle with 1 tablespoon coffee. 6 servings, less than 100 calories per serving.

Reprinted from Betty Crocker's Recipe Card Library, by permission of General Mills

PEACH FLUFF

1½ cups mashed peaches (3 – 4
   medium fresh or #303 can)
½ teaspoon almond flavor
2 cups miniature marshmallows

¼ cup sugar
2 tablespoons lemon juice
1 cup Milnot*, chilled

Combine marshmallows, sugar and lemon juice; heat over low heat until marshmallows are almost melted, remove from heat. Whip

Milnot until it will hold very stiff peaks. Stir peaches into marshmallow mixture; fold into whipped Milnot. Pour into shallow dish or bowl (approx. 2 qt.) or individual serving dishes. Chill several hours or freeze. Makes 8 servings.

May be garnished with peach slices (any left over is better frozen).

*Milnot Brand Dairy Vegetable Blend (no butterfat, virtually no cholesterol)

PEACH FROSTY

1 16-oz. can cling peach halves
¼ cup plain yogurt
1 egg

2 tablespoons sugar
1 tablespoon lemon juice

Drain peaches, chop coarsely and place in shallow pan or ice cube tray; freeze. A few minutes before serving, remove peaches from freezer. In blender or food processor, whirl together remaining ingredients. With motor running; drop in frozen peaches, several pieces at a time; whirl until mixture is thick and smooth. Spoon into individual dessert dishes. Serve at once or store in freezer, removing 10 minutes or so before serving to soften slightly. Serves 4.

Reprinted by permission of Cling Peach Advisory Board

PEACHES 'N CREAM

2 tablespoons sugar
¼ teaspoon ginger
2 cups peach slices
½ cup raspberries

1 pint vanilla ice cream, softened
1 cup mayonnaise
1 teaspoon almond extract

Combine sugar and ginger; toss lightly with fruit. Chill. Combine ice cream, mayonnaise and almond extract, mixing until blended. Pour into six 5-oz. custard cups; freeze. Spoon fruit into serving dishes. Unmold ice cream mixture; serve over fruit. Top with additional fruit, if desired. 6 servings.

CREAMY PEACH MOUSSE

1 envelope Knox unflavored
    gelatin
2 tablespoons sugar
2 cups peach nectar, heated to
    boiling

1 tablespoon lemon juice
½ cup whipping or heavy cream,
    whipped
1½ cups chopped fresh peaches*

In large bowl, mix unflavored gelatin with sugar; add hot peach nectar and stir until gelatin is completely dissolved. Stir in lemon juice. Chill, stirring occasionally, until mixture mounds slightly when dropped from spoon. Fold in whipping cream, then peaches. Turn into dessert dishes or 3-cup bowl; chill until firm. Makes 6 servings.

*Substitution: Use 1 16-oz. **can** sliced peaches in light syrup, drained and chopped.

Reprinted by permission of Thomas J. Lipton, Inc.

PEACH MOUSSE

4 to 5 medium peaches
1⅔ cups evaporated milk,
   chilled

⅛ teaspoon salt
½ cup sugar
2 tablespoons lemon juice

Peel peaches, stone and mash enough to make 1½ cups pulp. Add sugar and stir occasionally until sugar is dissolved. Whip milk very stiff. Fold in lemon juice, salt and peach mixture. Freeze until firm. Makes 1½ quarts.

Joseph P. DiBlasi, Market Investigator, Produce Marketing Association

LIGHT AND FRUITY TAPIOCA

2 cups skim milk
Sugar
¼ cup quick-cooking tapioca
¼ teaspoon salt

2 eggs, separated
1 teaspoon vanilla extract
2 cups sliced fresh peaches

Measure milk into 4-cup glass measuring cup; add ¼ cup sugar, tapioca, salt and egg yolks. Blend well. Cook in Radarange oven for 6 minutes or until mixture boils, stirring after 4 minutes. Beat egg whites in large bowl until frothy; add 2 tablespoons sugar gradually, beating until mixture forms soft peaks. Beat in vanilla. Fold into pudding mixture. Cool. Spoon fruit into 6 serving dishes; top with pudding. Yield: 6 servings/100 calories per serving.

Reprinted by permission of Favorite Recipes Press, Nashville, Tennessee

CREAMY PEACH PUDDING

1¾ cups cold milk
1 package (4-serving size) Jell-O
   vanilla flavor instant
   pudding and pie filling

¼ teaspoon almond extract
1¾ cups (4 oz.) Birds Eye Cool
   Whip non-dairy whipped
   topping, thawed
2 cups diced fresh peaches

Combine milk, pudding mix and almond extract in deep narrow-bottom bowl. Beat at lowest speed of electric mixer about 1 minute. Add 1½ cups of the whipped topping and beat about 1 minute longer. Fold in peaches. Spoon into dessert dishes. Garnish with remaining whipped topping. Makes 4 cups or 8 servings.

Reprinted by permission of General Foods

OLD-TIME FRESH PEACH CRUMB PUDDING

18 medium fresh peaches (4
   pounds)
1 cup sugar

1¼ cups sifted all-purpose flour
½ cup margarine
Sliced fresh peaches for garnish

Peel and cut peaches into quarters. Combine ½ cup of the sugar and 3 tablespoons of flour and mix with peaches. Turn into a 10 × 6 × 2-inch greased baking dish. Mix remaining sugar and flour; add margarine and cut into crumb consistency. Sprinkle crumbs over peaches. Bake in preheated oven at 375 degrees F. 1 hour or until peaches are tender and crumbs are brown. Garnish top as desired with sliced fresh peaches. Yield: 8 servings.

Reprinted by permission of Produce Marketing Association

PEACHES 'N BITS PUDDING

1 14-oz. can Eagle Brand
   Sweetened Condensed Milk
   (NOT evaporated milk)
1½ cups cold water
1 4-serving size package instant
   vanilla flavor pudding and
   pie filling mix

2 cups (1 pint) whipping or heavy
   cream, whipped
36 Nabisco Nilla Wafers
1 large can sliced peaches
¾ cup Nestle Little Bits Semi-
   Sweet Chocolate
Additional Little Bits, Nilla
   Wafers and peaches optional

In large bowl, combine Eagle Brand and water. Add pudding mix; beat well. Chill 5 minutes. Fold in whipped cream. Spoon 2 cups pudding into 3-quart glass serving bowl; top with half of each of the Nilla Wafers, peaches, Nestle Little Bits Semi-Sweet Chocolate and remaining pudding. Repeat layering. Garnish with additional Little Bits, Nilla Wafers and peaches if desired. Chill thoroughly. Refrigerate leftovers. Makes 8–10 servings.

PEACH CUSTARD CHAMPION

1½ cups all-purpose flour
½ cup butter or margarine,
   softened
½ teaspoon salt
1 1-pound 13-ounce can sliced
   peaches

½ cup sugar
1 teaspoon cinnamon
1 egg, slightly beaten
1 cup Pet Evaporated Milk

In a 1½-quart mixing bowl mix in with pastry blender or two knives until mixture resembles coarse meal: flour, butter and salt. With hands or back of spoon, press mixture firmly onto bottom and halfway up sides of greased 8-inch square baking pan. Drain peaches well, reserving ½ cup syrup. Arrange peaches on crust. Combine sugar and cinnamon. Sprinkle over peaches. Bake in 375-degree oven for 20 minutes. Mix together egg, reserved ½ cup peach syrup and evaporated milk. Pour over peaches. Return to oven. Bake 30 to 35 minutes more, or until custard is firm except in center. Center becomes firm upon standing. Total baking time 55 minutes. Serve warm or cold. Makes 9 servings.

Reprinted by permission of PET, An IC Industries Company

PEACH PARFAIT PUDDING

1 7-oz. pkg. Sun-Maid dried
   peaches
2 cups water
½ cup sugar
1 tablespoon lemon juice
Chopped Diamond walnuts
½ teaspoon cinnamon
1 3½-oz. pkg. vanilla
   pudding/pie filling
1½ cups milk
1 cup whipping cream, whipped

Cut peaches in half. Bring peaches, water, sugar, lemon juice and cinnamon to a boil. Stir, reduce to a medium heat and cook uncovered for 15 minutes. Whirl in blender until smooth. Set aside. Prepare pudding according to package directions using only 1½ cups milk. Cool to room temperature and fold in whipping cream. Layer peach sauce and pudding in bowl or individual serving dishes. Sprinkle with nuts. Serves 6 – 8.

Reprinted by permission of Sun Diamond Growers of California

EASY FRUIT WHIP

2 egg whites
1 cup drained sliced peaches
½ teaspoon lemon juice
Dash of salt

Beat egg whites in small bowl until stiff. Place remaining ingredients in blender container; cover and process at puree until smooth. Pour over egg whites; fold together gently. Pile into sherbet glasses; chill before serving. Yield: 4 servings. About 40 calories per serving.

Reprinted by permission of Favorite Recipes Press, Nashville, Tennessee

PEACH SNOW

1 pkg. frozen unsweetened
   peaches or 2 cups fresh
   peaches
1 pkg. unflavored gelatin
1 teaspoon liquid sweetener
½ cup nonfat dry milk powder
½ cup ice water
1 tablespoon lemon juice

Drain juice from peaches, add enough water to measure 1 cup liquid. Add gelatin; let stand to soften. Place over low heat; stir until gelatin is dissolved. Add peaches and sweetener; chill until syrupy. Chill small mixer bowl and beaters; place milk powder, ice water, and lemon juice in bowl. Beat until stiff peaks form. Fold in gelatin mixture; pour into 4-cup mold. Chill for 2 – 4 hours. Yield: 4 servings. Each ½ cup serving = ½ milk exchange.

Reprinted by permission of Favorite Recipe Press, Nashville, Tennessee

PEACHY PUDDING

2 tablespoons butter or
    margarine
6 slices Pepperidge Farm
    Sprouted Wheat Bread
2 tablespoons sugar
1 teaspoon ground cinnamon
4 eggs, separated

2 cups milk
½ cup shredded coconut
1 cup sugar
1 teaspoon vanilla extract
3 cups sliced fresh or frozen
    peaches

Spread butter on bread and sprinkle with sugar and cinnamon; cut into cubes. Combine egg yolks, milk, ½ cup sugar, coconut and vanilla. Place bread cubes in bottom of well-greased 1½-quart baking dish. Pour milk mixture over bread. Bake in pan of hot water at 350 degrees for 40 minutes. Remove from oven and arrange peach slices on custard. Beat egg whites until foamy; gradually beating in remaining ½ cup sugar. Continue beating until mixture holds stiff peaks. Spread over top of peach slices. Return to oven and bake 15 minutes longer or until meringue is golden brown. Serve warm or at room temperature. Makes 6 to 8 servings.

Reprinted by permission of Pepperidge Farm, Inc.

PEACHY BREAD PUDDING

4 slices bread, buttered
¼ cup raisins
1¼ cups milk
1 egg, beaten

2½ tablespoons sugar
1 4¾-oz. jar Gerber strained
    peaches
¼ teaspoon nutmeg

Make sandwiches with buttered bread. Cut bread into small squares and place in bottom of a buttered 1½-quart baking dish. Sprinkle raisins over the bread. Heat milk just to boiling; pour over egg. Stir in sugar, peaches and nutmeg. Pour custard over bread and let stand for ½ hour. Bake in preheated 325-degree oven 30 – 40 minutes, or until set. Makes 4 servings.

Reprinted by permission of Gerber Products Company

RICE 'N PEACHES 'N CREAM

1 cup uncooked Mahatma Long
  Grain Brown Rice
1 16-oz. can Freestone sliced
  peaches in heavy syrup
⅓ cup brown sugar

2 tablespoons butter or
  margarine
1 teaspoon lemon juice
¼ teaspoon ground cinnamon
¼ teaspoon ground nutmeg
½ cup heavy cream

Cook rice by package directions, using 1 teaspoon salt. Drain peaches and reserve ½ cup of the liquid and about 12 of the slices. Dice the remaining peaches. Stir the chopped peaches and reserved peach liquid, brown sugar, butter or margarine, lemon juice, cinnamon, and nutmeg into hot, cooked rice. Mix well and simmer about 5 minutes. Pour into a buttered 1½-quart casserole. Pour the cream over the rice. Arrange the remaining peaches over the top. Bake at 425 degrees F. for 15 minutes. Serve warm or cold. Makes 8 servings (about ½ cup each).

Reprinted by permission of Riviana Foods Inc.

PEACH PARFAITS

1 8-ounce carton peach yogurt
1½ cups chilled, cooked Uncle
  Ben's Converted Brand Rice

2 cups pared, coarsely chopped
  fresh peaches
Cinnamon or nutmeg (optional)

Stir yogurt into chilled rice. Layer peaches and rice mixture in parfait or dessert dishes. Sprinkle with cinnamon or nutmeg, if desired. Makes 6 servings.

Reprinted by permission of Uncle Ben's, Inc. Houston, Texas

PEACH BRITTLE RICE PUDDING

3 cups cooked rice
3 cups milk
⅓ cup sugar
1 teaspoon grated lemon peel
1 tablespoon butter or margarine
3 eggs, beaten
1 teaspoon vanilla extract

1 29-ounce can sliced peaches*
1 cup (½ pint) heavy cream,
  whipped
¼ teaspoon salt
1 teaspoon lemon juice
½ cup broken pieces of peanut
  brittle

Combine rice, milk, sugar, lemon peel, and butter in medium saucepan. Cook and stir over medium heat until thick and creamy —about 20 minutes. Mix some of the rice mixture into the beaten eggs; stir all into the hot mixture and cook 1 minute longer. Add vanilla. Pour into large serving dish or individual serving dishes. Chill until ready to serve. Drain peaches, reserving 10 of the slices for garnish. (Save the syrup for use another time.) Then combine remaining peach slices with whipped cream, salt and lemon juice. Spoon onto rice pudding. Garnish with reserved peach slices and pieces of peanut brittle. Makes 8 to 10 servings.

*Or use about 2½ cups sliced fresh peaches, sweetened to taste.

Reprinted by permission of
Rice Council for Market Development Home Economics Department

RICE PUDDING U.S.A.

5½ cups milk
1 cup uncooked Adolphus Rice
1 teaspoon salt
1 tablespoon butter or margarine

1 12-oz. jar peach preserves
1 teaspoon vanilla extract
¼ cup cream sherry
½ cup chopped nut meats

In a 3-quart saucepan combine milk, rice, salt, and butter. Bring to a boil, reduce heat, cover, and simmer 35 to 40 minutes, or until thickened, stirring occasionally. Remove from heat; fold in ½ cup preserves and vanilla. Heat the remaining preserves with sherry. Fold in the nut meats. Serve pudding warm or cold topped with preserve sauce. Makes 10 servings (½ cup each).

Reprinted by permission of Comet Rice, Inc.

CALIFORNIA PEACH PUDDING

3 cups cooked rice
3 cups milk
½ cup honey
Salt
1 teaspoon vanilla extract
2 tablespoons butter or
    margarine, divided
¼ cup firmly packed brown
    sugar

2 teaspoons cornstarch
½ teaspoon ground cinnamon
1 16-oz. can sliced peaches
2 tablespoons brandy or 1
    teaspoon brandy extract
6 tablespoons slivered almonds,
    toasted
Whipped or sour cream, optional

Combine rice, milk, honey, and ¼ teaspoon salt in saucepan. Cook over medium heat about 30 minutes, or until thickened, stirring often. Add vanilla and 1 tablespoon butter. Portion into serving dishes. Blend sugar, cornstarch, cinnamon, ¼ teaspoon salt, and peaches with syrup. Bring to a boil, reduce heat, and simmer 2 to 3 minutes, or until clear and thickened. Remove from heat. Add remaining butter and brandy. Spoon over rice pudding. Sprinkle with almonds. Serve warm or cold, topped with cream. Makes 6 servings.

Reprinted by permission of Rice Council for Market Development Home Economics Department

KASHA FRUIT FANTASIA

1 cup water
1 cup orange juice
½ cup kasha
1 teaspoon butter or margarine
1 cup heavy cream, whipped
3 tablespoons sugar

3 tablespoons orange-flavored
　liqueur (or rum or kirsch)
2½ cups well-drained canned or
　fresh fruit (such as mandarin
　oranges, peaches, apricots,
　pineapple)
Coconut (optional)

In saucepan, heat water and orange juice to boiling; add butter and kasha, and bring back to boiling. Then cover pan, reduce heat to simmer for 15 minutes or until kasha is tender. Drain thoroughly and set kasha aside to cool. Add sugar and liqueur to whipped cream. Fold in fruits and kasha. Chill several hours or overnight. May be topped with grated coconut before serving. Serves 8.

Reprinted by permission of The Burkett Mills

FRESH PEACH COMPOTE WITH TAPIOCA

1 cup fresh orange juice
6 tablespoons brandy
4 tablespoons sugar
¼ teaspoon ground cardamom
4 cinnamon sticks, halved

3 pounds fresh California
　peaches, peeled, pitted,
　sliced (6 cups)
8 servings vanilla-flavored
　tapioca

Combine all ingredients, *except* tapioca, and marinate in refrigerator at least 2 hours. Serve with tapioca, using cinnamon sticks as garnish. 8 servings.

Reprinted by permission of *The Houston Post*

FLUFFY PEACH ALMOND PUDDING

¾ cup dry Carnation Nonfat Dry
　Milk
½ cup sugar
1 envelope unflavored gelatin
1 cup water
4 beaten egg yolks

1½ cups fresh or frozen peach
　puree
½ teaspoon almond extract
½ teaspoon vanilla extract
4 egg whites
Toasted almonds

Combine dry nonfat milk, ¼ cup sugar, and gelatin in medium saucepan. Stir in water and egg yolks. Cook over medium heat, stirring constantly, until mixture coats a spoon. Remove from heat. Stir in peach puree and extracts. Chill until mixture mounds from spoon. (Place mixture in freezer for rapid chilling.) Beat with wire whisk to smooth mixture, if necessary. Beat egg whites in small mixer bowl on high speed until foamy. Gradually add remaining ¼ cup sugar, 1 tablespoon at a time. Continue beating until sugar is dissolved and meringue is stiff but not dry. Fold into peach mixture. Spoon into dessert dishes. Garnish with toasted almonds. Serve immediately, or chill for later use. Makes 6 cups.

Reprinted by permission of Carnation

Desserts

A PEACH PICKING

If you're looking for fun and good fruit, too,
Picking peaches is what you should do.
You can pick the amount and the kind,
The perfect activity to ease your mind.
A family occasion to have a good time,
And you get your money's worth to the dime.
When you get real tired 'cause you've picked a bunch,
It's time for a relaxing picnic lunch.
If you haven't tried it, you'll never know,
So organize a trip and get ready to go!

By Michael Freeman, Ennis, Texas, May 29, 1985

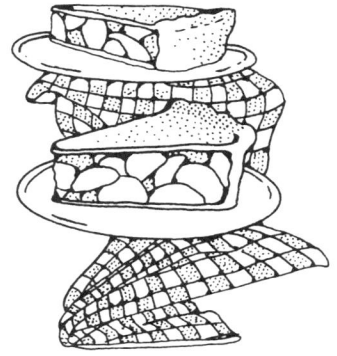

BAKED PEACH AMBROSIA

4 to 6 peaches, peeled*
¼ cup firmly packed brown
   sugar
¼ cup Widmer's Cocktail Sherry
   or orange juice

⅛ teaspoon French's Ground
   Cardamom Seed
½ cup dairy sour cream
¼ cup flaked coconut
1 tablespoon French's Cinnamon
   Sugar

Cut peaches in half; remove pits and place in shallow baking pan. Stir together brown sugar, sherry, and cardamom; spoon over peaches. Bake at 400 degrees for 20 to 30 minutes, until tender. Stir together sour cream, coconut, and cinnamon sugar; spoon over hot peaches. 4 to 6 servings.

*Or, use canned cling peach halves, drained.

Reprinted by permission of French's. The R. T. French Company

BAKED PEACHES

6 large ripe whole peaches
4 tablespoons butter
1 cup Jacquin's Peach Brandy
½ cup sugar

1 teaspoon mace
Grated rind and juice of ½ lemon
Sour cream, optional

Peel peaches and place in a baking dish greased with 1 tablespoon butter. Mix together Jacquin's Peach Brandy, sugar, mace, lemon rind and lemon juice; pour over peaches. Dot with remaining 3 tablespoons butter. Cover dish with lid or foil and bake in a 400-degree oven for 30 to 40 minutes. Baste several times while baking. Serve hot or cold, with or without sour cream. Serves 6.

Reprinted by permission of Charles Jacquin's ET CIE., Inc.

BROILED PEACHES

6 freestone peaches, peeled and
   cut in halves
¼ teaspoon allspice

1 tablespoon grated orange rind
3 tablespoons brown sugar
¼ cup chopped nuts

Scald peaches in boiling water 1 minute and remove; with tip of sharp knife, remove peel. Cut peaches in halves and place pit sides up in shallow baking dish. Combine remaining ingredients and place the mixture in hollow of peaches. Broil about 5 minutes, or until sugar mixture is bubbling and peaches are very hot. Nice accompaniment for meat dishes. Serves 6.

Reprinted by permission of June Towers, Imperial Sugar Company

DIXIE CANTALOUPE AND PEACHES

1 medium cantaloupe, pared and
   cut into ½-inch pieces (about
   3 cups)
4 fresh peaches, peeled and
   sliced (about 3 cups)
2 tablespoons lemon juice
1 cup all-purpose flour*

1 cup packed brown sugar
⅓ cup butter or margarine
½ teaspoon ground cinnamon
⅛ teaspoon salt
Ice cream or light cream
   (optional)

Heat oven to 375 degrees. Place cantaloupe and peaches in ungreased baking dish, 8 × 8 × 2-inches, or 1½-quart casserole; sprinkle with lemon juice. Mix remaining ingredients except ice cream with pastry blender or fork until crumbly; sprinkle over cantaloupe and peaches. Bake until cantaloupe and peaches are tender and topping is golden brown, about 30 minutes. Serve warm with ice cream. 6 servings.

*If using self-rising flour, omit salt.

Reprinted from Betty Crocker's Recipe Card Library, by permission of General Mills

PEACH DESSERT

1½ cups Bisquick baking mix
½ cup packed brown sugar
1 egg
½ cup milk
2 tablespoons shortening
1 teaspoon vanilla

1 8-oz. pkg. cream cheese,
   softened
¼ cup milk
2 tablespoons sugar, if desired
1 16-oz. can peach halves
Chopped nuts
Butterscotch Sauce (below)

Heat oven to 350 degrees. Grease and flour round layer pan, 9 × 1½ inches. Beat baking mix, brown sugar, egg, ½ cup milk, the shortening and vanilla in large mixer bowl on low speed, scraping bowl constantly, 30 seconds. Beat on medium speed, scraping bowl occasionally, 4 minutes. Pour into pan. Bake until wooden pick inserted in center comes out clean, 30 – 35 minutes. Cool completely (do not remove from pan). Beat cheese, ¼ cup milk and 2 tablespoons sugar until smooth; spread over cake. Pat peach halves dry; place cut sides down in circle on cream cheese mixture. Sprinkle nuts around edge of cake. Serve with Butterscotch Sauce. Refrigerate any remaining dessert.

Butterscotch Sauce: Heat ¾ cup packed brown sugar, ¼ cup light corn syrup and 2 tablespoons margarine or butter to boiling over low heat, stirring constantly. Stir in ¼ cup whipping cream and ½ teaspoon vanilla. Cool completely; stir before serving.

Jean Pryor, Houston, Texas

PEACHES 'N CREAM CHEESE OAT SCONES

⅔ cup Sun-Maid or Sunsweet
   dried peaches
1 cup water
1⅔ cups all-purpose flour
2 tablespoons granulated sugar
2½ teaspoons baking powder
½ teaspoon salt

½ cup quick cooking oats
1 tablespoon butter or margarine,
   softened
1 3-ounce package cream cheese,
   softened
2 eggs
¼ cup milk

In a saucepan, bring peaches and water to a boil: simmer uncovered about 20 minutes, or until fruit is tender. Cool, drain and dice peaches. In a bowl, sift together flour, sugar, baking powder and salt. Stir in oats. Cut in butter and cream cheese until consistency of coarse meal. Beat eggs; add milk and peaches. Stir into flour mixture just until all of flour is moistened. Turn out onto well-greased baking sheet. Pat out to an 8-inch circle about 1-inch thick. Bake at 375 degrees F. for 20–25 minutes or until baked through. Cut into 8 wedges and serve warm.

Reprinted by permission of Sun-Diamond Growers of California

PEACH REVEL MERINGUE

Meringue Shell (recipe follows)
1 can sliced peaches (drain,
   reserve syrup)
3 tablespoons cornstarch
1 cup chilled whipping cream

1 3-oz. pkg. cream cheese,
   softened
½ cup sugar
½ teaspoon vanilla
1 cup miniature marshmallows

Prepare meringue shell. Mix ¼ cup of reserved syrup and the cornstarch in saucepan. Add peaches and remaining syrup. Heat to boiling, stirring constantly. Boil and stir 1 minute. Cool at room temperature. Beat whipping cream in chilled bowl. Blend cream cheese, sugar and vanilla. Fold cheese mixture and marshmallows into whipped cream. Spread ⅓ of peach mixture in meringue shell. Spread half of cheese mixture over peach mixture, ½ of remaining peach mixture, the remaining cheese mixture. Top with remaining peach mixture. Refrigerate at least 2 hours but no longer than 24 hours.

Meringue Shell:
Heat oven to 250 degrees. Cover baking sheet with brown paper. Beat 4 egg whites and ¼ teaspoon cream of tartar in small mixer bowl until foamy. Beat in 1 cup of sugar, 1 tablespoon at a time; continue beating until stiff and glossy, about 4 minutes. Spread half the meringue mixture in an 8-inch circle on brown paper, building up sides. Drop remaining meringue mixture by rounded teaspoon-

fuls on edge of circle, making peaks. Bake 1½ hours. Turn off oven; leave meringue in oven with door closed 1 hour. Remove from oven; cool.

Adapted by Barbara Sisk, Hempstead, Texas, from Raspberry Revel Meringue.
Reprinted from Betty Crocker's Recipe Card Library, by permission of General Mills

PECAN ROULADE

6 eggs, separated
¾ cup sugar
¼ teaspoon cream of tartar, if using an electric mixer

1½ cups coarsely ground or finely chopped pecans
1 tablespoon baking powder

Filling:

Powdered sugar for sprinkling wax paper
2 cups heavy cream
¼ cup powdered sugar
2 drops vanilla extract, rum or brandy flavoring

1 cup sliced fresh peaches, bananas or strawberries
Optional fruit: kiwi fruits, peeled and sliced

Preheat the oven to 350 degrees. Oil a 10½ × 15½-inch jelly-roll pan and cover with oiled wax paper extending over the edges of the pan. Beat the egg yolks and sugar with an electric mixer until they are thick and light. In a separate bowl, beat the egg whites until they hold a stiff peak. (If you are using an electric mixer, add the cream of tartar.) Add the ground pecans and baking powder to the egg yolk mixture. With a rubber spatula, fold a large spoonful of the egg whites into the pecan/egg mixture, then fold this mixture into the egg whites. Do not over-fold. Pour into the prepared pan. Bake for 20 minutes. The roulade will be puffy and light; it is done when it springs back when touched and when a toothpick inserted in the center comes out clean. Remove the roulade from the oven and cool to room temperature. When cool, cover with a slightly damp towel to make the top soft but not wet. It may now be refrigerated for several days. To serve: Sprinkle a sheet of wax paper the length of the roulade with powdered sugar. Invert the roulade onto the paper. Peel off the wax paper backing in narrow strips. Whip the cream with flavorings and powdered sugar. Spread the roulade with the whipped cream and top with the sliced fruit; roll as you would a jelly-roll. Make a final roll to slide it from the wax paper onto the platter. Sprinkle with additional powdered sugar and decorate with whipped cream and fruit.

153

Note: The roulade may be frozen if peaches and/or strawberries are used as the fruit. Thaw it for several hours in the refrigerator and serve it while it is still almost icy in the center. Serves 8 to 10.

Reprinted by permission of The National Pecan Marketing Council, Inc.

STUFFED FRESH PEACHES

4 medium-size firm, ripe peaches
½ cup vanilla wafer crumbs, about 8 to 10 crushed wafers
1 tablespoon sugar
2 teaspoons freshly squeezed lemon or lime juice
½ teaspoon grated lemon or lime rind
¼ teaspoon ground cinnamon
2 tablespoons butter or margarine
2 tablespoons toasted slivered almonds

Peel peaches by submerging in boiling water for 1 to 2 minutes; skin should pull off easily with a paring knife. Cut peaches in half, remove pits and hollow out about 1 teaspoon of pulp per half; reserve. Chop reserved peach pulp (you should have about 2 tablespoons) and combine with crumbs, sugar, lemon or lime juice, lemon or lime rind, and cinnamon; mix well. Fill each peach half with crumb mixture. Dot with butter and sprinkle with toasted almonds. Bake in a 400-degree oven 15 minutes or until peaches are just tender. Serve warm or at room temperature. Makes 4 servings.

Reprinted by permission of United Fresh Fruit and Vegetable Association

FRESH FRUIT POLYNESIAN

1 quart vanilla ice cream
⅔ cup packed brown sugar
1 tablespoon cornstarch
½ cup butter or margarine
1 tablespoon lemon juice
2 teaspoons finely shredded orange peel
2 cups peaches, sliced
2 cups strawberries, sliced
¼ cup rum or apricot brandy

Shape ice cream into 6 to 8 balls. Place on waxed paper-covered baking sheet and freeze.

Mix brown sugar and cornstarch in chafing dish or skillet; add butter, lemon juice and orange peel. Cook over medium heat, stirring constantly, until mixture thickens and boils. Boil and stir 1 minute. Stir in fruit; heat until fruit is hot, about 2 minutes. Heat rum or brandy in a small saucepan just until warm; ignite and pour over fruit. Stir; spoon over each serving of ice cream. 6 to 8 servings.

Reprinted from Betty Crocker's Recipe Card Library, by permission of General Mills

PEACHES MARSALA

The Peaches:

6 medium-size ripe peaches   3 quarts boiling water

The Marsala Sauce:

¼ cup Marsala wine
⅓ cup polyunsaturated
    margarine, at room
    temperature
1 ¼ cups sifted confectioners'
    sugar

2 large eggs, separated
½ teaspoon grated lemon rind
⅛ teaspoon salt

To prepare the peaches: Immerse whole peaches in boiling water and poach for 5 minutes. Immediately drain and cover with cold water. When cool enough to handle, peel, cut in half, and remove pits. Set peaches aside. To prepare the Marsala sauce: Place Marsala in a small saucepan. Bring to a boil for one minute and remove from heat immediately. Set aside. In a large bowl, beat margarine, sugar, and egg yolks until blended smoothly. Transfer mixture to the top of a double boiler and cook over hot water, stirring constantly, until smooth and thickened. Remove from heat and stir in Marsala, lemon rind, and salt. In a separate bowl, beat egg whites until soft peaks form. Fold one-fourth of the whites into the sauce and then fold in the remaining whites. Place two peach halves, cut side down, in each serving dish and spoon sauce over peaches. Serve at once. Yield: 6 servings, 2 cups sauce.

Reprinted by permission of Gibson Wine Company

FROSTY PEACH COOLER

1 16-oz. can Diet Delight Cling
    Peach Slices, drained
    (reserve juice)
6 teaspoons sherry or brandy

1 envelope Knox Unflavored
    Gelatin
⅓ cup boiling water
2 tablespoons sugar
1 tablespoon lemon juice

Reserve 4 peach slices; drizzle with 1½ teaspoons sherry and chill. In a 5-cup blender, sprinkle gelatin over reserved juice; let stand until moistened. Add water and blend at low speed 2 minutes. Add remaining peaches and sherry, sugar, and lemon juice; blend at high speed 2 minutes. Pour into 4 dessert glasses and chill until set. Just before serving, garnish with reserved peaches. Makes 4 servings.

Tested recipe from The Lipton Kitchens. Reprinted by permission of Thomas J. Lipton, Inc.

FRUITS BRULÉE

1 17-oz. can peach halves in
  heavy syrup, drained,
  reserve 2 tablespoons syrup
1 16-oz. can pear halves in heavy
  syrup, drained
1 16½-oz. can pitted dark sweet
  cherries, drained

⅔ cup packed light brown sugar
3 tablespoons all-purpose flour
½ teaspoon ground cinnamon
2 tablespoons fresh lemon juice
Ground nutmeg
1 cup sour cream

Arrange peach and pear halves, cut side up, in single layer in broiler-safe dish. Top with cherries. Mix sugar, flour and cinnamon; sprinkle over fruits. Mix the 2 tablespoons reserved syrup with the lemon juice; sprinkle over sugar mixture. Broil until sugar bubbles and glazes fruits. Sprinkle with nutmeg; serve with sour cream. Makes 6 servings.

NO-BAKE PEACH SOUFFLE

1 quart peach halves or 1 28-oz.
  can peach halves
1 6-oz. pkg. peach gelatin

3 egg whites
½ pint whipping cream,
  whipped
½ cup peach preserves

Drain peaches, reserving juice. Add water to juice to make 1-½ cups. Set aside. Puree peaches in blender. Set aside. In a medium saucepan, bring juice mixture to a boil. Stir in gelatin. When gelatin is dissolved, blend in peach puree. Refrigerate until almost set, about 1 hour. In a medium bowl, beat egg whites until peaks form. Whip peach mixture until fluffy. Fold egg whites into peach mixture. Fold in whipped cream. Spoon about ⅓ of the peach mixture into 1½-quart souffle dish or casserole. Swirl ⅓ of the preserves through peach mixture. Repeat using half of remaining peach mixture and ½ preserves. Repeat using remaining ingredients. Chill until firm, at least 4 hours. Makes 8 servings.

Reprinted by permission of Barbara Sisk, Hempstead, Texas

PEACH-CHEESE CHIFFON

2 cups sliced, peeled, fresh
  peaches (4 or 5 peaches)
2 tablespoons sugar
1 3-oz. package Jell-O peach
  flavor gelatin
¾ cup boiling water

1 3-oz. package cream cheese,
  softened
1 cup thawed Birds Eye Cool
  Whip non-dairy whipped
  topping
1 cup crushed ice

Place 2 or 3 peach slices in each of 8 dessert glasses. Add sugar to remaining peaches; set aside. Combine gelatin and boiling water in blender container, cover and blend at low speed until gelatin is dissolved, about 1 minute. Add cheese and the peaches. Cover and blend at high speed until smooth. Add whipped topping and ice; blend until ice is melted and mixture is creamy. Pour into glasses. Chill until set, about 30 minutes. Garnish with additional whipped topping and peach slices, if desired. Makes about 4 cups or 8 servings.

Reprinted by permission of General Foods

PEACH FOAM

1½ pounds fresh California
    peaches, peeled, pitted,
    sliced (3 cups)
1 package unflavored gelatin

½ cup each cold water and
    orange juice
½ cup sugar
¼ teaspoon almond extract
3 large egg whites

In blender, puree enough peach slices to measure 1 cup. Reserve puree and remaining slices. Sprinkle gelatin over water and orange juice. Transfer gelatin mixture to saucepan; add sugar, peach puree and almond extract. Heat mixture only until sugar dissolves. Remove and cool until mixture starts to thicken. Line 6-cup mold with remaining peach slices. Beat egg whites until soft peaks form. Gently fold whites into cooled gelatin mixture. Pour into mold and chill until firm. To serve, unmold on serving dish. Garnish with additional peach slices. 8 servings.

Reprinted by permission of *The Houston Post*

PEACH CREAM DESSERT
An easy yet tasty dessert!

1 3⅛-oz. package vanilla
    pudding and pie filling
1 tall can (12 fluid ounces) Pet
    Evaporated Milk
⅓ cup water

12 graham crackers (each 2½
    inches square)
1 cup sliced peaches (about 2)
2 medium bananas, sliced

Empty pudding mix into saucepan. Gradually stir in evaporated milk and water. Heat to boiling. Boil 1 minute. Place 4 crackers in bottom of l-quart square casserole or baking pan. Place peaches on top. Pour over half of pudding. Layer crackers, spread with bananas, pour remaining pudding over, top with crackers. Cover. Refrigerate until firm. Serve chilled. Makes 4 – 6 servings.

Reprinted by permission of Pet, An IC Industries Company

PEACH DELIGHT

2 pounds sliced peaches (approx. 3 cups)
½ cup sugar
Few drops lemon juice
1 pound coconut macaroons (approx. 4 cups)
1 egg
1 cup powdered sugar
½ cup Milnot*
½ stick butter or margarine
2 teaspoons unflavored gelatin
⅓ cup syrup drained from peaches (or water)
1 cup Milnot, whipped
1 teaspoon almond flavoring

Sprinkle peaches with sugar and lemon juice and let stand. Crumble macaroons; reserve 1 cup, use remainder to line dish (approx. 7 × 11 × 2). Beat egg, blend in powdered sugar, add Milnot and butter; cook over low heat until slightly thickened. Pour over crumbs and allow to cool. Arrange peaches on top of custard. Soften gelatin in peach juice, melt over hot water then cool slightly. Add gelatin and flavoring to whipped Milnot; spread Milnot mixture over peaches and top with reserved macaroon crumbs. Chill several hours or overnight. Garnish with fruit and nuts if desired. 10 – 12 servings.

Note: Canned or **frozen** peaches may be used, but if sweetened fruit is used omit the ½ cup of sugar.

*Milnot Brand Dairy Vegetable Blend (no butterfat, virtually no cholesterol)

PEACH FROST

1 6-oz. package peach-flavored gelatin
1½ cups boiling water
1½ cups lemon-lime carbonated beverage or ginger ale
1 2.8-oz. envelope whipped topping mix
¾ cup chopped peaches
2 tablespoons pina colada cocktail mix

Dissolve gelatin in boiling water. Add lemon-lime beverage, stirring well. Pour 1 cup gelatin into a lightly oiled 8-inch square dish. Chill until set but not firm. Prepare whipped topping mix according to package directions; set aside. Add peaches and cocktail mix to remaining gelatin, stirring well; fold in whipped topping. Pour mixture over first layer. Chill until firm. Cut into squares to serve. Yield: 9 servings.

Mrs. L.H. Carter, Lexington, Kentucky. This recipe is from *Southern Living Annual Recipes*, 1984.

QUICK RUMTOPF

1 16-oz. can Del Monte Yellow
    Cling Sliced Peaches
1 16-oz. can Del Monte Bartlett
    Pear Halves
1 15½-oz. can Del Monte
    Pineapple Chunks

1 11-oz. can Del Monte Mandarin
    Oranges
1 cup Don Q Rum
1 cinnamon stick
½ cup Del Monte Natural
    Raisins

Drain fruit, reserving syrup in medium saucepan. Add rum and cinnamon stick to reserved syrup. Bring to boil, stirring occasionally. Cool. Layer fruit and raisins in rumtopf pot or large jars. Pour syrup mixture over fruit. Refrigerate. Allow 1 week to mellow. Serve as fruit compote or on ice cream or pound cake. 2 quarts.

Reprinted by permission of Del Monte Kitchens/Del Monte Corporation

RUBY PEACHES

6 canned peach halves
1 cup sugar-free strawberry-
    flavored carbonated
    beverage

¼ cup low-calorie raspberry
    preserves
1 tablespoon cornstarch
6 tablespoons low-calorie
    whipped topping

Place 1 peach half cut side up in each of 6 dessert dishes. Heat remaining ingredients except topping to boiling, stirring constantly. Boil and stir 1 minute. Cool; top each peach with 1 tablespoon whipped topping. Pour sauce on peach halves. Refrigerate 2 hours. 6 servings, less than 75 calories per serving.

Reprinted from Betty Crocker's Recipe Card Library, by permission of General Mills

SUMMER'S DELIGHT

1 store-bought angel food cake
1 6-oz. package peach gelatin

4 large peaches, sliced
1 carton of whipped topping

Break angel food cake into small pieces; put into 9 x 13-inch pan. Dissolve gelatin in 2 cups boiling water; add 2 cups of cold water. Stir peaches into gelatin; pour over angel food cake. Chill for at least 4 hours. Top with whipped topping.

Barbara Sisk, Hempstead, Texas

PEACH ROSETTES

Vegetable oil
1 egg
1 tablespoon sugar
½ teaspoon salt
½ cup all-purpose flour*
½ cup water or milk

1 tablespoon vegetable oil
⅓ cup sugar
½ teaspoon ground cinnamon
9 peaches, sliced
¼ cup sugar
Coffee Whipped Cream (recipe follows)

Heat oil (2 to 3 inches) to 400 degrees in small deep saucepan. Beat egg, 1 tablespoon sugar and the salt in small deep bowl. Beat in flour, water and 1 tablespoon oil until smooth. Heat rosette iron by placing in hot oil 1 minute. Tap excess oil from iron; dip hot iron in batter just to top edge, being careful not to go over top. Fry until golden brown, about 30 seconds. Immediately remove rosette, using fork if necessary; invert on paper towel to cool. (If rosette is not crisp, batter is too thick. Stir in small amount of water or milk.) Heat iron in hot oil before making each rosette. (If iron is not heated, batter will not stick to iron.) Mix ⅓ cup sugar and the cinnamon. Dip rosettes in sugar mixture. Mix peaches and ¼ cup sugar. Serve rosettes with sweetened peaches and Coffee Whipped Cream. Makes 18 rosettes.

*If using self-rising flour, omit salt.

Coffee Whipped Cream
Beat 1 cup chilled whipping cream, ¼ cup powdered sugar, 1 teaspoon instant coffee, ½ teaspoon vanilla and ⅛ teaspoon ground cardamom or ground cinnamon in chilled small mixer bowl.

Reprinted from Betty Crocker's Recipe Card Library, by permission of General Mills

PEACH WHIP

2 8-oz. cans unsweetened peach slices
1 envelope D-Zerta orange gelatin

1 cup boiling water
1 tablespoon lemon juice (optional)

Drain peaches, measuring juice; add enough water to juice to measure 1 cup liquid. Finely chop or crush peaches; set aside. Dissolve gelatin in boiling water; add peach liquid and lemon juice. Place bowl of gelatin in a larger bowl of ice and water; stir until thickened. Whip with rotary beater or electric mixer until fluffy and thick and about doubled in bulk. Fold in peaches. Pour into dessert dishes or individual molds. Chill for at least 2 hours or until firm. Garnish with mint sprigs, if desired. Yields 8 ½-cup servings / 25 calories per serving / ½ fruit exchange.

Reprinted by permission of Favorite Recipes Press, Nashville, Tennessee

DELICIOUS PEACH TORTE

1 1-lb. 2 ½ oz. package yellow
  cake mix
1 14-oz. package lemon creamy
  frosting mix
1 cup heavy cream
1 cup diced fresh or frozen
  peaches, drained
2 cups Durkee Flaked Coconut

Prepare cake mix according to package directions. Bake in two 9-inch layer pans as directed on package. Cool and split layers. Fold frosting mix into cream. Chill 10 minutes. Beat until thickened. Fold in diced peaches and coconut. Spread filling between layers and on top. Chill until served.

Reprinted by permission of Durkee Famous Foods Kitchens

PEACHES 'N CREAM POUND CAKE

½ cup dairy sour cream
1 tablespoon orange liqueur OR
  orange juice
1 cup sliced sweetened fresh
  peaches, strawberries, OR
  nectarines
½ cup fresh blueberries
6 slices, each ½-inch thick, Sara
  Lee Pound Cake, thawed

Stir together sour cream and liqueur. Fold in fruit. Spoon about ¼ cup fruit mixture over each pound cake slice. Makes 6 servings.

Reprinted by permission of Kitchens of Sara Lee

POUND CAKE TRIFLE

1 10¾-oz. Sara Lee Original All
  Butter Pound Cake, thawed
¼ cup liqueur, orange juice, rum
  OR sherry
½ cup fruit preserves
2 cups custard OR pudding
2 cups sweetened fresh OR
  canned peaches
Whipped cream, optional

Slice pound cake into 10 slices; cut each slice into 6 cubes. Place half of pound cake cubes in 2½-quart glass bowl; sprinkle with half of liqueur. Spoon half of preserves over pound cake cubes, then layer on half of custard and half of fruit. Repeat layers. Refrigerate covered 2 hours before serving to blend flavors. Garnish with whipped cream, if desired. Makes 10–12 servings.

Reprinted by permission of Kitchens of Sara Lee

MAGIC MARSHMALLOW PEACH-EASY PAVLOVA

2 egg whites
Dash of salt
1 7-oz. jar marshmallow creme
Pastry for 1-crust 9-inch pie,
   baked

1 8-oz. container (3 cups) La
   Creme whipped topping with
   real cream, thawed
1 cup peeled peach slices

Beat egg whites and salt until soft peaks form; gradually add marshmallow creme, beating until stiff peaks form. Spread mixture onto bottom and sides of pastry shell. Bake at 325 degrees, 15 to 20 minutes or until lightly browned. Cool. Top with whipped topping and peaches. 6 to 8 servings.

Variation: Substitute strawberries or blueberries for peaches.

PEACH MELBA PARFAIT

2 envelopes unflavored gelatin
½ cup cold milk
½ cup milk, heated to boiling
½ lemon, peeled and seeded
⅔ cup Domino Granulated Sugar
1 cup heavy cream
1 cup cracked ice

1 16-oz. can sliced peaches
   drained and cut-up or 1½
   cups fresh peaches
1 10-oz. package frozen
   raspberries, thawed
½ cup Domino Granulated Sugar

In 5-cup blender container, sprinkle gelatin over cold milk and let stand 3–4 minutes to soften. Add boiling milk and blend at low speed for 2 minutes. Add lemon, sugar and cream. Blend until smooth. Add ice 2 tablespoons at a time and process until mixture is smooth. If necessary, chill until slightly thickened. Fold in peaches.

Meanwhile, combine raspberries and remaining ½ cup sugar in blender container. Blend until smooth. Spoon alternate layers of peach mixture and raspberry puree into dessert glasses. Chill until firm. Makes 6 servings.

Reprinted by permission of Amstar

CHEESY FRUIT PIZZA

1 cup 3 Minute Brand Oats
¾ cup all-purpose flour
½ cup shredded cheddar cheese
6 tablespoons butter or
    margarine, melted
1 3-oz. pkg. cream cheese,
    softened
1 cup whipping cream
⅓ cup powdered sugar

1 teaspoon vanilla
Assorted fresh fruits such as:
    peach slices, pineapple
    tidbits, seedless grapes,
    strawberries, kiwi fruit,
    sliced. (All fruit should be
    drained very well.)
Additional shredded cheddar
    cheese optional

Stir together oats, flour, ½ cup cheese, and butter. Press onto greased pizza pan. Bake in 400-degree oven for 8 to 10 minutes. Cool. Beat cream cheese until smooth; blend in whipping cream, powdered sugar, and vanilla. Beat until thickened. Spread cream cheese mixture on crust. Arrange fruit pieces in attractive pattern on pizza. Sprinkle with additional cheddar cheese, if desired. Refrigerate until serving time.

Reprinted by permission of The National Oats Company, Cedar Rapids, Iowa

PEACHES 'N CREAM DESSERT PIZZA

½ cup butter or margarine,
    softened
½ cup firmly packed brown
    sugar
1 cup flour
½ cup quick oats
½ cup finely chopped walnuts

1 14-oz. can sweetened
    condensed milk
½ cup sour cream
¼ cup lemon juice
1 teaspoon vanilla
1 21-oz. can Thank You Peach
    Pie Filling

Cream butter and sugar, mix in flour, oats and nuts; blend thoroughly. Press mixture onto bottom and rim of oiled pizza pan. Bake at 350 degrees for 10 minutes or until golden brown. Cool. Combine milk, sour cream, lemon juice and vanilla, mix well. Chill. Spread over baked crust evenly. Spoon pie filling over top leaving rim of cream showing around edge. Chill. Serves 8 – 10.

Reprinted by permission of Michigan Fruit Canners

FRUIT FLAMBÉ

1 can peach halves
1 can pear halves
1 can sliced pineapple
1 can apricot halves

1 can pitted black cherries
1 cup Jacquin's Triple Sec
½ cup Jacquin's Vodka

Drain fruit and arrange in a shallow baking dish suitable for serving. Make a design of the fruit, arranging it artistically in orderly rings or scallops on a round or oval dish; or in strips on an oblong dish. Spoon Triple Sec over fruit and bake in a 325-degree oven for 30 minutes. Baste often. Remove from oven and pour on Jacquin's Vodka; ignite and serve immediately. Serves 6 to 8.

Reprinted by permission of Charles Jacquin's ET CIE., Inc.

BRANDIED PEACHES FLAMBÉ

½ cup sugar
1 cup water, divided
½ cup brandy, divided

4 large fresh peaches, peeled, pitted, sliced
2 teaspoons cornstarch

In medium saucepan or chafing dish combine sugar, ¾ cup water and ¼ cup brandy. Bring to a boil, stirring constantly, until sugar is dissolved. Add peaches. Simmer 10 minutes until tender. Combine cornstarch with remaining ¼ cup water. Stir into peaches. Cook until mixture boils and thickens. Warm remaining ¼ cup brandy; ignite. Pour over peaches. Serve in dessert dishes or spooned over ice cream. Makes 4 servings.

Variation: ¼ cup apricot jam may be added to sugar, water and brandy.

Reprinted by permission of United Fresh Fruit and Vegetable Association

COUPE MELBA

Place 3 peach slices in large wine glass or demi-snifter. Add 3 small scoops Haagen-Dazs vanilla ice cream and 1 tablespoon fresh or frozen raspberries. Drizzle with Hiram Walker Peach Flavored Brandy or Hiram Walker Amaretto or Hiram Walker Amaretto & Cognac. Repeat layers. Top with whipped cream. Serves one.

Reprinted by permission of Hiram Walker Inc.

MOLDED PEACHES MELBA

1 30-oz. can sliced peaches, drained
1½ cups drained juice

2 3-ounce packages orange-flavored gelatin
1 12-oz. can Milnot*
1 teaspoon almond flavor

Heat 1 cup peach juice to boiling; dissolve 1 package of gelatin in juice, add remaining cup juice, cool, pour into prepared mold (9–10 cup). Chill until syrupy. Arrange peach slices—about 15 —to make a design in gelatin; chill until firm. In the meantime, puree remainder of peaches (about 1 cup); heat with remaining gelatin until gelatin dissolves; chill until slightly thickened. Whip Milnot until it will hold stiff peaks, gradually whip in the gelatin and flavoring. Spoon over first layer in mold. Chill until firm (3 to 4 hours). Unmold and serve each slice with raspberry sauce:

164

Raspberry Sauce

1 package frozen raspberries, defrosted	¼ cup sugar 1 teaspoon cornstarch

Puree raspberries, discard seeds. Stir ingredients together in saucepan over low heat until mixture boils gently. Chill. 10 – 12 servings.

*Milnot Brand Dairy Vegetable Blend (no butterfat, virtually no cholesterol)

QUICK 'N EASY PEACH MELBA

1 16-oz. can sliced peaches in heavy syrup, drained (reserve syrup) 1 envelope Knox Unflavored Gelatin	½ cup milk 1 cup (8 oz.) lowfat plain or peach yogurt 6 teaspoons raspberry preserves

Reserve 6 peach slices for garnish.

Mix reserved syrup with enough water to equal ⅔ cup; bring to a boil. Meanwhile, in 5-cup blender, sprinkle unflavored gelatin over milk; let stand 3 to 4 minutes. Add boiling liquid and process at low speed until gelatin is completely dissolved, about 2 minutes. Add yogurt and peaches; process at high speed until blended. Pour into dessert dishes; chill until set. Top each dish with reserved peach slice and 1 teaspoon preserves. Makes 6 servings.

Tested recipe from The Lipton Kitchens. Reprinted by permission of Thomas J. Lipton, Inc.

PEACH RUM-BA

1 1 lb.-13 oz. can peach halves ⅔ cup peach syrup 3 tablespoons sugar 2 teaspoons cornstarch Pinch of salt	2 teaspoons margarine or butter 1 teaspoon Durkee Orange Extract 2 teaspoons Durkee Rum Flavor 1 pint vanilla ice cream Toasted Durkee Coconut

Drain peaches well and save ⅔ cup of the syrup for the sauce. Chill peaches. In a small saucepan, combine sugar, cornstarch and salt. Stir in peach syrup and cook until mixture has thickened and boiled for 1 minute. Remove from heat and stir in margarine and extracts. Cool. Place peach half in the bottom of a sherbet dish, top with ice cream and then rum sauce. Garnish with toasted coconut. Makes 8 servings.

Reprinted by permission of Durkee Famous Foods Kitchens

BRANDIED PEACHES

½ cup sugar
¼ cup (½ stick) butter
¼ cup water

8 fresh peach halves
3 tablespoons brandy

Heat sugar and butter until well blended; stir in water and add peeled peach halves. Cook over low heat 20 to 30 minutes. Add brandy (Grand Marnier is nice) and serve or store in refrigerator. Serves 4.

Reprinted by permission of June Towers, Imperial Sugar Company

BRANDIED PEACHES

1 1-lb. can peach halves
1 tablespoon cornstarch
¼ teaspoon French's Cinnamon
¼ teaspoon French's Nutmeg

¼ cup brandy
1 tablespoon honey
Maraschino cherries, if desired

Drain peaches, saving syrup; add water to syrup to make 1 cup. In a small saucepan, combine cornstarch, cinnamon, and nutmeg. Gradually stir in syrup, brandy, and honey. Cook over medium heat, stirring constantly, until mixture boils for one minute. Cool; pour over peach halves. Garnish with maraschino cherries. 6 servings.

Recipe reprinted by permission of FRENCH'S / The R. T. French Company

BRANDIED PEACH BLITZ TORTE

½ cup shortening
¾ cup sifted confectioners' sugar
4 eggs, separated
1 cup all-purpose flour
1 teaspoon baking powder

¼ teaspoon salt
3 tablespoons milk
1¼ cups granulated sugar
4 Raffetto Grand Marnier
   Brandied Peaches
½ cup heavy cream

Preheat oven at 325 degrees F. Grease and lightly flour two 9-inch cake pans. Cream together shortening and sugar until fluffy. Beat in egg yolks, one at a time. Sift together flour, baking powder and salt. Add to creamed mixture alternately with milk. Spread batter in prepared cake pans. Beat egg whites until foamy. Add granulated sugar, a little at a time, beating until stiff and glossy. Spread carefully over top of cake batter. Bake 30 minutes or until lightly browned. Let cake cool in pan about 5 minutes. Remove to cake racks and cool thoroughly. Dice 3 peaches. Place 1 layer on serving plate, meringue side down. Top with cut-up peaches. Place second layer on top of peaches, meringue side up. Whip cream with remaining sugar. Spoon over meringue. Slice remaining peach and arrange on top of cream. Chill before serving. Serves 8.

Reprinted by permission of Iroquois Grocery Products, Inc.

DRAMBUIE FRUIT COCKTAIL

2 tablespoons sugar
1 teaspoon grated lime zest
2 bananas, ripe but firm, peeled
    and sliced
2 peaches, peeled and sliced

3 navel oranges, peeled and
    sectioned
⅓ cup orange juice
⅓ cup Drambuie
¼ cup seedless raisins

Simmer sugar and juice in a small saucepan for 4 minutes. Remove from heat, add Drambuie and lime zest; let cool. Pour the syrup over the slices of fruit; mix gently with raisins and chill. Makes 4 servings.

Recipe reprinted by permission of W. A. Taylor and Company

DRAMBUIE OVER PEARS OR PEACHES

Warmed, spicy pears or peaches laced with Drambuie make a dessert sensation guests cannot resist.

4 large pears or peaches
1 cup sugar
2 ounces sweet butter

2 cups heavy cream, at room
    temperature
1 cup Drambuie

Peel fruit and slice in half lengthwise. Remove the core or pits and slice each half into four wedges. Set aside. In a large deep skillet or saucepan, heat the sugar over medium high heat until sugar dissolves and turns golden. Add the butter and stir until melted. Add the heavy cream and stir. Cook for 2 minutes over high heat to reduce mixture. Add the pear or peach slices and cook for 2 to 3 minutes more. Pour Drambuie over fruit, but do not stir. Working carefully, take a long-stemmed match and ignite mixture. Serves 4.

Recipe reprinted by permission of W. A. Taylor and Company

BAKED PEACH PECAN ALASKA

SHORTCAKE:

1½ cups flour
1 tablespoon baking powder
¼ cup sugar
¼ teaspoon salt

4 ounces cold, unsalted butter,
    cut in ½-inch squares
½ cup finely chopped pecans
1 cup whipping cream

Sift together dry ingredients. Cut in butter, add pecans, then add cream, blending lightly, producing soft dough.

CLING PEACH FILLING:

¼ cup sugar
½ teaspoon cinnamon
Dash of nutmeg
1 cup whipping cream

2 tablespoons powdered sugar
½ teaspoon vanilla
16 ounces frozen California cling
    peach slices, defrosted

Toss peaches with sugar, cinnamon and nutmeg. Whip cream stiffly with powdered sugar and vanilla. Cut shortcakes in half and cover bottom with peaches and cream; replace top, and cover with whipped cream. Refrigerate while making meringue.

MERINGUE:

6 large egg whites   ¾ cup powdered sugar

Whip whites to soft peaks, then add sugar. Encase each short-cake with meringue. Place under broiler until golden and serve immediately.

Variation: Substitute liqueur-flavored cream or ice cream for the whipped cream.

Reprinted by permission of Chef Steve Froman, Campton Place Hotel
California Canning Peach Association/California Cling Peach Advisory Board

POACHED SUMMER FRUIT

1 cup Del Monte Orange Juice
1 cup sugar
Julienne peel of one lemon
Juice of one lemon
1 lb. small plums, pitted and
    quartered

1 16-oz. can Del Monte Yellow
    Cling Peach Halves, drained
1 17-oz. can Del Monte Unpeeled
    Apricot Halves, drained
¼ cup cognac or brandy
Sprigs of mint

In saucepan, combine orange juice, sugar, lemon peel and juice. Boil until thick syrup forms (drops heavily from a spoon). Reduce heat. Add plums; simmer 5 minutes. Add peaches and apricots; simmer 2 minutes more. With slotted spoon, place fruit in serving bowl. Bring syrup to boil. Remove from heat. Add cognac and mint; pour over fruit; chill. 8 servings.

Helpful Hint: When reducing syrup, cook at full rolling boil. Can be made a day ahead.

Recipe reprinted by permission of Del Monte Kitchens, Del Monte Corporation

SHERRIED PEACHES

2 17-oz. cans S&W Halves Yellow
  Cling Peaches
1 teaspoon lemon juice
¼ cup sherry
Nutmeg

¼ cup margarine or butter
¾ cup firmly packed brown
  sugar
Whipping cream, whipped

Drain peaches and reserve ⅓ cup syrup. In a large saucepan, melt margarine or butter, then stir in peach syrup, lemon juice and sugar. Bring to boil. Add peaches and simmer for 10 minutes; basting frequently. Add sherry and simmer for 5 more minutes. Serve peaches warm with whipping cream and a dash of nutmeg. Serves 6.

Reprinted by permission of S&W Fine Foods, Inc.

SPICED PEACH BLEND 'N GEL

1 16-oz. can sliced peaches in
  heavy syrup, drained
  (reserve syrup)
½ teaspoon whole cloves
1 cinnamon stick, broken

1 envelope Knox Unflavored
  Gelatin
½ cup cold peach nectar
¼ cup sherry
1½ cups ice cubes

In small saucepan, combine reserved peach syrup with enough water to equal 1¼ cups, cloves, and cinnamon. Simmer 5 minutes, then bring quickly to a boil.

In 5-cup blender, sprinkle Knox Unflavored Gelatin over peach nectar; let stand until moistened. Strain boiling syrup over gelatin and process at low speed 2 minutes. Add peaches, sherry, and ice cubes one at a time and process at high speed until ice is melted. Pour into 8 dessert dishes and chill until set, about 40 minutes. Makes 8 servings, 60 calories each.

Variation: Substitute 1 16-oz. can water-pack sliced peaches. Add artificial sweetener to equal 2 tablespoons sugar. 35 calories per serving.

Tested recipe from The Lipton Kitchens. Reprinted by permission of Thomas J. Lipton, Inc.

GINGER PEACHES WITH RUM

1 16-oz. can peach halves,
  drained
1 tablespoon butter or margarine

2½ tablespoons brown sugar
½ teaspoon ground ginger
2 tablespoons light rum

Place peaches in a 1-quart casserole; set aside. Place butter in a 2-cup glass measure. Microwave at HIGH 35 seconds or until melted. Add remaining ingredients to butter, stirring well; pour over peaches. Cover with heavy-duty plastic wrap, and microwave at HIGH 3 to 5 minutes or until peaches are hot. Let stand 2 minutes, basting peaches occasionally with juice mixture. Serve hot. Yield: about 6 servings.

This recipe is from *Southern Living Annual Recipes*, 1984.

KAHLUA SPICED PEACHES

2 29-oz. cans cling peach halves	¼ cup tarragon white wine
½ cup Kahlua	vinegar
½ cup brown sugar (packed)	2 sticks cinnamon
	3 thin 4-inch strips each orange and lemon peel

Drain 1½ cups syrup from peaches into saucepan. Add Kahlua, sugar, vinegar, cinnamon and peels. Simmer 5 minutes. Pour over drained peaches. Cool. Refrigerate. Will keep up to several weeks. Makes 12 to 14 spiced peaches.

Reprinted by permission of Maidstone Wine and Spirits, Inc.

PEACHES IN SPICED WINE

¼ cup dry Sauterne	Dash of cinnamon
2 tablespoons sugar	Dash of cloves
1 tablespoon lemon juice	2 cups peeled and sliced peaches

Combine Sauterne, sugar and lemon juice in small saucepan; cook, stirring until sugar is dissolved. Do not boil. Stir in cinnamon and cloves. Pour hot wine mixture over peaches in deep bowl. Chill thoroughly. Yield: 4 servings; 62 calories per serving.

Reprinted by permission of Favorite Recipes Press, Nashville, Tennessee

SPICED PEACHES

2 29-oz. cans yellow cling peach halves	½ teaspoon ground cloves
	¼ teaspoon ground ginger
1½ cups brown sugar	Dash salt
Juice of 2 Sunkist lemons	Whole cloves
2 sticks cinnamon	

Drain peaches, reserving syrup from one can (about 1¼ cups syrup). In large saucepan, combine reserved syrup, brown sugar, lemon juice, cinnamon, ground cloves, ginger and salt; heat to boiling. Reduce heat; simmer 10 minutes. Meanwhile, stud each peach half with 1 or 2 whole cloves. Add peaches to syrup; heat. Refrigerate peaches in syrup in covered container 1 to 2 days before serving. Makes 6 servings, about 6 cups.

Reprinted by permission of Sunkist Growers, Inc.

SPICED PEACHES

1½ cups Sun-Maid or Sunsweet
    dried peaches
1½ cups water
½ teaspoon cinnamon

¼ teaspoon allspice
⅛ teaspoon cloves
½ cup brown sugar, packed
2 tablespoons lemon juice

In a saucepan, combine all ingredients. Heat to boiling, simmer uncovered 20 minutes. Remove from heat. Cool thoroughly. Makes about 2½ cups. Flavor improves when refrigerated at least 24 hours.

Recipe reprinted by permission of Sun-Diamond Growers of California

JIFFY SPICED FRUIT

1 1 lb.-13 oz. can peach or pear
    halves*
¼ cup Heinz Apple Cider
    Vinegar

½ teaspoon whole cloves
1 3-inch cinnamon stick

Drain fruit, reserving syrup. Add vinegar, cloves and cinnamon stick to fruit syrup; simmer 10 minutes. Add fruit; simmer an additional 5 minutes. Cover; refrigerate overnight to blend flavors. Serve chilled as a meat accompaniment or on the relish tray. Makes 8 servings.

*1 1 lb.-14 oz. can apricots may be substituted.
NOTE: Fruit will keep up to one month in refrigerator. Remove spices at the end of the second week.

Reprinted by permission of Heinz U.S.A.

ORANGE AND SPICE PEACHES

1 16-oz. can peach slices
1 10-oz. jar orange marmalade

1 cinnamon stick
¼ teaspoon whole cloves

Drain peaches, reserving liquid. Combine marmalade, reserved liquid and enough water to measure 1 cup and spices. Bring to boil; reduce heat. Simmer, uncovered, 10 minutes. Add peaches; simmer 5 minutes. Remove spices; serve warm. 4 to 6 servings.

NOTE: May be served with ice cream or topped with whipped cream cheese.

PEACHES IN SPICED CREAM

1 29-oz. can peach halves, well
   drained
2 tablespoons packed brown
   sugar
½ teaspoon cardamom or ginger
½ cup sour cream
1 cup softened vanilla ice cream
½ cup toasted slivered almonds

Place peaches, rounded side up, in single layer in shallow glass dish. In small bowl mix brown sugar, cardamom and sour cream until sugar dissolves. Fold in ice cream; spoon sauce over peaches. Sprinkle with almonds; serve immediately. Makes 5 servings.

Tina Montalvo, Hempstead, Texas

SUNRISE PEACH PUFFS

ALMOND PASTRY CREAM:

26-oz. pastry cream
18 oz. commercial almond paste
18 oz. sugar
6 eggs
2 oz. cornstarch
2 oz. dark rum
18 oz. butter or margarine

Mix the almond paste and sugar. Blend in butter until creamy. Add pastry cream, eggs, rum and cornstarch.

48 drained California cling peach
   halves
48 each 4 – 5″ puff dough discs,
   depending on peach size
48 oz. Almond Pastry Cream
Apricot or peach glaze or
   thinned jam

For each puff pastry disc place approximately 1 oz. of cream in center. Place cling peach half over the cream, cut side down. Fold the puff dough over and around the peach. Allow to rest for 30 minutes. Bake at 375 to 385 degrees until the puff dough is golden. Cool and glaze, or dust with powdered sugar. Yield: 48 servings.

Reprinted by permission of California Canning Peach Association,
California Cling Peach Advisory Board

172

Beverages, Sauces And Miscellaneous

LIFE

Life is something we take for granted,
Which started from the seed God planted.
Losing life is something we can't afford,
For this reason we should praise the Lord.
Even bad times always seem to change,
When asked, help is what God can arrange.
With Jesus as your Savior, a new life you can lead,
He can help you as a friend in need.
So you should live your life as much as you can,
Through the years whether you're a woman or a man.
Animals have these same feelings too,
So treat them as though they were like you.
There are only two reasons to make a kill,
You wouldn't want to die without a will.
When they are harmful you have the right,
To end their life without a fight.
The other reason is for food,
Any other explanation would be crude.
So the next time you wish a life to end,
If you have no reason, your guilt won't mend.

By Michael Ray Freeman, Ennis, Texas, August 18, 1985

FRESH PEACH COOLER

4 medium-size fresh peaches
  (about 1 pound)
1 tablespoon fresh lemon or lime
  juice

Sugar
1 quart lemon-lime carbonated
  beverage, well chilled
1 pint orange sherbet

Peel and pit peaches. Puree in food processor or blender. Stir in lemon or lime juice. (There should be about 1½ cups.) Sweeten to taste with sugar. Chill until serving time. Gradually stir in lemon-lime beverage. Place a scoop of sherbet in each of eight 8-ounce glasses. Add peach mixture. Makes 8 servings.

TEXAS PEACH COOLER
(Low Calorie)

1 cup cold skimmed milk
1 medium Texas peach, sliced
  with skin on

⅛ teaspoon vanilla
Dash cinnamon

Combine in electric blender and blend until smooth. Serves 1.

Reprinted by permission of Texas Department of Agriculture

PEACH FROST

1 medium peach, peeled and
  chunked
1 egg

½ cup lemon-flavored yogurt
3 ice cubes
¼ teaspoon cinnamon

Combine all ingredients in blender container and blend about 45 seconds or until smooth. Pour into tall glass and serve immediately. 1 serving or 1⅓ cups.

Reprinted by permission of American Egg Board

FRESH PEACH MALTED

1 fresh California peach, sliced
1 egg

1 scoop vanilla ice cream
½ tablespoon instant malted
  milk

In blender jar, blend all ingredients. Pour into tall glass. Serve with spoon and straw. For shake, leave out the malt and add ¼ teaspoon almond or vanilla extract. Makes one 8-ounce serving.

Reprinted by permission of California Tree Fruit Agreement

A PEACH OF A SHAKE

1 8-oz. container vanilla low-fat
  yogurt
1 16-oz. can peach halves or
  slices in extra light syrup,
  drained

1 cup skim or whole milk
⅓ cup crushed ice

Place all ingredients in blender or food processor and process until smooth. Serve immediately in chilled glasses. Makes 3 servings. Per 8-ounce serving: 79 calories with skim milk; 136 calories with whole milk.

Reprinted by permission of National Food Processors Association

HONEYED PEACH MILK SHAKES

1 cup diced fresh peaches
¼ cup honey
½ teaspoon vanilla

1½ cups milk
1 pint vanilla ice cream

Mix peaches and honey. (Honey keeps peaches from darkening as well as sweetening them.) Add remaining ingredients and mix in blender to a smooth cream. Serve in tall glasses. Makes 4 servings.

Beverly Levandowski, Hempstead, Texas

PEACHY-NANA SHAKE

1 cup fresh peaches
1 medium banana
1 egg

1 cup buttermilk
1 to 2 teaspoons sugar (to taste)

Process all ingredients in blender until smooth. 2 servings.

PEACH-STRAWBERRY MILK SHAKE

¼ cup sliced fresh peaches
¼ cup strawberries
3 tablespoons sugar
1 tablespoon Grand Marnier, if
  desired

¼ cup light cream
½ cup milk
½ cup chipped ice

Combine all ingredients in blender; cover and buzz until thoroughly blended. Pour into tall glass. Makes 1 generous serving or 2 smaller ones.

Reprinted by permission of June Towers, Imperial Sugar Company

COOL PEACH SHAKE

1 cup cold milk
1 cup (½ pint) vanilla ice cream
1 10-oz. package frozen peaches,
    thawed
1 egg

3 tablespoons Kretschmer Wheat
    Germ, Regular or Brown
    Sugar and Honey
Nutmeg

Put all ingredients in blender container. Cover and blend at high speed about 1 minute. Refrigerate before serving if desired. Sprinkle with nutmeg if desired. Makes 3½ cups.

Reprinted by permission of International Multifoods/Kretschmer Wheat Germ

ZIPPY PEACH SHAKE

2 cups (16-ounce can) peach
    halves and syrup
1 cup chilled lemon-lime soda or
    club soda

½ cup dry Carnation Nonfat Dry
    Milk
½ teaspoon vanilla

Puree peaches and syrup in blender container. Pour peach puree into ice cube tray or 8-inch metal pan. Freeze until firm. Remove from freezer; allow to stand at room temperature 10 minutes. Cut frozen puree into cubes. Place cubes, lemon-lime soda, dry nonfat milk, and vanilla in blender container. Blend on high speed, stirring as necessary, until mixture is smooth. Makes 3 cups.

Reprinted by permission of Carnation

FRUITY EGGNOG

1 quart pasteurized eggnog

2 7½-oz. jars Gerber Junior
    Peaches

Pour eggnog into 2-quart pitcher. Add peaches and blend thoroughly. Chill before serving. Yield: 6 cups.

Recipe reprinted by permission of Gerber Products Company

PEACH BLEND
A creamy peach drink made in the blender!

1 cup (1 large) sliced fresh or
    thawed frozen peaches
1 cup plain yogurt

1 small can (5 fluid ounces) Pet
    Evaporated Milk
1 tablespoon sugar or honey

Combine all ingredients in blender container. Whirl until thick and smooth. Serve immediately over ice. Makes 2 servings.

Recipe reprinted by permission of Pet / An IC Industries Company

PEACH YOGURT FRAPPE

1 16-oz. package frozen sliced
  peaches, partially thawed (2½
  cups)
2 teaspoons French's Vanilla
½ teaspoon French's Almond
  Extract

3 to 4 tablespoons sugar
1 8-oz. carton plain or peach low-
  fat yogurt
1 cup skim milk

Using blender or mixer, puree 1 cup of the peaches along with vanilla and almond extracts and sugar. Add yogurt and milk; blend a few seconds on high. Add remaining peaches and blend so that small pieces of peach remain. Makes about four 1-cup servings. 135 calories in each serving.

Reprinted by permission of The R. T. French Company

PEACH REFRESHER

2 cups sliced peeled peaches
  (about 5)
2 cups water

3 scoops Country Time lemonade-
  flavor drink mix
1 28 fl. oz. bottle ginger ale,
  chilled

Place peaches, water and drink mix in blender. Blend on high speed until smooth, about 1 minute. Pour into nonmetal pitcher and chill. Just before serving, stir in ginger ale. Serve over ice; garnish with mint sprigs and additional peach slices, if desired. Makes about 9 cups or 9 servings.

Reprinted by permission of General Foods

7-UP CANDLELIGHT PUNCH

1 46-oz. can apricot nectar
12 7-oz. bottles 7-Up
2 6-oz. cans frozen, concentrated
  orange juice, thawed

2 12-oz. packages frozen peaches,
  slightly thawed
1 pint vanilla ice cream

Chill the apricot nectar and 7-Up. Just before serving time, combine the apricot nectar and the concentrated orange juice in punch bowl. Slowly pour in chilled 7-Up. Add the peaches and float generous spoonfuls of ice cream on top of the punch. Makes about 35 servings.

Reprinted by permission of The Seven-Up Company

ALMOND PEACH LIQUEUR
Almond tastefully highlights the subtle fresh peach flavor.

1½ pounds peaches, unpeeled, pitted and sliced

2 cups vodka

1 cup sugar

4 teaspoons Durkee Almond Extract

In a glass jar with tight-fitting lid, thoroughly combine all ingredients. Let stand 1 week; shake occasionally. (For a richer flavor blend, let stand 3 to 4 weeks.) Pour through a coffee filter to strain. Store liqueur in jar covered with tight-fitting lid. Strained peaches may be used for compote or as an ice cream topping. Makes about 2½ cups.

Reprinted by permission of Durkee Famous Foods Kitchens

FRESH PEACH MARGARITAS

9 frozen peach cubes

3 ounces tequila

3 ounces orange-flavored liqueur

1 ounce (2 tablespoons) lime juice

2 tablespoons sugar

10 ice cubes

Granulated sugar

Peach slices

Lime slices

Put peach cubes in blender container. Add tequila, liqueur, lime juice and sugar. Blend smooth. Add ice cubes, one at a time, blending until smooth. Pour into stemmed glasses with rims first dipped in granulated sugar. Garnish with peach and lime slices. Makes 4 (5-ounce) drinks.

Frozen Peach Cubes:
Halve and pit 1 pound fresh unpeeled peaches (there should be about 3 cups). Slice into blender container. Add 1 tablespoon lemon juice; puree. Pour into ice cube tray; freeze. When solid, store in freezer container until used. Makes 18.

For a nonalcoholic version, substitute 4 ounces lemon and lime flavored cocktail mix for tequila and liqueur. Pour into glasses. Add a splash of ginger ale.

Reprinted by permission of Jean Pryor, Houston, Texas

FROZEN GEORGIA PEACH

2 eggs

2 tablespoons honey

2 tablespoons lemon juice

½ cup Haagen-Dazs vanilla ice cream

1½ cups sliced peaches

½ cup cracked ice

2 oz. Hiram Walker Peach Flavored Brandy

Combine in blender until smooth. Pour into parfait glasses. Set in freezer until firm. Garnish with shaved chocolate.

Reprinted by permission of Hiram Walker Inc.

FROZEN PEACH DAIQUIRI

1 oz. Hiram Walker Peach
   Flavored Brandy
½ oz. Hiram Walker Triple Sec

1 oz. light rum
2 oz. Sweet & Sour Mix
½ fresh or canned peach

Blend with cracked ice until smooth. Serve in on-the-rocks glass. Variation: Add a scoop of Haagen-Dazs vanilla ice cream and blend.

Reprinted by permission of Hiram Walker, Inc.

PEACH FROSTY

1 cup peach ice cream
½ cup light rum
3 tablespoons powdered sugar

3 fresh peeled peaches, sliced
Cracked ice

Combine ice cream, rum, sugar and peaches in container of electric blender. Process until smooth. Add ice to within 1 inch of container top; blend well. Yield: 5 cups.

Jean Pryor, Houston, Texas

PEACHY PUNCH

2 10-oz. packages frozen sliced
   peaches
2 cups dry white wine, chilled
   (optional)
1 cup lemon juice, chilled

1 6-oz. can frozen red fruit punch
   concentrate, thawed
2 quarts ginger ale, chilled
Mint sprigs

Thaw 1 package frozen peaches. Mix thawed peaches, wine, lemon juice and fruit punch concentrate; pour on frozen peaches in chilled punch bowl. Just before serving, stir in ginger ale; garnish with mint sprigs. (To keep punch cold, another package of frozen peaches can be added.) About 24 servings (½ cup each).

Reprinted from Betty Crocker's Recipe Card Library, by permission of General Mills

PLANTERS PUNCH

2 large, fresh California peaches
2 cups apricot nectar
¼ cup lime juice
¼ cup grenadine syrup

2 oz. dark rum (optional)
Crushed ice
Extra peach slices

Wash peaches and remove pits. Quarter and puree in blender to measure 2 cups. Combine puree, apricot nectar, lime juice, grenadine and rum in large pitcher. Add plenty of crushed ice and float peach slices in bowl, if desired. Makes 1 quart.

Recipe reprinted by permission of California Tree Fruit Agreement

LAHAINA SUNSET

2 fresh California peaches,
  washed
1 cup coconut milk*

¼ cup pineapple juice
3 ice cubes, cracked
¼ cup dark rum, optional

Halve and pit peaches. Combine peaches, coconut milk and pineapple juice in blender. Whirl until smooth. Add ice and rum and whirl until smooth and fluffy. Serve immediately. Makes 3½ cups.

*If coconut milk is not available, combine 1 cup half-and-half and ⅔ cup flaked coconut in saucepan. Heat to simmering. Remove from heat and cool to room temperature. Strain through wire sieve, pressing with spoon to extract all of milk from coconut. Discard coconut.

Recipe reprinted by permission of California Tree Fruit Agreement

SPICED PEACH LIQUEUR

3 pounds peaches, unpeeled,
  pitted and sliced
2 cups sugar
4 strips of lemon peel, 2 inches
  long

2 Durkee Stick Cinnamon,
  broken in half
6 Durkee Whole Cloves
1 quart bourbon

In a gallon container, combine peaches, sugar, lemon peel, stick cinnamon, and cloves. Pour in bourbon. Adjust cap. Invert container daily for about 4 days or until sugar is dissolved. Store in cool, dark place for 2 months. Strain through cheesecloth or coffee filter paper and rebottle. Makes 1½ quarts.

Recipe reprinted by permission of Durkee Foods

BEST BBQ SAUCE

1 cup chopped onion
2 tablespoons vegetable oil
1 12-oz. jar chili sauce
1 12-oz. jar peach or apricot
  preserves
1 cup catsup
1 cup chopped fresh parsley
2 tablespoons Worcestershire
  sauce
½ teaspoon celery seed
¾ teaspoon cinnamon
¼ teaspoon pepper

Sauté onion in oil in 3-qt. saucepan until tender. Add remaining ingredients; mix well. Bring mixture to a boil. Reduce heat; simmer until thickened, about 20 minutes, stirring occasionally. Makes about 1 quart sauce. (Recipe may be doubled.)

Reprinted by permission of M&M/Mars / A Division of Mars, Inc.

INDIAN COCONUT CURRY WITH BEEF AND PEACHES

2 cups half-and-half
1½ cups (4 ounces) flaked
  coconut
2 cloves garlic, finely chopped
½ teaspoon ground ginger
2 teaspoons freshly squeezed
  lemon juice
2 teaspoons curry powder
¼ teaspoon salt
⅓ cup golden seedless raisins
2 large fresh peaches, pitted and
  cut into wedges (2 cups)
1 tablespoon cornstarch
2 tablespoons cold water

Combine half-and-half in saucepan with coconut; heat just to boiling point. Remove from heat and cool to room temperature. Strain through a sieve, pressing with spoon to extract all the milk from coconut. Discard coconut. Return coconut milk to saucepan. Add garlic, ginger, lemon juice, curry powder, salt, raisins and peaches; heat to simmering. Blend cornstarch with cold water and stir into curry sauce. Cook, stirring constantly, until thickened. Serve with barbecued steak (strip or flank steak.) Makes 4 servings.

FRUIT FONDUE

1 17-oz. can Larsen Peach Puree
1½ teaspoons cornstarch
¼ teaspoon ground cinnamon
⅛ teaspoon ground allspice
½ teaspoon vanilla

Mix ingredients until well blended; pour into saucepan. Cook and stir until thickened. Transfer to fondue pot and use with fresh fruit as dippers.

Recipe reprinted by permission of The Larsen Company

HOT PEACH SAUCE

2 tablespoons butter or
  margarine
3 tablespoons packed brown
  sugar

1 tablespoon lemon juice
3 medium-firm ripe peaches,
  sliced
1 teaspoon vanilla

In small heavy skillet over medium heat, stir butter, sugar and juice until hot and bubbly. Add peaches and cook about 4 minutes or until peaches are heated through but still keep their shape. Remove from heat; stir in vanilla. Serve warm over ice cream, plain cake or pancakes, or serve in small bowls and top with heavy cream or milk. Makes 4 servings.

Nutritional information per sauce serving:
calories — 118; protein — 1 gram; fat — 6 grams; cholesterol — 18 mg with butter, 0 with margarine; carbohydrates — 17 grams.

For microwave oven combine butter, sugar and lemon juice in 1½-quart casserole. Cover and cook on high, stirring once, 2 minutes. Add peaches; cover and, stirring once, cook 3 minutes.

Jean Pryor, Houston, Texas

PEACH SAUCE

1 cup chopped, dried peaches
3 cups water or white wine

⅓ cup sugar

Mix peaches and water in a saucepan. Bring to a boil and lower heat. Simmer for 15 minutes, or until peaches are tender. Stir in sugar.

Recipe reprinted by permission of N. Dorman and Company, Inc.

PEACHES AU COURVOISIER OVER CAKE

3 fresh ripe peaches
2 teaspoons Courvoisier
2 cups water

3 teaspoons sugar
1 teaspoon lemon juice
1 cinnamon stick

Peel, halve and core peaches. Heat the water in a 3-quart saucepan over medium heat. Add sugar and stir until dissolved. Add remaining ingredients, including peaches. When mixture boils, lower heat, cover, and poach peaches gently for 5 minutes per side until tender but not soft. Remove from heat, cool in liquid. (Not necessary if using canned peaches.) To serve, place peach half over a piece of pound cake or vanilla ice cream, if desired. Top with Chocolate Sauce Courvoisier:

Chocolate Sauce Courvoisier

10 oz. semi-sweet chocolate
½ cup Courvoisier

1⅓ cups sour cream

Melt chocolate in double boiler. Add Courvoisier and sour cream and blend well. This is wonderful as a topping for crepes.

Recipe reprinted by permission of W. A. Taylor and Company

BLUSHING PEACH ICE CREAM TOPPING

1 29-oz. can Del Monte Yellow Cling Sliced Peaches
2 tablespoons cornstarch
⅔ cup Hawaiian Punch Concentrate

6 tablespoons butter or margarine
½ teaspoon vanilla extract
Vanilla ice cream

Drain peaches reserving syrup in large saucepan. Dissolve cornstarch in reserved syrup. Add punch concentrate and butter. Cook, stirring constantly, until thickened. Stir in peaches and vanilla extract. Serve warm over ice cream or pour into jars and cover tightly. Cool and refrigerate. Reheat before serving. 1 quart (8 to 10 servings).

Variation: Substitute 1 30-oz. can Del Monte Unpeeled Apricot Halves for Peaches.

Recipe reprinted by permission of Del Monte Kitchens/Del Monte Corporation

BUTTERSCOTCH PEACHES WITH ICE CREAM

1 tablespoon butter or margarine
½ cup brown sugar
Dash of salt

2 tablespoons milk
4 fresh peach halves, poached
Vanilla ice cream

Melt butter in small saucepan over low heat. Add brown sugar, salt, and milk. Cook about 4 minutes, stirring constantly. Add cooked peach halves and heat well. Serve warm with vanilla ice cream. Serves 2.

Reprinted by permission of June Towers, Imperial Sugar Company

PEACH LEMON SAUCE FOR CHICKEN

2 lemons
3 medium-size fresh California peaches, pitted and quartered

3 tablespoons chicken stock
Salt and pepper

Thinly peel one of the lemons, reserve peel. Squeeze both the lemons as needed to get ¼ cup juice. Combine the juice and peaches in a saucepan. Cover and cook for 20 minutes or until the peaches are very tender. Meanwhile, cut the reserved lemon peel into fine julienne strips and cut in half. Boil strips in water for 7 or 8 minutes.

Drain and set aside. Combine the cooked peaches and chicken stock in an electric blender. Whirl until smooth. Stir in julienne lemon strips and salt and pepper to taste. Serve hot over grilled chicken. Makes 2½ cups.

Reprinted by permission of California Tree Fruit Agreement

CANDIED FRUITS:
Peaches, Pears, Plums and Cherries

2 cups sugar
1 cup water

⅓ cup light corn syrup

Boil together until syrup spins a thread when dropped from spoon (234 degrees). Pare, core, slice or otherwise. Have fruit drained, clear of all juices, and add to boiling syrup. Do not crowd. Simmer until clear. Remove skim from syrup, drain, and spread on a screen to dry until they are no longer sticky. Pack between sheets of wax paper. Store in tin box or jar.

Jean Pryor, Houston, Texas

PEACH BURRITOS

2 cups peaches, coarsely
    chopped
½ cup sugar
¼ cup flour

3 tablespoons margarine
1 teaspoon cinnamon
½ teaspoon nutmeg
8 to 10 large flour tortillas

Combine peaches, sugar, flour, margarine, cinnamon and nutmeg in saucepan. Cook over medium heat until thick. Remove from heat and set aside. Soften flour tortillas in melted butter in skillet, turning once. Put peach filling on tortillas and roll. Place on greased tray of broiler pan. Sprinkle with cinnamon sugar and broil for 3 minutes.

Barbara Sisk, Hempstead, Texas

PEACH-CHEESE APPETIZER TWIST

1 16-oz. loaf frozen light rye
    bread dough
1 egg, beaten
1 tablespoon water

1 8-oz. piece brick, colby or
    cheddar cheese
1 21-oz. can Wilderness Peach
    Fruit Filling

Thaw dough and let rise until double in size, about 1 hour. Punch dough down; divide into 2 equal pieces. Roll each piece into log about 15 inches long and 1 inch in diameter. Pinch one end of logs together; twist logs together, pinching ends to seal. Remove Peach Fruit Filling from can and reserve; remove paper from can. Wash and dry can; place in center of greased cookie sheet. Arrange twisted dough in ring around can; pinch to seal ends. Mix egg and water; brush over dough. Let rise, covered, until dough is double in size; about 45 minutes.

Bake bread at 375 degrees until golden, about 30 minutes. Remove can; place cheese in bread, trimming to fit. Bake at 375 degrees until cheese is warm, but not melted, about 5 minutes. Remove to serving plate. Heat Peach Fruit Filling in saucepan until bubbly; spoon over bread and cheese. To serve, slice bread and spread with cheese mixture. 8 servings.

Reprinted by permission of Wilderness Foods, Inc.

KAHLUA DESSERT QUICHE

Butter Pastry (recipe follows)
1 8-oz. package cream cheese
2 teaspoons sugar
¼ teaspoon salt
⅛ teaspoon mace
4 large eggs
¼ cup Kahlua
1½ cups thin cream (half-and-half)
Fresh fruit (grapes, peaches, apricots, plums)

Prepare butter pastry and line pan; chill 1 hour. Set rack below oven center. Place cookie sheet on rack; preheat oven to 375 degrees F. Have all ingredients at room temperature (or warm cream). Beat cream cheese with sugar, salt and mace in small bowl until soft. With mixer running, beat in 1 egg at a time. Add Kahlua. When mixture is smooth, stir in cream. Carefully pour filling into chilled crust. Set filled pan on cookie sheet and bake till filling is barely set in center and golden brown on top (40 to 45 minutes). Cool on wire rack. Serve warm or at room temperature with fruit in season. Makes 8 servings.

Butter Pastry:

Mix 1¼ cups sifted all-purpose flour with ¼ teaspoon salt. Cut in ⅓ cup shortening and 2 tablespoons firm butter. Add about 3 tablespoons cold milk, just enough to make stiff dough. Shape into ball and roll out on floured board to an 11-inch circle. Gently fit into cake pan, 8 × 1½ inches. Trim pastry ¼ inch above rim of pan. Turn edge in, shape into rim about ⅛ inch above pan edge.

Reprinted by permission of Maidstone Wine and Spirits, Inc.

MUENSTER-WHEAT GERM QUICHE

6 oz. Dorman's Muenster Cheese, grated in blender (use Dorman's Natural Muenster sticks)
8 to 10 slices white bread, crusts removed
1 cup peach jam
2 cups milk
½ cup wheat germ
¼ cup firmly packed light brown sugar
4 eggs
¼ teaspoon salt
Whipped cream (optional)

Fit 2 slices and 4 triangular half-slices of bread on greased 8-inch springform pan. Use small pieces to cover bottom. Cut remaining bread in half. Place around edge to form side crust. Press firmly and evenly. Spread jam over bread crust. Mix remaining ingredients. Pour into crust. Bake, 375 degrees, 20 minutes. Cool. Gently remove side of pan. Serve with whipped cream. Serves 6 to 8.

Reprinted by permission of N. Dorman and Company Inc.

SUGAR PUFF TRAIL MIX

2 cups Malt-O-Meal Sugar Puffs
1 cup shaved unsweetened coconut
1 cup date pieces
2 cups broken nuts *
1 cup dried peaches

Toss all ingredients together. Store in an airtight container. *Walnuts, pecans, brazil nuts, peanuts or a combination. Dried apricots, figs, prunes, dried papaya or dried pineapple cut up may be substituted for dates.

Recipe reprinted by permission of Malt-O-Meal Co.

GRANOLA AND PEACHES

1 cup uncooked old-fashioned oats
½ cup graham cracker crumbs
½ cup slivered blanched almonds
1 teaspoon vanilla extract
¾ cup sliced peaches
1 cup wheat germ
½ cup flaked coconut
1 to 2 tablespoons light brown sugar
Milk

Combine oats, wheat germ, cracker crumbs, coconut, almonds, brown sugar and vanilla in shallow baking pan; mix well. Bake in 275-degree oven for 1 hour, stirring occasionally. Cool. Store granola in tightly covered container in refrigerator. Combine ½ cup milk and about ¾ cup sliced peaches for each serving. Recipe may be doubled, if desired.

PEACH RAISIN CHUTNEY

1 1 lb. 13-oz. can peach halves, drained
⅓ cup firmly packed light brown sugar
⅓ cup seedless raisins
⅓ cup honey
½ cup Heinz Apple Cider Vinegar
⅛ teaspoon ground mace
6 whole cloves
1 3- to 4-inch cinnamon stick, broken

Coarsely chop peaches; combine with brown sugar and next 4 ingredients in saucepan. Tie cloves and cinnamon in cheesecloth bag; add to peach mixture. Simmer 30 minutes, stirring occasionally. Remove spice bag. Pour chutney into glass bowl; cover; chill. Serve as a meat accompaniment with roast pork, ham or poultry. Makes about 2⅓ cups.

Reprinted by permission of Heinz U.S.A.

CALIFORNIA PEACH CHEESE SPREAD

1 16-oz. can peach slices in juice or extra light syrup
2 8-oz. packages cream cheese, softened
2 tablespoons minced green onions
2 teaspoons garlic salt
1 teaspoon dill weed
Crisp crackers or party rye bread

Drain peaches, reserving 2 tablespoons juice; save remainder for other uses. Chop peach slices finely; set aside. Combine softened cream cheese, reserved peach juice, onions, garlic salt and dill weed in food processor bowl or mixer bowl. Process until smooth. Fold in chopped peaches. Turn into serving bowls and chill well. Serve with crisp crackers or party rye. Makes approximately 3 cups spread.

Reprinted by permission of S & W Fine Foods, Inc. and Cling Peach Advisory Board

FRESH PEACHES

WHEN PICKING, handle fruit carefully because peaches BRUISE VERY EASILY and decay develops rapidly.

WHEN SELECTING, look for peaches with a creamy to gold undercolor that best indicates ripeness. The amount of red blush on fruit depends on the variety and is not always a sign of ripeness. Two other indicators of ripeness are a well-defined crease and a good fragrance. Select fruit that has begun to soften for immediate use. Firm ripe fruit can be held a few days at room temperature and ripened further. Never pick peaches with a green undercolor since they will not ripen well. They will shrivel, become flabby, and never achieve a good flavor.

WHEN STORING, peaches should be held at 32°–35° F. and high humidity. Fully ripened peaches should be refrigerated immediately and kept there until ready for consumption. Sound and mature but not overripe peaches can be expected to hold 1–2 weeks at 32°–35°F. with little adverse effect. Peaches deteriorate rapidly when stored for periods longer than this.

WHEN RIPENING mature peaches a room temperature of 65°–70°F. is best. There is no gain in sugar content once a peach is picked from a tree. Its ripening process consists primarily of softening, development of juiciness and development of flavor. So the riper a peach is at harvest, the more sugar it will contain. Remember once a mature peach begins to ripen it never stops, but you can slow the rate of ripening by using low temperatures.

WHEN PREPARING, wash peaches gently, peel and remove pits. Handle carefully to avoid bruising.

Reprinted by permission of North Carolina Department of Agriculture

COMMON WEIGHTS AND MEASURES

3 teaspoons	=	1 tablespoon
4 tablespoons	=	¼ cup
8 tablespoons	=	½ cup
12 tablespoons	=	¾ cup
16 tablespoons	=	1 cup
1 cup	=	8 fluid ounces
1 cup	=	½ pint
2 cups	=	1 pint
4 cups	=	1 quart
4 quarts	=	1 gallon
8 quarts	=	1 peck
4 pecks	=	1 bushel

Equivalents

1 bushel peaches	=	48 pounds
1 bushel peaches	=	30 – 40 pints
		15 – 20 quarts
1 pound peaches	=	2 large or 3 medium peaches
		2 cups peeled and sliced
		1⅔ cups peeled and diced
		1½ cups peeled and pureed

Imaginative ways with leftover syrup

Don't throw that leftover syrup away! Creative cooks can use canned cling peach or fruit cocktail syrup as a versatile ingredient in gelatin salads, pancake syrup, beverages and sauces.

Gelatin Salads and Desserts: Substitute syrup for part of the liquid in gelatin recipes.

Pancake Syrup: Simmer heavy syrup from sliced peaches until reduced by half. Add ½ cup maple syrup and peaches, then heat through. Serve over French toast, pancakes or waffles.

Beverages: Use syrup in fruit punch or to extend and sweeten orange and grapefruit juices. Canned fruit syrup also is a good base for shakes, blender drinks and nogs.

Tangy Sauce: Flavor syrup and currant jelly, mustard, horseradish, ginger or curry; add vinegar and thicken with cornstarch. Serve sauce with chicken, pork or ham.

Dessert Sauce: Add lemon juice, orange juice or other flavorings to syrup and thicken with cornstarch; spoon over gingerbread, cakes, crepes or ice cream.

Reprinted by permission of Cling Peach Advisory Board

TIP

IF A RECIPE CALLS FOR PEELED PEACHES, USE THE "TOMATO" METHOD. PUT PEACHES INTO BOILING WATER FOR ABOUT 30 SECONDS, THEN TRANSFER IMMEDIATELY TO COLD WATER. THE SKIN WILL SLIP RIGHT OFF.

Reprinted by permission of California Tree Fruit Agreement

Garnishing With Peaches

Hot or cold, filled or plain, cling peaches are an attractive garnish for main dishes. Their golden color, firm texture and simple shape lend eye appeal to everything from entrees to salads and desserts.

Filled cling peach halves make a particularly attractive garnish. For pork, beef, poultry, seafood or casseroles, fill hot or cold halves with:

sour cream	steak sauce	chopped green onion
horseradish	cranberry sauce	diced green chilies
capers	grated cheese	mint or currant jelly
chutney	a ripe olive	toasted sesame seeds
soy sauce	toasted almonds	crumbled blue cheese

As a chilled garnish for breakfast items, salads, sandwiches and desserts, fill halves with:

yogurt	salad dressing	grated lemon peel
berries	chopped chives	orange marmalade
fresh mint	cottage cheese	shaved chocolate
parsley	chopped nuts	whipped cream
sprouts	cream cheese	toasted coconut

Some Like Them Hot . . . Some Like Them Cold

Either way, cling peaches are delicious.

Hot peaches can be poached, broiled, baked or sautéed. Heating actually enhances their characteristic flavor and aroma, and peaches retain their shape, color and juiciness when heated. Hot peaches are delicious flavored with brandy, sherry, liqueur, flavoring extracts or herbs and spices.

To Poach: In a skillet or pan, gently heat peach halves in their syrup. A flavoring extract or liqueur may be added to the syrup after the peaches are heated through.

To Broil: Brush peaches cup side up with melted butter and sprinkle the tops with brown sugar. Season if desired and broil until slightly colored.

To Bake: Brush peaches with melted butter and bake in a moderate oven until heated through.

To Sauté: In a skillet, turn peaches cup side down in melted butter, season if desired, and heat until peaches are slightly colored.

Chilled, cling peaches are marvelous served straight from the can, as a garnish, or in salads, beverages and desserts. For a delightful instant dessert ice, freeze peaches right in the can and then whirl in the blender with one tablespoon lemon juice until smooth.

Reprinted by permission of Cling Peach Advisory Board

Index

BREADS, PASTRIES AND COBBLERS

CAKES, COOKIES AND BARS

197